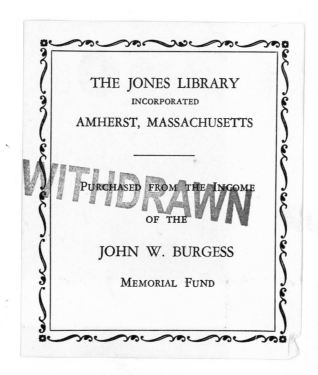

PORCELAIN
TRADITIONS AND NEW VISIONS

PORC

TRADITIONS AND NEW VISIONS

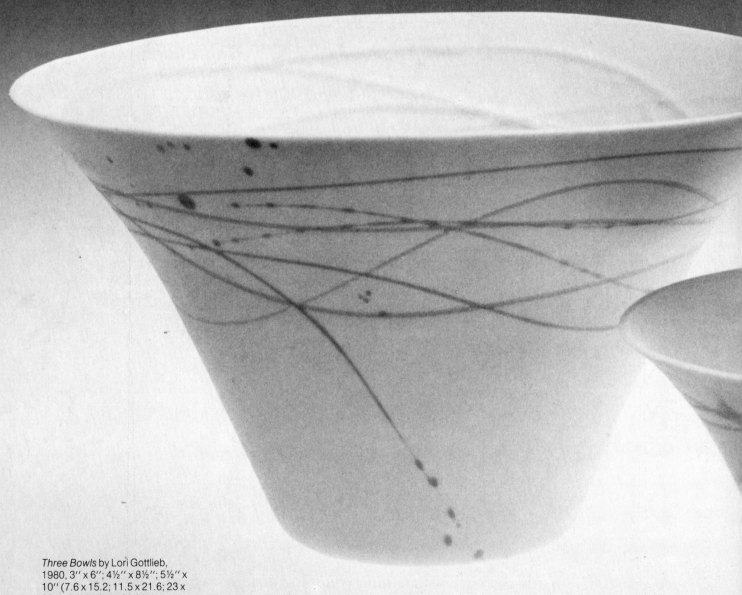

Three Bowls by Lori Gottlieb, 1980, 3'' x 6''; 4½'' x 8½''; 5½'' x 10'' (7.6 x 15.2; 11.5 x 21.6; 23 x 25.4 cm). In these highly trans-lucent cast bowls inlaid with col-ored clays, Gottlieb is seeking a cross between clay and glass. Though elegant and delicate, they are intended for use. Photo: Jim Kiernan.

ELAIN

BY JAN AXEL AND KAREN MCCREADY

WATSON-GUPTILL PUBLICATIONS/NEW YORK

For Bob—for everything. –J.A.

In memory of my friend Laura Garza,
who believed in the magic of beauty. –K.M.

Copyright © 1981 by Jan Axel and Karen McCready

First published 1981 in New York by Watson-Guptill Publications,
a division of Billboard Publications, Inc.,
1515 Broadway, New York, N.Y. 10036

Library of Congress Cataloging in Publication Data

Axel, Jan.
    Porcelain, traditions and new visions.

    Bibliography: p.
    Includes index.
    1. Porcelain—20th century. I. McCready, Karen.
II. Title.
NK4373.A93   738.2'09'04   81–4971
ISBN 0–8230–4091–7   AACR2

Manufactured in U.S.A.

First Printing, 1981

Edited by Betty Vera
Designed by Bob Fillie
Graphic Production by Ellen Greene
Text set in 10-point Medallion

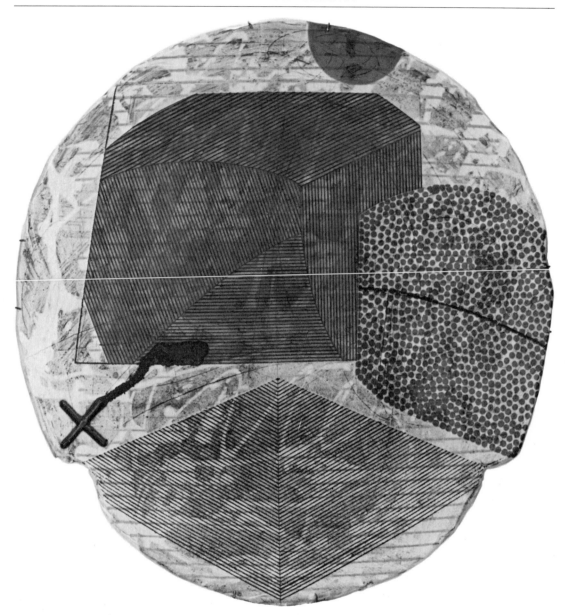

Meidum by Walter Hall, 1977, 21″ (53.3 cm) diam. The drawing on this wall piece was influenced by aerial photographs of the massive pyramid and ruins at Meidum, Egypt. Photo: John Vignoli.

Porcelain: Traditions and New Visions is the result of a collaboration between two authors, but it would not have been possible without the responsiveness and cooperation of many other individuals, whom we most heartily thank.

Our special thanks to Michael McTwigan and Betty Vera for their excellent editorial guidance in shaping this book, and to David McFadden for his fine historical chapter and advice throughout the project. Thanks also to Lee Ryder, who initially proposed the project, and to Susan Loesser for her editorial advice and assistance.

We are most grateful to all the artists who generously offered both information and photographs of their work. We also wish to thank the following people for additional assistance in compiling the material for this book: Rena Bransten, Ruth Braunstein, Hazel Bray, Judith Carrington, Helen Williams Drutt, Irene Friedman, Lee Goler, Lynn Gull, Eleanor Haas, Tony Hepburn, Lloyd Herman, Bryce Holcombe, Daniel Jacobs, Jim Kiernan, Ruth DeYoung Kohler, Malcolm and Sue Knapp, Tom Lasher, Olivia Murray, Kristin Olive, Robert and Jean Pfannebecker, Joanne Polster, Jacqueline Poncelet, Elsa Rady, Nicholas Rodriguez, Jim and Shelley Rothrock, Michael Sullivan, Edward and Ruth Tanenhaus, and Lisa Tundry.

A note of personal thanks to Bob Axel, Sandy Gellis, Lori Gottlieb, Judy Harney, Wendy Insinger, Susan Larsen, Kathryn Markel, Diane Villani, Paula Winokur, and Lynn Schrurnberger for their friendship and encouragement throughout the process of giving form to our particular vision of contemporary porcelain.

THIS BOOK was born from an evolving dialogue between maker and viewer: joined by our mutual love of porcelain, our respective viewpoints are also polarized by our different perceptions and experiences of the material.

While history and porcelain are inextricably bound, the contemporary ceramist may choose to accept, modify, or defy the limitations of historical porcelain aesthetics. It can be said that some objects exude porcelain, and it is from them that a porcelain aesthetic arises. In these objects both substance and subject matter unite to fulfill our traditional expectations of the material. We may question the issue of a specific porcelain aesthetic when porcelain is used as a point of departure for making a statement rather than as the end in itself. Then it becomes part of a larger scheme, though it is still valued for its qualities.

For the ceramist, porcelain is the most demanding ceramic material because it is the one that is most limited by technical considerations. Lacking the plasticity and toughness of most stonewares and earthenwares during the forming process, porcelain demands special attention. A common attitude that porcelain is an "unworkable" clay stems from this fact, as well as from associations with industrially made objects such as thin teacups, and contributes to many ceramists' hesitancy in attempting to use it in a studio situation. True, porcelain is an unforgiving material, one with a memory for every touch. Because of its sensitivity and tendency to lose shape, it requires a decisive, sure-handed approach. But once its particular characteristics are taken into consideration, porcelain is simply another clay for the ceramist to explore.

The broadened aesthetic scope of works within all the ceramic media in recent years has caused a change in the identity of the maker. With this new identity has come the tendency to categorize and label both art and artist, debating the particular issues germane to various styles and splitting the ceramics community into factions. The pre-industrial potter suffered no identity crisis; but with the Industrial Revolution and division of labor, the question of the artisan's role was raised. At that time the controversy revolved around the titles (and with this, the roles and status) of *technician* versus *designer*—not so different from today's controversy over *artist* versus *craftsperson*. But semantic debates about nomenclature are symptomatic of a broader issue facing the ceramist and viewer alike today: Where do these new ceramic objects belong in the hierarchy of all art objects? The

dialogue is a healthy one. It symbolizes the growing pains of a field energized by fresh aesthetic approaches. With the debate comes the development of a new vocabulary, new criticism, and new aesthetic standards to accommodate all that ceramic art, of which porcelain is an important part, is today.

The common denominator that unites the diverse works in this book is the material of which they are made—porcelain. Though these works of art may share the same medium and sometimes even technique, that may be all they have in common. Those with stylistic or formal similarities should be judged accordingly and be valued for their own unique qualities, despite inclusion of many different approaches under the same ceramic umbrella—which can be, admittedly, confusing. Our attempt, however, is not to equate different styles or offer a single current alternative definition of porcelain, but rather to survey and document the enormous scope of creative approaches to the material today. We believe that porcelain is a never-ending challenge to all who encounter it. As ceramist Tony Hepburn has declared in lecturing and writing about clays as an expressive medium, the material is "so susceptible to change in one state and so resistant in another that those paradoxes will sustain man's interest in it forever."

At the outset of this project, we thought porcelain would be a straightforward subject about which to write a book. In trying to grasp its essence, however, as perceived in the vast array of objects before us (and now before you), we discovered that the forms porcelain can take are as varied as the talents of those who work with it. Its tactile and visual qualities, as seen in contemporary works, whether they are functional or purely expressive pieces, express only part of porcelain's potential. In order to treat the subject in its totality, we found it necessary to consider the porcelain industry and the material's technological uses, both in and out of the artist's studio, as well. No creative process is complete without an appreciative audience—connoisseurs, collectors, patrons, and the average gallery visitor. For this reason, we have not only discussed the viewer's perspective throughout the book, but also devoted a chapter to the role of the collector throughout history and today.

This book, then, is a survey of quality work by potters, ceramists, and artists (let each choose his or her own title). We investigate, through the eyes of ceramist and viewer, those who use porcelain to express their fantasies, dreams, and visions in old, new, and newer ways.

CONTENTS

THE EVOLUTION OF PORCELAIN

THE EVOLUTION

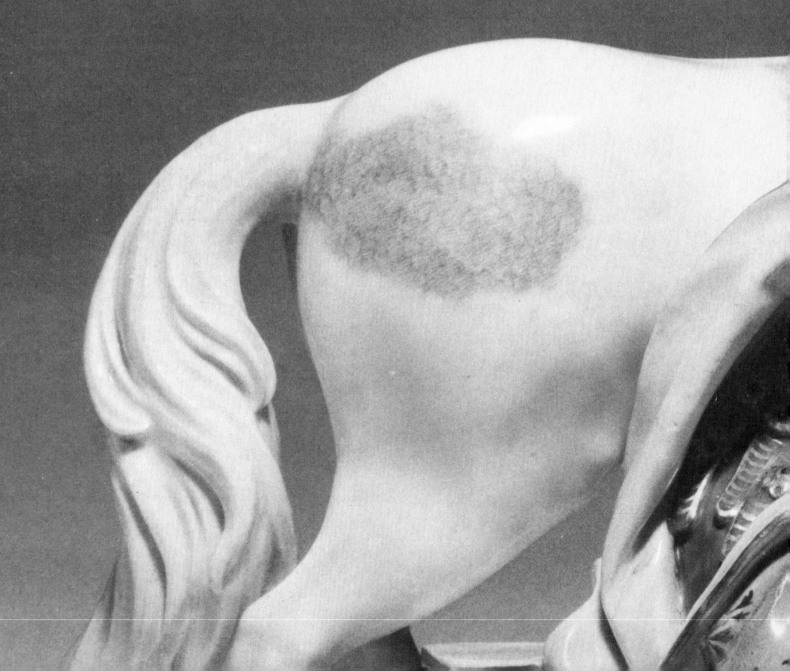

OF PORCELAIN

Europe, one of the *Allegories of the Four Continents,* Meissen factory, Germany, about 1750, hard-paste porcelain with enamels and gilding. Courtesy Cooper-Hewitt Museum, the Smithsonian Institution's National Museum of Design.

CHAPTER ONE

EARLY PORCELAIN IN EUROPE

BY DAVID REVERE McFADDEN

ITHIN THE DIVERSE range of ceramic products that have developed over the millenia, porcelain has enjoyed a distinct and unusual history. The inherent characteristics of this material—resilience even in its thin fragility, potential for translucency, resonance when struck, and purity of texture and color—have made it one of the rarest and most highly desirable, expensive, and technically demanding of mediums for artists and craftspeople. It is little wonder that both the East and West developed highly sophisticated methods and techniques for fashioning this precious substance, and that the techniques for forming, firing, and decorating porcelain require specialized knowledge, manual dexterity, and sensitivity to material unequaled by any other ceramic product. By the time Westerners were able to manufacture true porcelain, the Chinese had already left behind them an impressive legacy of porcelain design, and had created masterpieces of the porcelain maker's art for well over five hundred years. The history of porcelain, from its initial development in Asia through the culmination of the art of porcelain in eighteenth-century Europe, provides both a richly textured background for the aesthetics of contemporary porcelain and insights into the development of a design vocabulary of form and decoration in this revitalized field.

In the East porcelain developed logically within the highly competent and specialized ceramic tradition of China, whereas in the West there was a more self-conscious and intentional search for the materials and methods of porcelain production. It is possible to trace the origins of Chinese porcelain to an early knowledge and understanding of the particular ingredients necessary to make true porcelain—most notably, a special clay called kaolin, used to make a near-white stoneware as early as the Han dynasty (206 B.C. to A.D. 220). A second essential ingredient in porcelain was petuntse, a fusible feldspathic stone that, when mixed with the clay and fired, produced a ceramic body with an unusual degree of vitrification. Such fusion was dependent upon extremely high firing temperatures and the technological understanding of kiln construction. The ingredients and the process were used to produce fused porcelaneous wares at least as early as the T'ang dynasty (A.D. 618 to 906). Much later, European awareness of porcelain stimulated great artistic and scientific interest in the nature of the material. The search for the secret of its manufacture—the arcanum—encouraged highly competitive investigations into the properties of various ceramic mixtures, completely altering the course of ceramic history in Europe.

Porcelain Comes to Europe

Europeans had been aware of Chinese porcelain for centuries before the treasured wares were readily available in the West, and certainly long before the techniques of production were even partially understood. The Greeks and Romans knew of the existence of China, but the long and perilous journey nec-

Vase, China, Han dynasty (206 B.C.–A.D. 220). This porcelaneous stoneware is an early example of a refined stoneware that developed into true or hard-paste porcelain. Courtesy The Metropolitan Museum of Art, Bequest of Mrs. H. O. Havemeyer, 1929.

essary to reach the East prevented extensive exploration of trade possibilities between the distant parts of the globe. The southern tip of India was the most important point of contact between East and West during the classical period, and a certain amount of trade goods in the form of textiles and spices reached the West by this route.

By the time of the Roman emperor Augustus, geographers and historians were compiling information about the unknown and mysterious East; much of the "factual" data was fictitious and unproved by direct observation. The lands to the East were called Seres—the "Land of Silk"—in homage to one of Asia's most luxurious and desirable products.

The early development of porcelain in China meant that Marco Polo, who traveled in the East for seventeen years during the thirteenth century, encountered this magical material and recorded its existence in his journal. Marco Polo's description of the material as *alla porcella*, or having the appearance of a delicate, shiny seashell, is said to have given porcelain its common name in the West. Contact with Asia during the succeeding centuries after Polo's visit remained sporadic and difficult. It can be safely assumed that during the fourteenth, fifteenth, and sixteenth centuries, the amount of porcelain that filtered into Europe was small but far from negligible. However, goods and luxuries that were unobtainable from Western weavers, potters, and spice growers continued to haunt the imaginations of Westerners; to those who had access to silk, pepper, cinnamon, lacquer, tea, and porcelain, wealth and prestige logically followed, and Europeans never completely abandoned the idea of establishing a sea route to reach the East. It was not until the late sixteenth century that extensive and adventurous seafaring expeditions made possible a viable trade route between East and West. By the end of the century, Portuguese traders and merchants had established a secure trading post at Macao, China, a port connected to Canton by the Pearl River. Within a relatively short period of time Dutch, Spanish, English, French, Swedish, and Danish (and later, American) entrepreneurs had made similar arrangements for continued trade activities with the Chinese. Throughout the centuries of active East–West trade, porcelain remained a vital and lucrative export product for China and a secure "blue chip" commodity for European merchants and collectors.

Japan and Korea both developed strong and vital traditions of porcelain design. Japanese production began in the early seventeenth century; in Korea, however, porcelaneous wares were being produced as early

Left
Winepot, China, Sung dynasty
(960–1279). This winepot is gray-
ish white, porcelaneous ware with
Honan celadon glaze. Courtesy
The Metropolitan Museum of Art,
Gift of Samuel T. Peters, 1926.

Bottom
Bowl, Japan, Edo period
(1615–1868). This bowl is in the
Kakiemon style. Courtesy Freer
Gallery of Art, Washington, D.C.

Right
Vase, China, Ming dynasty, Wan Li
period (1573–1619), 13⅝″ (34.6
cm) high. Rare imported porcelains were often mounted in silver
gilt to emphasize the porcelain and
to protect them from damage.
Courtesy The Metropolitan Museum of Art, Rogers fund, 1944.

as the Koryo dynasty (A.D. 918–1392).

Porcelain imported into Europe in the early days of East–West trade included the ubiquitous blue-and-white wares of the Ming and Ch'ing dynasties. These enduringly popular porcelains, painted in a brilliant and rich underglaze cobalt blue on a pristine white ceramic body, were eagerly collected by the wealthy aristocrats of Europe. Due to the rarity and expense of imported blue-and-white porcelain, few examples actually appeared in European collections during the sixteenth century in comparison with the thousands that were made in China for domestic use or for export to other Eastern countries. The few prized blue-and-white wares that did find their way into Europe were treated with the care and concern generally given to precious jewels. Porcelains were frequently mounted in elaborate silver-gilt mounts to emphasize their rarity and preciousness and also to protect the fragile treasures from damage. Mounts were applied at the most vulnerable areas of a piece, such as the lip, foot, and handles. Although such mounts often radically altered the appearance of the porcelains—a vase might be transformed into a pitcher—the effect was similar to the setting of a rare gemstone.

The supply of Chinese blue-and-white porcelain could never meet the demand of eager European collectors and connoisseurs, and it was obvious that anyone who could discover the secret of its manufacture would enjoy untold wealth. Numerous ceramic artisans, accustomed to working with standard pottery and stoneware bodies, imitated the surface appearance of porcelain by covering humble pottery objects with a white skin of tin oxide glaze; in combination with cobalt blue decoration, such approximations were the closest European equivalent to authentic blue-and-white ware. Faience, majolica, and delftware factories throughout Europe concentrated on such imitative wares, but the prized and incomprehensible porcelain eluded analysis.

There were several serious attempts to uncover the secret of true porcelain, primarily through using combinations of ingredients that were assumed to make up the porcelain body. One of the earliest attempts to manufacture porcelain occurred in Italy, under the patronage of the Medici family of Florence. Since true porcelain was shiny and translucent, it was incorrectly assumed that the recipe must include glass. Medici potters used a white clay as the base for their peculiar mixture and added to it a substantial amount of glass frit. This intractable material was potted, decorated with underglaze blue or manganese purple, and fired—with limited success. The Medici mixture had an understandable tendency to lose its shape during

firing, and the number of kiln wasters far exceeded that of the few objects that emerged intact. In fact, there are only about sixty pieces of the Medici porcelain extant, which gives some indication of the problems that plagued the enterprise. The Medici factory was in existence for only about twelve years, from 1575 to 1587; it was not until the late seventeenth century that further attempts to make porcelain resulted in a more successful, though still inaccurate, equivalent of the Chinese rarity.

Both Medici porcelain and the products of the seventeenth-century French innovators used a mixture of ingredients other than kaolin and petuntse, and thus they are classified as "artificial" or "soft-paste" porcelain. Nevertheless, these products had a tremendous impact on the history of ceramics in Europe, and soft-paste porcelain became the vehicle of genius in the hands of the potters at the factory of Sèvres in France. The tradition of French soft-paste porcelain can be traced at least to the 1670s, when Louis Poterat, a potter from Rouen, succeeded in producing a limited number of clear-glazed vessels with a bluish green body. The second factory to carry on important experiments on the nature of the porcelaneous body was founded slightly later in Saint-Cloud. At this factory, delightful forms and designs were produced in spite of the difficult and laborious process needed to work the artificial porcelain mixture. Early experimental porcelain enterprises combined functional forms with sculptural interest, a feature of porcelain design that has been maintained to the present.

Meissen: Europe Reinvents True Porcelain

It was in the early years of the eighteenth century that true porcelain was produced for the first time in Europe. Following centuries of wonder and amazement at the marvelous material, and countless futile experiments, both the materials and the methods of fabricating true porcelain were realized in the workshops patronized by Augustus the Strong, King of Poland and Elector of Saxony. For the next hundred years porcelain remained supreme among European ceramics, and the Asian mystery was challenged by the West.

Two personalities were closely associated with the discovery of the proper combination of ingredients equal to the Chinese formula during the first decade of the 1700s: Ehrenfried Walther von Tschirnhausen, economic advisor to Augustus the Strong, and Johann Friedrich Böttger, a recalcitrant but brilliant alchemist who claimed he could transform base metal into gold. These two unlikely colleagues worked together in numerous experiments on the nature and prop-

Right
Dish, Medici factory, Italy, sixteenth century, 13⅛″ (33.3 cm) diam. This soft-paste porcelain dish depicting the death of King Saul is a product of one of the earliest attempts to produce porcelain in Europe at the short-lived Medici factory. Courtesy The Metropolitan Museum of Art, Samuel D. Lee Fund, 1941.

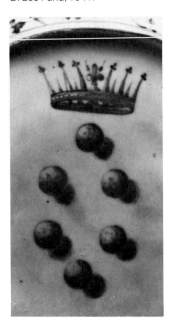

Above
The Medici coat of arms appears on the reverse side of the dish from the Medici factory.

Right
Tea and Chocolate Service, Meissen factory, Germany, about 1730. This piece is made of hard-paste porcelain with gilding. Courtesy Cooper-Hewitt Museum, Smithsonian Institution.

erties of refractory clays found in Saxony, and their work laid the foundations of the porcelain industry in the West. Early experiments with ceramic materials resulted in the production of a superbly hard, fine-grained red stoneware that resembled the stoneware produced in the I-hsing area of China. The stoneware was so thoroughly fused by firing at high temperatures that it could be polished to a high luster and even cut or engraved on a lapidary wheel. Early wares produced from

this hard, reddish brown, porcelaneous material included not only ornamental vases and urns, but also an important repertoire of useful domestic objects such as teapots, cups and saucers, and tankards. This emphasis on the production of both functional and decorative wares at the Saxon factory continued throughout the century. The workshops in which this important breakthrough had occurred were located at the royal fortress at Meissen, and the manufactory soon became known by this name. Even today, the Meissen name evokes the grandeur of baroque

porcelain, and it is the one name nearly everyone associates with the material.

Subsequent to the development of the red stoneware—a material that remained in the factory's output for a considerable period of time—there were further experiments with white clays that shared similar properties of fusibility and plasticity. These resulted in a less-than-perfect, but nonetheless white, ceramic body. Early white wares sometimes incorporated alabaster in the clay mixture, but a suitable clay for making porcelain was discovered in Colditz. Potters at Meissen were now able to extract from the high-temperature kilns objects that were snowy white, translucent, and delicate. Among the best known early wares from the nascent industry at Meissen were utilitarian "production" objects: handleless cups with accompanying saucers, tall and elegant coffee pots, and precisely modeled tea caddies. Often these were decorated with underglaze cobalt blue in patterns derived from Chinese examples. Some services were enriched with lively, imaginative gilded scenes of Chinese inspiration, known as *chinoiseries*. Augustus the Strong had long been a collector of imported Chinese porcelains; with his own private factory he was able to pursue his expensive hobby with abandon. Augustus commissioned the factory to produce hundreds of monumental pieces of porcelain for his palaces and his favorites, including life-size porcelain representations of the animals he kept in the royal menagerie! These personal expenses, however, were balanced by the enormous number of porcelain pieces that were being exported from Saxony; a steady income for the factory was assured, since Meissen was the sole supplier of true porcelain for the whole of the West. The sale of Meissen porcelain to an eager and affluent audience of European collectors meant tremendous financial improvement for the Saxon budget.

The repertoire of decorative designs used at Meissen was greatly expanded by the factory's extensive use of overglaze enamel colors. The brilliant hues made possible by enamels contrasted dramatically with the pure white body of the wares, bringing an added richness to the product. Visual opulence was the goal, and plain surfaces were frequently painted with representational polychrome vignettes and motifs such as landscapes, seascapes, and figural groups. Among the skilled, specialized enamelers who worked for the factory during its early period, Johann Gregor Höroldt excelled in the painting of detailed landscape vistas, and he often incorporated figures of Chinese inspiration into his scenes. Often the entire body of a vessel was decorated with color ap-

Above
Coffee Pot designed by J. F. Böttger for Meissen factory, Germany, about 1709. Böttger's early experiments in the search for porcelain resulted in a dense red stoneware clay body, used to create useful wares like this coffee pot, as well as ornamental vases.

Left
Clock Case designed by J. C. Kirchner for Meissen factory, Germany, about 1732. Elaborate sculptural forms such as this hard-paste porcelain clock case, decorated with enamels and gilding, were produced at Meissen. Courtesy Cooper-Hewitt Museum, Smithsonian Institution.

Opposite page
Two of the *Allegories of the Four Continents: Asia, Africa, Europe, America*, Meissen factory, Germany, about 1750. Figures such as these, in hard-paste porcelain with enamels and gilding, were a major emphasis of the Meissen factory and often depicted theatrical figures or allegories. Courtesy Cooper-Hewitt Museum, Smithsonian Institution.

plied over patterns that protected white "reserve" areas on the form. These pristine white panels on teapots, cups, and saucers were filled with exotic harbor scenes, sometimes showing the unloading of cargo ships by brilliantly clad figures. Höroldt was a major force in refining the possibilities for using porcelain as a "canvas" for painted decoration, a tradition that has remained vital to the present day.

A second tradition that flourished at Meissen—and has had an enormous impact on the aesthetics of porcelain design throughout the centuries until the present—was the treatment of the material as a vehicle of purely sculptural form. Sculptors and modelers were engaged at the factory, and two figures active at the factory in the 1730s—J. G. Kirchner and Johann Joachim Kändler—were major contributors to the sculptural tradition of porcelain. Kirchner began work at the factory around 1727 and was responsible for the design of numerous ornamental vases and three-dimensional animal figures. He was joined and eventually eclipsed by the talented sculptor Kändler. In Kändler's hands, the raw material became the means of achieving a sculptural unity and precision that had previously been outside the realm of ceramics. Particularly noteworthy are the animal figures modeled by Kändler, in which the sculptural veracity of form and subject is joined by his unmistakably lively imagination and vitality. Meissen porcelain rapidly became the rage in Europe, and crowned heads vied with one another to obtain it. Collecting and using porcelain were still the prerogatives of the rich, and the competition to acquire and display the expensive products was instrumental in encouraging important commissions, as well as swelling the coffers of the factory. Many distinguished clients placed special orders with the factory, including those for extensive services of porcelain to be used at table. Following the death of Augustus, his son (whose interest in porcelain was secondary to his passion for paintings) turned over the administration of the manufactory to his father's trusted chief minister, Count Heinrich von Brühl. Shortly after assuming his duties as head of the factory, the Count commissioned Kändler to design a dinner service of truly staggering quantity and unequaled quality. In this justly famous "Swan" service, Kändler achieved a brilliant synthesis of function and ornament; each of the more than two thousand pieces in the service—plates, bowls, platters, tureens, sugar casters, and even spoons—incorporated motifs of swans, rippling water, and aquatic plant life, meticulously integrated with the functional form.

Meissen's supremacy in the field of Euro-

pean hard-paste porcelain was based on the inventiveness and variety of forms to which factory artists dedicated their efforts, and also, importantly, on the fact that no one else in Europe had discovered the correct ingredients and techniques for making true porcelain. Consequently, every effort was made at the factory to protect the arcanum, or secret, from entering the sphere of general information. It is customarily reported that the workmen at Meissen were permitted knowledge of only a part of the fabrication process so that they could not desert the factory and begin their own businesses or sell their knowledge to those in a position to capitalize on it.

Porcelain Technology Spreads Throughout Europe

As with most well-kept secrets, however, only a short period of time passed before the process was known in other areas. By about 1719, one of the kiln masters at Meissen had already left Saxony and carried the necessary information to Vienna. There, under the sponsorship of Claudius Innocentius du Pacquier, the second porcelain factory to be built in Europe came into being. Vienna porcelain began to enter the European market as a competitor to Meissen, and this new factory was only the first in an enormous series of rivals to appear throughout Europe. By the middle of the century, factories had been established in centers such as Höchst-am-Main, Berlin, Nymphenburg, Frankenthal, Furstenburg, and Ludwigsburg, to mention only a few. Each factory contributed its own special character to the material itself, and the history of porcelain in eighteenth-century Europe is enriched by the seemingly endless array of functional items and ornamental products that emanated from these active centers of production.

By mid-century, Meissen was facing stiff competition from the many German and

Left
Plate, from the Swan Service, Meissen factory, Germany, 1737–1741. Created for Count von Brühl, the Swan Service, made of hard-paste porcelain with enamels and gilding, is one of the masterpieces of the Meissen factory. Courtesy Cooper-Hewitt Museum, Smithsonian Institution.

Far left
Saucer, Vienna factory, Austria, about 1730. The factory that produced this hard-paste porcelain with enamel and gilding was an early rival of the Meissen factory in Germany. Courtesy Cooper-Hewitt Museum, Smithsonian Institution.

Left
Saucer, Chantilly factory, France, about 1740. This piece is made of soft-paste porcelain and decorated with enamel. Courtesy Cooper-Hewitt Museum, Smithsonian Institution.

Above
Candlestick with Seated Chinese Figure, Höchst factory, Germany, about 1760. This piece is made of hard-paste porcelain decorated with enamel and gilding. Courtesy Cooper-Hewitt Museum, Smithsonian Institution, Gift of Mr. and Mrs. Edward M. Pflueger.

Right
Cup and Saucer, Berlin factory, Germany, about 1800. These pieces are made of hard-paste porcelain decorated with enamel and gilding. Courtesy Cooper-Hewitt Museum, Smithsonian Institution.

Austrian manufacturers that had sprung up virtually overnight and begun flooding the market with their luxurious wares. Meissen also faced other difficulties directly related to its survival. In 1756 the Seven Years War broke out, pitting the Saxon troops against the mighty armies of Frederick the Great of Prussia. The factory was, in fact, occupied by Frederick's troops, and it never again regained its preeminence as the leading source of porcelain design in Europe.

In addition to the rival firms within the immediate area, another challenge to leadership in the field of porcelain came from France.

The early experiments at Rouen and Saint-Cloud on the nature of porcelain have already been discussed; contrary to experiments with artificial or soft-paste porcelain bodies that had been a form of preliminary research in other countries, the factories of France developed their soft-paste compositions to the point of perfection and did not abandon them until the late eighteenth century. The role that the aristocracy played in the growth of a native porcelain industry in France was similar to the developments in Germany. Two factories deserve special attention, both for their history and for the

Far left
Cache-pot, Sèvres factory, France, 1782. This is made of soft-paste porcelain with modeled decoration, enamel, and gilding. Courtesy Cooper-Hewitt Museum, Smithsonian Institution.

Left
Wine Cooler, Sèvres factory, France, 1755–1760. The decoration here is done with enamel and gilding on an apple-green ground. © Sotheby Parke-Bernet. Agent: Editorial Photocolor Archives.

Verrière and Drawing, Sèvres factory, France, 1772. This is a rare example of a drawing, probably made for the Sèvres factory, and the existing piece made from it of soft-paste porcelain decorated with enamel and gilding. Courtesy Cooper-Hewitt Museum, Smithsonian Institution.

quality of their wares—the factory patronized by the Prince de Condé and that of the Duc de Villeroy.

Around 1725, the Prince de Condé, an avid collector of Japanese porcelain, established a factory at Chantilly. Although the body paste developed for use at the factory was a soft, artificial variety, an effort to make the wares as white and pure as possible led the artisans of the factory to cover the soft-paste body with a glaze of tin oxide not unlike that used by faience potters. Chantilly porcelain reflects the taste of the factory owner in that many designs were inspired by Japanese prototypes. Even when the form was a purely European one, it was generally decorated with polychrome flowers arranged in asymmetrical patterns derived from the porcelains of Arita: sparkling white punctuated by brilliant turquoise, brick red, soft ocher, and a startling orange.

Another factory that lent distinction to the tradition of soft-paste porcelain in France was the one patronized by the Duc de Villeroy. This factory, located at Mennecy, produced finely modeled domestic wares painted in the most delicate of enamel colors—pale rose, soft greens, and blues.

The Ascendancy of Sèvres

The greatest triumph of French soft-paste porcelain was to occur at the factory founded at the royal château of Vincennes. As in German centers, workmen from the factories in France traveled to new sites to start porcelain factories; it was two workmen from the factory at Chantilly—Robert and Gilles Dubois—who were responsible for the works being set up at Vincennes. The factory later moved to Sèvres, near the château of Madame de Pompadour. The products of Sèvres, ranging from diminutive breakfast services to dazzling tour-de-force ornaments for the mantelpiece, are among the most beautiful and desirable in the entire history of European porcelain. Working with the soft white paste of the clay body, the artists at Sèvres created superior and refined shapes, the surfaces of which were painted with brilliant ground colors of yellow, green, rose, turquoise, or deep blue. Plainer white wares and white reserves on ground-color wares were enlivened with delicate floral sprays, and the borders and edges of the decorations were enriched by the lavish use of gold. The gilding at Sèvres was an art unto itself—the gold was not only thickly applied but also, upon completion of the gilding, painstakingly chased and tooled to indicate the surface textures and patterns of leaves and flowers.

Sèvres, like Meissen, was responsible for the production of enormous commissioned services. Clients of the factory included most of the fashionable crowned heads of Europe, such as Catherine the Great of Russia, the Empress Maria Theresa, and even clients in Scandinavia, England, and America. The sale of Sèvres wares provided a lucrative income for the crown, since the factory had been taken over by Louis XV in 1759. This was, of course, the period in which Meissen suffered its great and irretrievable decline, and Sèvres capitalized on the insatiable European demand for lustrous porcelain for table use and display. Due to the difficulties of working with the body mixture, the problems of firing and decorating the wares, and the consistently high standards of quality insisted upon by the manufactories' artistic directors, the number of kiln wasters and rejected pieces was always high. However, Sèvres countered the expense of this quality control by successfully marketing wares throughout the length and breadth of the "civilized" world. Sèvres merchants even prepared full-color pattern books that could be shown to potential clients to give them an accurate idea of the appearance of their costly investments. In rare cases, these drawings have survived to the present day and can be compared, point for point, with the actual pieces of porcelain. This distinctly modern form of "catalog" marketing indicates the level of business acumen that was always involved in the production and distribution of porcelain. At the same time, the drawings give us a glimpse into the methods of the artists at Sèvres—working within strictly defined rules and standards, each artist in the assembly line of production was ultimately responsible for the quality of his or her craftsmanship. In many cases, painters were even allowed to sign their work, and the amount of biographical material that exists in the Sèvres archives far exceeds that of any other European factory.

Porcelain in England

The third great force in the development of the porcelain aesthetic in eighteenth-century Europe was England. Like most European countries, England had enjoyed a vital and active ceramic tradition; from the late medieval period English ceramics developed a national character that distinguished them from the products of other countries. English potters were adept at integrating ornamental design with relatively ordinary useful forms, and this inherent talent for the aesthetic consistency of form and decoration was not lost when English potters began working in the new material of porcelain. The clay bodies used at the firms of Chelsea, Bow, Derby, Bristol, and Worcester, to mention only a few, were generally of the soft-paste variety. The Bristol firm and the later Worcester com-

Candlesticks, Chelsea factory, England, about 1758–1770. This soft-paste porcelain, modeled with birds in a bower, is decorated with enamel and gilding. Courtesy National Museum of American History, Smithsonian Institution.

Plate, Chamberlain's Worcester factory, England, about 1800. The plate is made of soft-paste porcelain decorated with enamel and gilding. Courtesy National Museum of American History, Smithsonian Institution.

pany incorporated steatite or soapstone into their mixtures, giving an added malleability to the mixture. True or hard-paste porcelain was, in fact, produced at the Plymouth factory, which was transferred to Bristol in 1770, and later at the firm of New Hall. However, most of the masterpieces of English porcelain were created in soft paste, indicating the popularity of this mixture.

The firm of Chelsea, which produced some of the most splendid examples of the potter's art in the mid-eighteenth century, was actually supervised by a silversmith, Nicholas Sprimont, whose abilities as a modeler of three-dimensional form were utilized to great advantage in the factory wares of the early period. In addition to the competence of modeling shown in Chelsea wares there are exceptional examples of the painting style.

One of the earliest factories in England was founded at Bow. By about 1749, the ingredients used there for the production of body paste included ground animal bones, which had been burned and powdered before being mixed with the clay. This recipe became extremely popular, and by the nineteenth century many firms were using a "bone china" formula for their wares.

Porcelain Fever Peaks, then Passes

By the third quarter of the eighteenth century, the porcelain craze in Europe had reached truly monumental proportions. The list of factories active and successful in Western Europe alone (from 1750 to 1800) is impressive and seemingly endless. In addition to those in Germany and Austria, factories sprang up in Scandinivia, Spain, Italy, the Netherlands, and Russia. By the late 1760s a porcelain factory had even been started in Philadelphia by the firm of Bonnin and Morris, the beginning of an indigenous American tradition of porcelain-making that has remained alive to the present day, as indicated by the many contemporary Americans working in this medium.

Ironically, it was during these last decades of the eighteenth century that the awesome reputation of European porcelain began to wane. Factories existed in nearly every country, and the sheer number of porcelain pieces that flooded the market reduced the special appeal of the material. No longer in the position of supplying the rare to the elite, factories entered a period of intense competition; to survive economically meant that new markets for porcelain had to be found, such as the rising middle classes, and production costs had to be cut to the minimum. Although porcelain had always been produced on a proto-industrial level, mass production was essential by the end of the century. Industrialization of the craft reduced the importance of individual artists and artisans, new techniques to speed up production were introduced, and processes such as transfer printing were adopted to assure rapidity and standardization. The glamour of porcelain during the eighteenth century had also been consistent with general aesthetic trends, and as the rococo style was replaced with neoclassicism, many designers looked toward the classical world for inspiration. Although much neoclassical porcelain was produced, the inherent nature of the material was inconsistent with neoclassical principles. Forms that echoed the ceramics of the ancient world were more logically produced in earthenware and stoneware than in porcelain, and great geniuses of design like Josiah Wedgwood altered the taste and climate for ceramics to the point that porcelain became a secondary interest.

It is somehow ironic that within the course of only one century, this prized substance emerged, flowered, and withered in the Western world. By the nineteenth century, many porcelain factories had resorted to revivals of earlier styles, and porcelain disappeared as a major force in design, although it continued to be commercially produced in great quantity. During the nineteenth century, however, this special material once again entered the realm of the individual artist/potter to become, in the present century, an important tributary of the mainstream of contemporary ceramics.

CHAPTER TWO

THE RISE OF THE CERAMICS INDUSTRY

CERAMIC PRODUCTION as an industry took root well before the beginning of Western manufacturing, which resulted from the Industrial Revolution in the eighteenth century. Multiple production on a relatively large scale, division of labor, and even specialized training had, in fact, emerged centuries before in China.

China

Industrial ceramic methods developed alongside trade, and in China they can be traced as far back as the T'ang dynasty (A.D. 618–906). During the dynasty's three-hundred-year span, kilns owned by individual craftsmen operated only when agricultural demands for laborers did not take precedence over those of pottery production. Later on, during the Sung dynasty (A.D. 960–1279), there was an organizational change in kilns: for the first time, they were owned and operated by families entirely concerned with the making of pottery. People trained in various aspects of the ceramic process now worked full time, supplanting the part-time field worker. The resulting division of labor meant that porcelain passed through as many as seventy pairs of hands during its transformation from raw clay to finished piece. It was at this point that ceramics as an industry was established, and with it, other new subsidiary industries developed to meet demands for materials, transport, and trade, thereby creating more jobs.

By the thirteenth and fourteenth centuries, the kilns of Northern Kiangsi province, particularly Ching-tê-Chên, were transformed from small individual potteries into industrial complexes. A larger market for porcelain, due to increasing foreign trade, made new demands on production methods and created a need for uniform production standards. The rapid expansion of porcelain trade forced a transfer of ownership from private hands to commercial syndicates that capitalized, expanded, and eventually owned the kilns—a scale of operation we do not usually associate with the Chinese ceramics housed in museums today. The commercial sophistication of this industry seems incongruous with the wares we revere as rare, treasured art objects.

In the individual potteries, skills were now specialized, broken down into a series of tasks that included the preparation of materials, shaping, decorating, firing, and shipping among others. Within these basic categories were many smaller tasks, for working methods had to be refined in order to standardize the wares for export. Changing techniques, coupled with greater production demands, eventually affected the quality of the finished objects. Although they were executed more proficiently, their aesthetic quality diminished. Furthermore, fulfilling the burgeoning demands for wares by the "foreign devils," as the Chinese viewed their Western consumers, always took second place to "official wares" commissioned for the imperial court. European trade was simply an economic necessity.

Vase, Meissen factory, Germany, about 1745, 9¼" (23.2 cm) high. This elaborate hard-paste vase is painted in the style of Watteau with polychrome scenes of lovers on a gold ground. Courtesy The Metropolitan Museum of Art, gift of Mrs. Charles Wrightsman, 1970.

Below
A Chinese potter is shown here decorating a large vase.

The Demand for Porcelain in Europe

Although the Chinese people's true aesthetic interest did not lie with the pieces they made for export, this does not mean these wares were of low quality. When porcelains began to make their way to Europe, they were celebrated for their whiteness and translucency. The superior quality of the material was recognized early by travelers to China such as Marco Polo. After seventeen years in China (from 1275 to 1292), he returned to Venice with some *porcellana*, the Italian word for cowrie shells, which the substance resembled. And so began a five-hundred-year quest for its formula.

At the end of the fifteenth century, porcelain trade with China began; during the next two hundred years it gradually escalated to a frenzied pace. Several factors contributed to this ever-growing demand for porcelain. The importation of tea from China, coffee from the Muslim world, and chocolate from Mexico created both new trade and new customs. Until this time, such beverages had not been available in Europe. Both tea and teacup were unheard of; the first cargoes of tea arrived in Amsterdam in 1606, on ships of the Oost Indische Companie. What is now thought of as "typically English," namely the ritual of teatime, in fact stems from the Japanese tea ceremony. The tea ceremony (Cha-no-yu) has religious overtones, and the English formal tea is bound in propriety, and though formally different, each has its own code of etiquette. In Europe proper, coffee was the favored drink, with chocolate being the special favorite of the Spanish.

Until the second half of the seventeenth century, pottery was not used in Europe except by the lowest classes. Made of earthenware and stoneware, these European ceramics fulfilled everyday needs and were the product of the local potter who lived in each village. Imported porcelain bore no resemblance to this folk pottery.

At this time the social status of the European potter was low, and it remained so even with the introduction of porcelain and the new appreciation of ceramic materials it engendered. Only those who modeled the porcelain and engraved the plates used for decorative transfers held an elevated social position, as shown in etchings of the time depicting their clean working environments and gentlemanly clothing. Bevis Hillier notes that "potting scarcely demanded classical erudition. It did not even demand complete sanity."[1] And Simeon Shaw retells the legend that "an idiot was employed to turn the potter's wheel."[2] The reason offered for the employ of a feeble-minded person was that it was to protect the secrets of porcelain's formula; nevertheless, meager intelligence certainly sufficed.

Dinnerware used by the upper classes at that time was made of gold, silver, or pewter until the new beverages created the demand for porcelain cups and services. In addition, the War of 1691 between France and Germany emptied the treasuries, and metals once used to make tableware were melted down for armaments, creating a real need for dishes of some other substance. Porcelain was an economical substitute for metal, and

Chinese Teabowl (part of a tea set attributed to Cornelius Pronk, 1691–1759), 2⅞″ (7.3 cm) diam. This is an example of eighteenth-century Chinese export ware, probably for the Dutch market, made of hard-paste porcelain with underglaze and enamel decoration. Courtesy The Metropolitan Museum of Art, Winfield Foundation Gift, 1961.

Right
This engraving depicts Böttger's ceramics laboratory at Dresden.

its relative ease of manufacture (once the clay formula had been perfected) made it an attractive alternative. Porcelain dinner services eventually replaced their metal counterparts. Although porcelain's inherent value was only that of processed earth, its perceived value skyrocketed until it equaled that of silver and gold. These historical wares are at least as highly valued today, and many Chinese porcelains are setting record auction prices. The importation of porcelain, and subsequently its manufacture in Europe, has had a long-lasting economic impact on the West.

Meissen: The Beginning of the European Porcelain Industry

When Europeans began trying to produce their own porcelain, the raw materials they found locally were a far cry from those of China. The clays that were made from them were neither as strong nor as plastic as Chinese porcelains, and they were difficult to work by hand. In order to duplicate the fluent forms of the East, Europeans needed to develop new manufacturing methods. Furthermore, Europe's ever-growing need for utilitarian wares in great quantities and at reasonable cost could be more effectively met by mass production. Slip casting was the most important of the many processes instituted during this century. In China, slip casting had existed as early as the T'ang dynasty, though it was practiced to a limited extent. There, the slip was poured into bisqued clay molds; it was not until much later, in Europe, that plaster of paris was used to make the molds.

European manufacture began in 1710, when Augustus the Strong established the Meissen factory. He did so not only to satisfy his own voracious appetite for porcelain (he has been called the bleeding bowl of China), but also to create a profitable industry for Saxony. (By 1733 there were 104 dealers in 32 towns selling the works of the factory.)

Johann Friederich Böttger, whose research led to the discovery of porcelain's formula, was held captive by Augustus in order to protect his coveted discovery. The secret of the formula did not last, however, and once it was no longer of prime importance (it reached Vienna in 1719, Venice in 1720), the technical and aesthetic accomplishments of artists such as Johann Gregor Höroldt (1696–1775) and Johann Joachim Kändler (1706–1775) were openly acknowledged. Kändler's remarkable abilities quickly eclipsed the achievements of the previous *modellmeister*, Höroldt, who had concentrated his creative energies on the perfection of glazes.

Kändler, perhaps more than any other artist, influenced the direction of Meissen porcelain. Trained as a sculptor, he joined the factory in 1731 (becoming *modellmeister* in 1733) and was responsible for creating the first distinctively European porcelain figure. Kändler was interested in the plastic nature of porcelain, and his forte was modeling large animals and figures for Augustus's Japanese Palace. Believing anything could be made of "china," Kändler precisely sculpted a pair of goats, a pelican swallowing a fish, an eagle, a turkey, a cock, a parrot, peacocks, sheep, leopards, and other animals—using real animals from Augustus's menagerie as live models—all life-size.[3] These animal forms not only exhibited Kändler's uncanny powers of observation, but they also placed immense demands on the porcelain medium. But Kändler not only was a genius at creating animal forms, he also made a set of dinnerware called the Swan Service, a tour de force

comprised of 2,200 pieces. Many pieces of this famous service are now scattered throughout European museums.

Specialized modelers and decorators were paid a salary as much as six times that of the other factory workers, who generally were shunned by society and the factory's management and were considered frivolous bohemians. They were also believed to be difficult to control, and rules were imposed upon them, including one forbidding marriage before the age of twenty-five. Some workers surreptitiously took "seconds" (imperfect, unpainted wares) from the factory and either decorated and sold them or else sold them to independent painters (*hausmalerei*). Of course, the factory did not approve, and occasionally someone was dismissed for the deed; but most often these practices were overlooked for fear that once a worker left the factory he might go to another country and reveal the secrets of Meissen manufacture. Indeed, this *was* a major factor in the spread of porcelain through Europe.

At first Meissen copied Chinese porcelains and German silver forms, but the factory quickly developed designs better suited to European taste, particularly that of the French, who were valued customers of Meissen before their own porcelain industry was fully developed. Not only decorative motifs but also the forms themselves were altered to suit European requirements. The slop basin and tea caddy, in particular, were popular European items that had no Chinese precedents.

Meissen continued to grow, its wares rising to ever higher levels of achievement, until 1756, when the Seven Years' War interrupted production and caused the factory great financial loss. Even though production was quickly resumed, the factory never again rose to its previous status. Prussia (which would eventually become Germany) was a war-torn country and had to concentrate on essentials; factory workers trained to produce porcelain luxuries sought work elsewhere. Many were forced to emigrate to other countries, and as a consequence, Meissen's technical and economic dominance ceased.

Expansion of the European Industry
During the Seven Years' War, numerous porcelain factories sprang up throughout Europe. By this time the Sèvres factory, in

France, had invented new forms and perfected glazes that began to capture the imagination of Europe. For the next twenty years, its rococo and, subsequently, neoclassical porcelains held sway over the continent.

England differed from the other European countries in the development of its porcelain industry. In England, ceramics was the business of local potters and middle-class entrepreneurs; it never received the royal patronage common throughout the continent. Therefore the English were late to develop porcelain, although in doing so, they accidentally discovered bone china. It was developed at the Bow Factory by Edward Heylyn and Thomas Frye in 1749, well after the man-

fact, the painting styles of the day inspired the paintings on ceramics). By the latter part of the century, porcelain factories had been established in virtually all Western countries.

Wedgwood and the Industrial Revolution

The establishment of manufacturing facilities marked the decline of royal and aristocratic patronage, and a new era began. The development of so many new machines in the nineteenth century altered the traditional roles of both artist and craftsman, while transforming the aesthetic content of items that previously had been crafted by hand.

The invention of the camera[4] meant the

Left
Mother Goat and Suckling Kid,
hard-paste porcelain from Meissen factory, Germany, about 1732, 19½″ x 25½″ x 13½″ (49.5 x 64.8 x 34.3 cm). Courtesy The Metropolitan Museum of Art, gift of Mrs. Jean Mauzé, 1962.

Pair of Plates, Chelsea factory, England, 1753–1756, 9″ (23 cm) diam. These soft-paste porcelain, deep-well plates are colorfully decorated with enamel. Courtesy Cooper-Hewitt Museum, Smithsonian Institution.

ufacture of "true" porcelain had already been established on the continent. More like soft-paste porcelain, bone china is fritted and less expensive to produce, though it lacks the durability of hard-paste porcelain. It was then, and still is, considered a "false" or "artificial" porcelain by some people. Its extreme translucency is due to the high percentage of bone ash used to lower the firing temperature. But because of its high bisque and low glaze firing, the clay and glaze do not fuse at the same high temperature, one of the requirements of "true" porcelain. The designations of "true" and "false" have unfortunate implications; the fact is, bone china and soft-paste porcelains have always shared the aesthetic of hard-paste porcelain. The shapes and decorations of bone china mimicked those of other porcelains. It soon became popular in England and was adopted as that country's version of porcelain.

The first half of the eighteenth century was the golden age of porcelain in Europe. The material and its techniques, forms, and aesthetic possibilities inspired artists to produce their greatest achievements. During this period the decorative arts as a whole were more vital than most academy paintings (in

role of the artist in reproducing and preserving history was supplanted by a mechanical device, thereby changing the artist's raison d'être. Because of this, by the 1860s, painting (with Manet) became more single-mindedly concerned with pictorial value and artistic interpretation, and so art for art's sake was born. For craftsmen involved with the practical arts something similar occurred. Mass-produced objects replaced hand-crafted ones. Though the aristocracy still demanded handmade objects, the machine met the demands of the greatest market, which was created by the growing middle class. Skills of the porcelain modeler and the furniture maker became unnecessary, as everyday needs could be satisfied so easily by the affordable, uniform, durable products of industry. Progress in the form of a "better" standard of living for a greater number of people—made possible by mass production—left many craftsmen unemployed or working in factories as opposed to producing their individual wares.

Descended from a long line of potters, Josiah Wedgwood (1730–1795) aspired to make ceramics more than a cottage industry. His genius lay in his organizational abilities. In the rigid system of specialization he established in his factory, each person became responsible for a single aspect of production: one man threw, another trimmed, another made handles, and so on throughout the ceramic process. In spite of the workers' reluctance to acclimate to division of labor, their resistance did not withstand it. "It was not then obvious that men would not willingly give up their independence," writes Anthony Burton of Wedgwood's thrust toward mechanization. "They worked long hours, [and] the way in which those hours were spent was of great significance. The old worker had his range of skills to use—the new was offered only greater monotony in the name of efficiency that brought very little benefit to the individual's own life."[5] Wedgwood constantly pushed toward greater accuracy and more stringent standards, while overlooking the dehumanizing aspects of mechanization. As he himself stated, his goal was to "make such machines of men as cannot err."[6] Wedgwood utilized new methods, such as transfer printing onto ceramics, and invented instruments such as the pyrometer (which measures kiln temperatures) to make his operation more efficient. He also systematically refined his clay bodies and glazes, the potter's wheel, and the kiln. He employed tools such as the lathe for refining ceramic forms and the scale for weighing clay, all in order to perfect and standardize his products.

The individual and the machine were at odds, but from industry's vantage point, the machine represented the apex of cultural progress and forward thinking. The notion of "progress" was the very thing that inspired the innovative ceramic methods of Wedgwood. He also respected the humanities, however, and he often attended the meetings of an intellectual group of about a dozen men known as the Lunar Society (so called because they met on the full moon, when nighttime travel was easier and safer). The society's members included James Watt, inventor of the steam engine, Erasmus Darwin (grandfather of Charles Darwin), Matthew Boulton, and Dr. William Withering, to name a few.

Most important of Wedgwood's accomplishments was the creation of a market for porcelain that had not previously existed. He did so by making his famous Queen's ware accessible to the masses. A version of creamware, it symbolized eighteenth-century progress, as it was of good quality, reasonable in cost, and could be produced in quantity. Because Wedgwood believed ancient Greek pottery had been the highest expression of artistic genius, he determined to raise the pottery of his own day to the standard he saw embodied in the Greek urn. Unfortunately, to achieve this end he merely copied classical

Left
Portland Vase, Wedgwood factory, England. This nineteenth-century blue-and-white jasper vase is a copy of a Roman glass vase and depicts Peleus and Thetis on Mount Pelion. Courtesy The Metropolitan Museum of Art, gift of Ged Frye, 1908.

Right
Vellum Vase with Wisteria Blossoms designed by Carl Schmidt for Rookwood Pottery, Cincinnati, Ohio, 1915, 12½" (31.7 cm) high. This vase is representative of the work that emerged from Rookwood Pottery during the Art Pottery movement in America. Courtesy Jordan-Volpe Gallery, New York. Photo: Scott Hyde.

Below
This nineteenth-century engraving illustrates a factory worker shaping plates with a jigger.

forms. Though a great commercial success, his neoclassical vases, busts, cameos, and other wares were sterile and lifeless. Wedgwood was truly a product of his time—a burgeoning industrialist with the intelligence to know, as Herbert Read states, that "art pays."[7]

But as Michael McTwigan discerned, Wedgwood's aesthetic "legacy for today's ceramic artist [is] both inescapable and negligible."[8] His ceramics were made for a middle-class audience seeking well-behaved art that was always in Good Taste, and this kind of taste is still with us.

As the eighteenth century ended, the Industrial Revolution was rolling ahead at full speed. Automation entered every realm of production, stifling the development of new styles in favor of those distilled largely from ancient and Renaissance sources. By this time both process and design had been taken completely from the hands of the craftsman and artist. Design became theoretical and was created on the drawing board. What was drawn for machine production, though, did not reflect the new set of tools industry provided. These works lacked originality and spirit, which is often the case when previous styles are revived and handmade products are expediently duplicated by machine. Such processes marked a decline in design standards, as was widely recognized at the Greek Exhibition of 1851. The stage was set for revolt. The neoclassical style that dominated the exhibition drove home "the fallaciousness of that Mechanical Fallacy that to Know was better than to Feel, that the mission of modern leadership lay more in improved mechanization than in a search for an aesthetic principle."[9]

The Arts and Crafts Movements
In England, when the Industrial Revolution took the hand from handcraft and dehumanized the quality of life, the result was social revolution. The philosophical underpinnings of this revolt, which would come to be known as the English Arts and Crafts Movement, were first formulated by the influential theorist and art critic John Ruskin (1819–1900), who could not accept the machine as compatible with art. His writings on industrialization were pungent and direct: "It is not, truly speaking, the labour that is divided; but the men—divided into mere segments of men—broken into small fragments and crumbs of life; so that all the little piece of intelligence that is left in a man is not enough to make a pin, or a nail, but exhausts itself in making the point of a pin, or the head of a nail."[10]

A member of the Romantic School, he viewed the artist as an inspired prophet and teacher producing works of art with high moral content. Ruskin upheld an ideal Gothic attitude in which a work's nobility exists in its being less than perfect. He was clearly opposed to industrial standardization. He added to the worship of beauty a concern for social, economic, and political issues. In his own words: "We are not sent into this world to do anything to which we cannot put our hearts. . . . [H]e who would form the creations of his own mind by any other instrument than his own hand, would also, if he might, give grinding organs to Heaven's angels, to make their music easier. . . . [S]ince our life must be at best a vapor that appears for a little time and then vanishes away, let it at least appear as a cloud in the height of Heaven, not as the thick darkness that broods over the blast of the Furnace, and rolling of the Wheel.[11]

In addition to being a brilliant theorist, Ruskin was an art critic who championed the Pre-Raphaelite Brotherhood (1848–1855), a group of painters and poets stylistically opposed to the academic painting of the day and also involved with designing decorative objects. At first they made the objects to use as props for their own paintings because they considered machine-made furniture and accessories morally tainted. They believed in the handmade object and in exercising their creative talents within an environment of cooperative living.

Ruskin was a philosopher, a visionary who influenced social thought, design, and architecture. But it is his disciple William Morris who is credited with having started the English Arts and Crafts Movement based on Ruskin's doctrine. Committing himself to restore dignity to craft, which under industrialization had become merely undignified labor, he studied the works and writings of previous periods in history that came closer to his ideals. This, as well as his own marriage—when he could find no manufactured furniture good enough to use in his own home—inspired Morris's impulse to create decorative household wares. By 1861 he had formed Morris, Faulkner and Co., makers of domestic furnishings, paintings, and decorative objects. Other Pre-Raphaelites joined with Morris in designing practical household objects. Though never an accomplished painter, Morris excelled in designing wallpaper and furniture, notably the Morris chair. Equal to his success as a designer were his achievements as poet, lecturer on art and politics, and critic of medieval crafts.

Morris was not a scholar like his predecessor Ruskin. Having no patience for language, he merely aimed to be heard, and his last coherent words were: "I want to get the mumbo-jumbo out of the world."[12] His energies were so great that when he died at the age of sixty-two, his doctor noted the cause of death as simply "being William Morris, and doing more than any ten men."[13]

Morris's most important achievement was his plea for decorative artists to concern themselves with national character and the quality of life. "[The artists'] endeavours were directed, ultimately, towards a social end, the establishment of a society in which all men would enjoy the freedom to be creative. Their concern, therefore, was not focused exclusively on end-products but on the society that shaped them, the men who designed and made them and on the people who bought them."[14] Or, as it was aptly stated by C. R. Ashbee in 1908: "The Arts and Crafts Movement means standards, whether of work or life; the protection of standards, whether in the product or the producer, and it means that these things must be taken together."[15] The machine was clearly the enemy. The "gush of power that spurted from the factory boiler without a stop"[16] was raping nature, and members of the movement saw their own intellectual and emotional resources being abused.

The movement was an idealistic one which professed theories abounding with wholesome intentions. Unfortunately, it took the form of a mass temper tantrum characterized by fear of change. The movement retarded the marriage between the ceramist and industry, which could have been fortuitous for both. Instead, lack of communication between the two caused the aesthetic quality of machine-made objects to suffer. Well into the 1950s, English industrial design ranked lowest in Europe, lagging far behind that of Germany, Scandinavia, and Italy.

The movement's effect on industry notwithstanding, Ruskin, Morris, Stickley, and others established the integrity of handmade work and its importance to the quality of life. In the words of William Morris, the decorative arts "are part of a great system invented for the expression of a man's delight in beauty: all peoples and times have used them; they have been the joy of free nations and the solace of oppressed nations. . . they are the sweetness of human labor, both to the handicraftsman, whose life is spent working them, and to people in general who are influenced by the sight of them at every turn of the day's work: they make our toil happy, our rest fruitful."[17] Without this cry of despair from those committed to restoring what they considered a better existence for all, the craftsman might have forever been lost to the machine. And though the Arts and Crafts Movement was only minimally successful in its own time, it did set an example for modern ceramists participating in the crafts re-

Staircase, Tassle House by Victor
Horta, 1893, Brussels, Belgium.
This is a superb example of Art
Nouveau ornamentation. Courtesy
The Museum of Modern Art.

vival of the late twentieth century which attracted a new generation with the same romantic ideals.

The Arts and Crafts Movement in America in the nineteenth century, however, did not really share the same premises as its British namesake. The aesthetic of American Art Pottery was closer to that of Art Nouveau. The American movement was a gentler reaction to burgeoning industry and mass-produced commercial wares, and it has had a subtle, lasting meaning for women as china painters and for the twentieth-century artist-potter.

Among the art potteries started in America at that time, the most prominent was Rookwood Pottery of Cincinnati, Ohio. Started by Mary Louise McLaughlin, of a prominent Cincinnati family, Rookwood prided itself on freedom of artistic expression, although it accepted the fashionable influences of Europe and Japan. Rookwood artists concentrated on the ornamentation of their one-of-a-kind vessels, with great effort devoted to glaze chemistry and the systematic exploration of unusual effects. Decoration consisted largely of flora and fauna interpreted with an Asian flavor. Ironically, in order to survive, Rookwood eventually became a commercial pottery. By 1920 the Art Pottery movement had virtually come to an end in America, overcome by industrial competition and a change in taste.

Art Nouveau

Like Ruskin, William Morris looked to Gothic art as the truest and best expression of beauty. His own designs, however—for wallpaper or book illustrations, for example—possessed an organic spirit akin to Art Nouveau. Proponents of Art Nouveau based their art on imagination and what they perceived as visions of universal happiness and fancy. Art Nouveau's stylistic tenets were elegance, beauty, and decorativeness. Many artists of the Pre-Raphaelite era—including Dante Gabriel Rossetti and John Everett Millais—were critical of Art Nouveau and likened it to a strange disease. Primarily an ornamental style, Art Nouveau achieved its greatest success in architecture, the applied arts, graphics, and illustration. Curiously, in spite of its unabashed decorativeness, Art Nouveau (which was called Jugendstil in Northern Europe) influenced the early practitioners of modern functional design and architecture, such as the Belgian Henry Van de Velde[18] (1863–1957). In Van de Velde's hands Jugendstil combined Art Nouveau's sinuous, plantlike motifs with geometric designs as decoration on spare, functional forms. Van de Velde's influence was most strongly felt in the 1890s, in Germany, where he toured from 1900 to 1901 to spread his design philosophy. But soon after, he began to refute all Art Nouveau principles in favor of functionalism, a theory based on strict functional tenets. He then "proclaimed the engineer as the true architect of our times, and announced that the new materials developed by modern science, such as steel, reinforced concrete, aluminum and linoleum, called for a new type of logical structure."[19]

Simultaneous with Van de Velde's proclamation, Viennese architect Adolf Loos (1870-1933) banished all ornamentation from his buildings. In America, a country characterized by technical efficiency, Louis Sullivan (1856-1924) made a declaration that would become the catch-phrase for the first three quarters of the twentieth century: "Form should follow function." His own belief notwithstanding, Sullivan, like Van de Velde, did not always practice what he preached. While expounding the virtues of rationalism and functionalism in design, he too applied sinuous, organic ornamentation to his buildings.

In 1907, German architect Hermann Muthesius (1861-1927) furthered modern design by founding the Deutscher Werkbund. Originally a follower of William Morris, he sought a synthesis between machine style and the ideals of the Arts and Crafts Movement. He hoped to create a climate for the production of quality objects in a world dominated by mass production and division of labor. His ideal was not achieved by the romantic individualists of the Werkbund, however, and the spirit of art was not yet integrated, either aesthetically or physically, with engineering.

The Bauhaus

It was Walter Gropius (1883-1969), the youngest member of the Werkbund, who finally effected a coalescence of the arts, craftsmanship, and technology. In order to combine these into an organic whole, Gropius founded the Bauhaus (1919-1933), a school for training the new practitioners. Its unique method was to educate each student in the two vital aspects of all creative processes—art and craft—in order to tune the mind and the hand as inseparable tools. Gropius brought his ideals into reality: "Modern artists, familiar with science and economics, began to unite creative imagination with a practical knowledge of craftsmanship, and thus to develop a new sense of functional design."[20] The Weimar Bauhaus proclaimed that "art is not a profession. There is no essential difference between the artist and craftsman. The artist is an exalted craftsman. In rare moments of inspiration, moments beyond his will, the grace of

heaven may cause his work to blossom into art. But proficiency in his craft is essential to every artist. Therein lies the source of creative imagination. Let us create a new guild of craftsmen, without the class distinctions which raise an arrogant border between craftsman and artist."[21] With one major exception—its openly embracing the machine as an accepted vehicle for creativity—the Bauhaus's concepts for the new century still reverberated with the ideals of Ruskin and Morris.

Gropius's words were prophetic. In his ideals lay the foundation for today's abiding relationship between the artist and industry. Because porcelain has always been an object of commerce, it offers a long historical legacy for the relationship between artist and industry—an endowment that provides both with not only a wealth of technical information but also a wide range of aesthetic possibilities.

Rosenthal

Rosenthal of Selb, West Germany, is one contemporary firm whose dedication to collaboration with artists is extensive. While Rosenthal's philosophy grew from the Bauhaus heritage, it differs from the Bauhaus's strict idea of only one possible design solution for a particular functional form. Instead, Rosenthal believes there are numerous contemporary forms that are not only functional but also can express diverse and personal aesthetic sensibilities while maintaining high standards of design.

When Philip Rosenthal, Jr., inherited the company from his father, it was a conservative producer of traditional wares. In 1950, under his direction, Rosenthal set out to create a new concept in porcelain and to raise the aesthetic standards for everyday objects. Since then Rosenthal has become one of the most advanced companies of its time, producing numerous lines of outstanding dinnerware and decorative objects.

Unlike the first German porcelains made in the eighteenth century at Meissen, which concentrated on surface decoration, Rosenthal's products fuse form, function, and decoration. The company's image has evolved through the efforts of a group of international artists, who are encouraged to abide by no rules, to follow no recognized styles, but rather to strive for complete originality and diversity: "The guiding principle is—and always has been—the recognition that over the centuries, the only creative endeavour of continuing value is that which truly reflects the spirit of its own age," as Rosenthal himself has succinctly put it. Each new design is first submitted to a panel of historians, curators, artists, and instructors from museums

Cubic Condiment Set designed by M. Mori for Hakusan-Toki, Japan, 3½''; 3''; 3'' (8.2; 7.6; 7.6 cm) high. This set is cast porcelain with a cobalt blue underglaze.

Plate from *The Magic Flute* dinnerware designed by Bjorn Wiinblad for Rosenthal Studio Line. Scenes from the Mozart opera are represented in relief on alternating matte and glossy surfaces. Excerpts from the arias are reproduced in gold on the undersurfaces of the plates. Courtesy Rosenthal.

and educational institutions for their critical assessment before being manufactured.

Rosenthal does not make distinctions between *artist, craftsman,* or *designer,* words which, as Richard Latham has noted, all translate into a single word—*Kunst*—in German. Latham is an American who, along with Philip Rosenthal, formulated the studio concept at Rosenthal in the 1950s. Aside from acting as an initial proponent of the concept and as a consultant to the firm, he has designed a broad range of forms. Among these are *E Form,* Rosenthal's first "new" form, which is still in use as hotel ware, cookware, glassware, and silverware.

The "Gropius Service," one of the designs to emerge from Rosenthal's studio line, was designed in 1968 by Walter Gropius and Louis A. McMillan. All elements are based first on functional considerations, in an attempt to fuse the practical and the aesthetic—an ideal pursued throughout Rosenthal's line.

Bjorn Wiinblad, painter, illustrator, stage-set designer, and ceramist from Denmark, began collaborating with Rosenthal in 1957. One of the firm's major designers, he moves easily from one material to another, whether it be porcelain, glass, or silver. Through carving or painting, he portrays onion-headed fairy-tale characters (his distinctive trademark) on clean, curvacious forms that reflect characteristic Danish modern design.

A newer member of the Rosenthal design team is Timo Sarpaneva of Finland. Sarpaneva's design talents are diverse, ranging from textiles to graphics to package design. He worked four years in developing "Suomi," a line of dinnerware combining porcelain and metal. The forms are simultaneously structural and sculptural, with clean lines and soft contours. Sarpaneva's design was awarded the Italian Republic's Presidential Gold Medal, the highest honor given for excellence of design for manufactured porcelain forms.

Artists with no primary connection to ceramics have also collaborated with the Rosenthal company. Some have designed surface treatments for already existing forms, while others have created limited-edition reliefs and plates. More than thirty artists, including Henry Moore, Victor Vasarely, Salvador Dali, Jean Cocteau, and Niki de Saint Phalle, have made editions ranging from 6 to 5,000 pieces.

Franciscan (Interpace)

Collaboration between artist and industry took place on a smaller scale in Los Angeles at Franciscan (a division of Interpace) during the 1960s and '70s. Craft artists were hired by this tile and dinnerware manufacturer as an outgrowth of a program set up between Chouinard School of Art (now defunct) and Franciscan. Students were given an opportunity to work in the factory, where they not only designed but learned about factory methods and materials as well. Some students were later hired by Franciscan as designers, for both production items and special projects such as a mural commissioned by and made for Disneyland in 1967. Unfortunately, this arrangement was not a lasting one, and in 1980 the firm was bought by Wedgwood to serve as a manufacturing facility for its American production (40 percent of Wedgwood's market is in the United States).

Arabia

The relationship of artist-potters to industry in Scandinavia is exemplified by Arabia, a company based in Helsinki, Finland. Intermittently since the 1940s, Arabia has offered artists a salary, private studios, and materials. While working in the factory the artists may freely use its facilities for their own experimentation; objects made there are owned by Arabia and sold under the artist's name; occasionally a design will be mass-produced, at which time the artist receives a commission on sales.

Scandinavia's continuous relationship between artist and industry, as provided by factories like Arabia, has allowed modern design to evolve without the necessity for delving into historical styles that is so prevalent in European, Japanese, English, and American factories. Implicit in Scandinavia's modern design aesthetic of clean form and functionalism is a breakdown of the distinction between formal and kitchen wares for special and everyday occasions respectively. When functional versatility is emphasized, a single vessel may suffice for cooking, storing, and serving food—without sacrificing pleasing design. Such an aesthetic reflects the artist-potter's influence. It is also an indication of our changing attitudes toward the ritual of eating. Though we still find a place for formal dining in our lives, today eating customs have for the most part been democratized, and distinctions between formal and informal occasions have blurred. The dining room is no longer a focal point in the home; in fact, its diminished importance is reflected in the very word *dinette,* which has replaced the dining room in some newer, smaller homes and apartments of the late twentieth century. The bar or counter top that now functions as today's groaning board is usually set with "everyday china," accumulated as gifts or bought with the groceries at the neighborhood supermarket, while the "good china" made of porcelain is saved for a few special occasions.

Gropius Service designed by Walter Gropius, 1969, for Rosenthal Studio Line. The fusion of practicality and aesthetics typical of Rosenthal is clearly seen in this set. Courtesy Rosenthal.

Suomi designed by Timo Sarpaneva for Rosenthal Studio Line. This design embodies the simple forms and clean lines for which Rosenthal is known. Courtesy Rosenthal.

Cunard Teaset by Foley, Liverpool, England, for the Cunard Steamship Co. Ltd. These bone china pieces are cast with overglaze decoration added. Photo: Michael McTwigan.

Assorted Chemical Porcelains produced by Coors Porcelain Works, Golden, Colorado. These pieces illustrate the beauty and clean design possible in chemical wares. Courtesy Coors Porcelain Works.

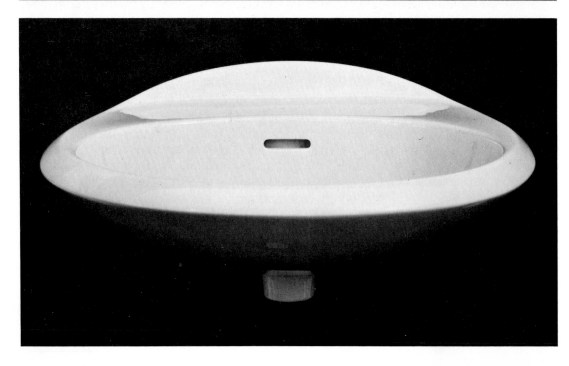

Washbowl designed by Scott Douglas for Ideal Standard, Italy, 1963, 10¼'' (27.2 cm) high. This is a good example of the high aesthetic standards of some contemporary porcelain sanitary ware. Collection The Museum of Modern Art.

Technological Porcelain

The manufacture of porcelain is not restricted to the decorative arts but has far-reaching applications. Only half of Rosenthal's production today is devoted to dinnerware. The firm's other involvements are in the production of porcelain for use in microelectronics and as computer memories and chemical ceramics. Major industries exist that are concerned not with porcelain's creative potential, but with its scientific and technological uses. These products—such as those used for dental, laboratory, and heat-resistant purposes—are known in the industry as *fine ceramics*, which are defined as ceramic substances with a controlled structure, whether glazed or unglazed.

One very significant industry to benefit from Böttger's discovery at Meissen is dentistry. The use of porcelain in dentistry was first attempted by the French in 1851. Although early dental porcelains used for artificial teeth were of an inferior quality, they marked the beginning of an entirely new industry. Porcelain is ideal as a restorative material, for it not only closely resembles the natural tooth but is equal to the demands of stress. Porcelain can mock the tooth's hardness, natural translucency, and subtle variations in color; beyond this, the nonconductivity of porcelain tends to insure against shocks from temperature changes. Because it is unaffected by acid conditions, dental porcelain maintains its original surface and quality indefinitely.

Chemical porcelains (those used in a laboratory) developed in eighteenth-century Germany simultaneously with porcelain dinnerware and figures. "Chemical porcelain ware is impermeable, compact, of vitreous fracture, smooth, and cannot be scratched by steel. Chemically, it is a mixture of various compound silicates. The final product must meet rigid dimensional tolerances, year after year."[22] Chemical porcelain has always been indispensable in the laboratory, since it is the most chemical- and heat-resistant material known. In the United States, porcelains from Berlin were considered the standard of quality until the embargo of World War I prevented the entry of German products into this country. Japanese chemical porcelains soon flooded the market but were of inferior quality, and so wartime conditions forced Americans to develop their own chemical porcelains to meet the necessary high standards. Adolph Coors, a German immigrant to the United States, indirectly began manufacturing laboratory porcelain when he founded a brewery. To furnish bottles for the brewery, he had to establish his own factory until outside sources became more economical. Almost twenty years later (1910), the previous bottle manufactory was redesigned to produce ovenware, dinnerware, and the then-popular art pottery. World War I placed growing demands on the Coors pottery to supply chemical porcelains, which the company has been producing ever since. The forms of these wares—chemical trays, dishes, and beakers—are aesthetically clean, even beautiful and, in fact, are included in the design collection of the Museum of Modern Art in New York. Though the laboratory is an area where function is certainly primary, Coors is proof that design need not be sacrificed for function.

Porcelain's resistance and nonconductivity make it extremely useful in many other fields. It is important as an insulating material for numerous types of electrical sockets, spark plugs, and other electrical parts. The nose cones of spacecraft are coated with a head shield of what is referred to by the industry as "near-porcelain." Upon reentering the earth's atmosphere, the shields are meant to burn off at a controlled rate, shedding the intense heat as the ship approaches the earth. Other near-porcelain materials are being developed as heat-resistant coverings for space shuttles. Aeronautic ceramic materials are fired to extremely high temperatures, and they still function and hold their shape at 2300°F, a temperature at which the porcelain known to studio ceramists is molten. Other highly resistant porcelains are used to line glass and steel melting tanks or used as heat exchangers in turbine engines. Aside from electrical outlets and such, porcelain is familiar to most people in their everyday lives. Plumbingware, now present in virtually every kitchen and bathroom, was developed at the time of the Industrial Revolution. Typhoid and other diseases resulting from poor sanitation were prevalent then, and for the first time products concerned with sanitation and health were produced. The paper industry uses porcelain (in the form of alum) as a coating and sizing substance; it is used in paint as a filler; and the cosmetics industry uses various clays, including porcelain—"rare earth"[23] and Porcelana[24] to name two—in beauty products. In many unexpected forms, porcelain's functional value extends into the world at large.

THE QUALITIES

Three Bottles by Elsa Rady, 1976, 8'' x 4''; 9'' x 4''; 8'' x 5½'' (20.3 x 10.2; 22.9 x 10.2; 3 x 14 cm). A spider-web effect is created by a white crackle glaze on these wheel-thrown forms. Photo: Bob Lopez.

CHAPTER THREE

THE NATURE OF PORCELAIN

THE WORD *porcelain* evokes a wealth of associations that both include and transcend its physical characteristics. Taking a variety of forms throughout history—dinnerware, figurines, urns, vases, curios, industrial products, handmade art objects—porcelain has profoundly influenced commerce, art, politics, and culture itself. This book explores porcelain's expanding definitions through the work being made by artists today. It is easier to understand the blurring of traditional boundaries, both material and aesthetic, if we explore the special qualities that emanate from porcelain's physical properties.

Porcelain is a dense, white, vitreous, and at times translucent ceramic material. True porcelain was developed in China from porcelaneous stoneware clay during the Sung dynasty (A.D. 960–1279). Unlike other clays, porcelain is never found in nature but is made up of a blend of materials. Chinese porcelain in particular was a combination of two local ingredients: kaolin and petuntse. W. B. Honey, the British historian, defines the original Chinese porcelain as a variety of translucent, vitrified stoneware made from a white-burning refractory clay produced by the decay of a feldspar called kaolin, meaning "high on the ridge," the location where it was found.[1] "This is fired into porcelain with the help of a less-decayed, fusible form of the same feldspathic rock, called *pai-ṭun-tzŭ* (or petunse in the French eighteenth-century equivalent), meaning 'little white blocks,' from the form in which it was sent to the pot-

ter after being pulverized and refined from the district where it was found."[2] During firing "petunse fuses to form a glassy cement holding together the particles of relatively unfusible kaolin; the Chinese speak of the two ingredients as the 'bones and flesh' of the ware."[3] Chinese porcelain must have been a highly plastic clay, for wheel-thrown forms were often quite large (three to four feet tall). These wares, which at times were made in multiple parts, were once-fired, and because they were formed paper-thin and apparently transported great distances to kiln sites, the clay must have been extremely strong in both its wet and dry states.

Petuntse was never found outside of China, and so when the Europeans formulated it themselves, they combined kaolin with silica (flint) and feldspar. These three ingredients have remained the essential components of porcelain to the present day. Kaolin, silica, and feldspar translate into clay, glass, and flux (which enables them to melt and fuse) respectively. The ideal porcelain clay body is workable, high in silica, and free from impurities. Unlike stoneware, porcelain is a homogeneous type of clay—its particles are relatively similar in size. This causes porcelain to dry out quickly, which in turn causes more stress in the clay during the forming process. But because porcelain is so homogeneous and generally does not contain heavy particles of grog and sand, it is capable of more complete fusion. Traditionally porcelain is fired at a high temperature of at least 1300°C (2372°F).

Twenty-Four-Cell Compression Sphere by Bradley R. Miller, 1980, 6½'' (16.5 cm) diam. Miller's undulant forms made of unglazed porcelain are the ultimate foil for light and shadow.

Kaolin

China clays, or kaolins, are the purest natural clays. Being the actual clay within porcelain, they are white in color and highly refractory, that is, resistant to the extreme temperatures to which porcelain is fired. Kaolins have always been the aristocrats of clays. They are primary or residual clays, which means they are found where they are formed and are thus relatively free from impurities. Most other clays are secondary, or sedimentary, clays that have been removed from their site of origin through the forces of nature and deposited elsewhere, picking up impurities along the way. Kaolins, low in impurities, are also unfortunately low in workability. This shortcoming can be counteracted by adding other clays, however. Often a small percentage of bentonite, a highly plastic clay with very fine particles, may be added to the body. Ball clays, which also have small particles, increase workability and plasticity, as well as dry strength. High in iron content, they are particularly useful where absolute whiteness is not crucial.

Silica

Silica, or flint, which turns to glass in firing, is the substance that causes both clay body and glaze to vitrify. It is found not only in pure form but is also contained within feldspars and kaolins. Considerable amounts of silica fortify the porcelain clay so that it can withstand extreme temperatures while becoming glassy and translucent. Unlike earthenware and stoneware, which have as little as 5 percent silica in their compositions, porcelain usually contains as much as 20 to 35 percent.

It is silica that gives porcelain its glowing, light-receptive quality. However, silica also causes problems during firing, when the chemical changes that it undergoes are responsible for a high percentage of loss due to stress. During silica inversion, silica's high rate of expansion and contraction puts the clay through "thermal shock." Porcelain, being dense, does not easily absorb the marked and sudden changes in size that silica undergoes; cracking is likely to occur as a result.

Feldspar

Because the clay and the glass substances in a clay body fuse at such extremely high temperatures, fluxing materials are used to lower the melting temperatures. Most suitable are feldspars, which are slow and even in fluxing, create less distortion in the temperature range at which porcelain is fired, and are more reliable than substances with narrower melting ranges. Soda and potash feldspars are appropriate, as are related substances used interchangeably such as neph-

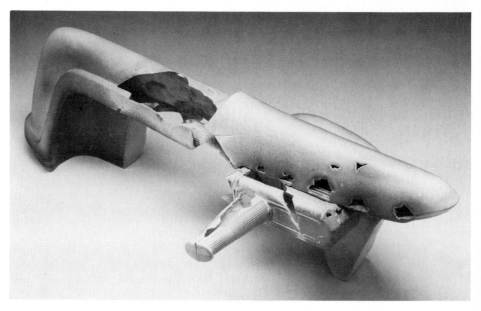

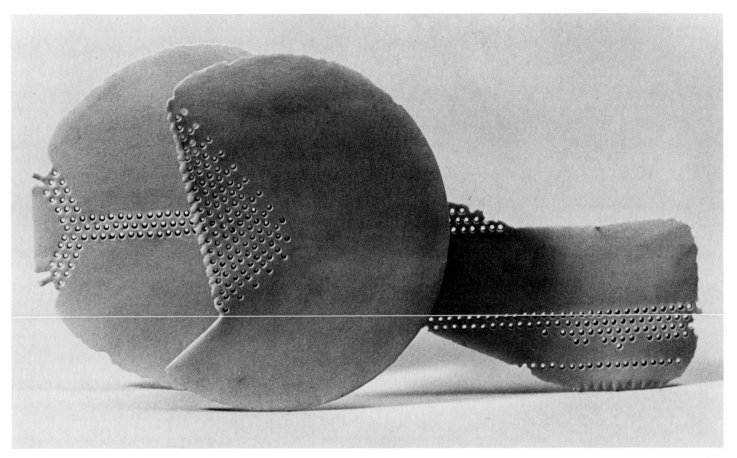

eline syenite and cornwall stone. Feldspars act as catalysts for the fluxing action,
which creates the desirable vitrification in
porcelain clay bodies.

When the feldspar or flux is increased,
translucency is heightened, though warpage
in the clay form is also more likely to occur.
Because kaolin opacifies the clay body, it can
also be said that the less kaolin present, the
higher the degree of translucency. But kaolin
acts as a plasticizer; by reducing its proportion in the clay body, the ceramist gains
translucency but loses workability. By manipulating these ingredients and weighing
their benefits and disadvantages, however, it
is possible to achieve a desirable clay body.

Because porcelain is comprised of just a
few ingredients—various types of kaolins, si-
licas, and feldspars—its characteristics are
considerably altered by making only slight
changes in their proportions—deviations that
would not affect clays with a greater number
of constituents.

Porcelain's Special Qualities

Porcelain's unique qualities—its whiteness,
translucency, fluidity, and smooth surface—
attract ceramists and connoisseurs alike.
Each of these characteristics is progressive,
that is, it is capable of being present to varying degrees. Whether a given quality is

heightened or diminished in a particular
piece depends greatly on what the ceramist
chooses to emphasize through manipulation
of the clay formula, the forming process,
glazing, and firing. Porcelain's qualities are
present to varying degrees during the different stages of creating a piece, changing as the
clay is transformed from its wet state to the
highly vitrified final work. Consequently,
maker and viewer are likely to have different
perceptions of porcelain that arise from their
involvement with process and product.

Whiteness is a quality that is central to porcelain's essence, and it is present from start to
finish, from the plastic to fired states. Translucency may be of primary importance to a
ceramist's aesthetic intentions, but it is evident only after the clay has been transformed
by heat in the firing process. Porcelain's sensuous fluidity when wet is experienced primarily by the ceramist who works with it, but
it also can be expressed visually through line
and form. Porcelain's unique surface, while
certainly of importance to the ceramist, is the
quality most readily appreciated in the finished work, and it is this aspect of the medium that draws such a large audience. An
exploration of these qualities, as expressed
in the varied work illustrated throughout this
book, bears testimony to the richness of porcelain's aesthetic potential.

CHAPTER FOUR

WHITENESS

BECAUSE VIRTUALLY all connoisseurs of porcelain—whether they are makers or viewers—are drawn to porcelain because of its color, it is appropriate to explore this quality first. Whiteness is so basic to porcelain that when some ceramists are asked for a contemporary definition, they explain it in terms of color alone—simply as white clay.

Although there is a variety of white materials with which an artist may choose to work—plaster, stone, bone, and white earthenware and stoneware among them—none has the particular whiteness of porcelain. Whether fully vitrified or underfired, glazed or unglazed, its special whiteness comes from the blend of relatively pure materials that chemically combine and are fixed in firing.

The singularity of porcelain's whiteness is attested to by the fact that ceramists past and present have often left the clay body unadorned or have covered it only with a clear glaze. Porcelain's whiteness, however, has a unique luminosity that is evident even when covered by a dark, opaque glaze such as temmoku (which is nearly black at times). This is best understood by comparing two pieces glazed alike, one of porcelain and one of earth-colored stoneware. The piece made from white porcelain will have a brilliant quality, while the other will be dull by comparison. This distinctive luster derives not only from porcelain's color but also from the fusion of clay and glaze, which brings this color closer to the surface.

Blanc de Chine

Before the development of true porcelain, it was not uncommon for the Chinese to cover ceramic surfaces with a white slip. Although this technique produced the desired white color, it was merely a surface coating that put an intermediate layer between clay and glaze, masking the clay's natural color. The creation of Te'hua wares (called *blanc de chine* by the French) marked Chinese porcelain's zenith between A.D. 1650 and 1725. Numerous vessels and objects for the writing table were made of *blanc de chine*, but the most striking and important objects were some figurative pieces[1] that relied solely on exquisite modeling and the satiny surface of the clear-glazed material for their visual impact. Although actually hollow, the figures appeared solid and massive. *Blanc de chine* wares particularly emphasized form, and in their time they were regarded as masterpieces of the modeler's art.

Blanc de chine also caught the eye of European royal patrons and aristocratic collectors and ultimately became the prime model for the development and definition of porcelain in Europe. Augustus the Strong's extensive collection of *blanc de chine* wares, housed in his Japanese Palace, numbered well over a thousand pieces. From his own potters, Augustus demanded a porcelain that was equally fine-grained, dense, vitreous, and of the same luminous whiteness. Although porcelain is by definition white to one degree or another, eighteenth-century Europeans focused undue attention on perfecting this as-

Goddess of Mercy Kuan Yin with Child, Fukien, China, Ch'ing dynasty, K'ang Hsi period, 1662–1722, 11¾″ (30 cm) high. The exquisite modeling and satiny surface of this goddess figure reveal the qualities for which *blanc de chine* was so admired. Courtesy Cooper-Hewitt Museum, Smithsonian Institution.

pect of the material. They were intolerant of the color impurities that added richness to many of the Chinese wares. The refined white objects brought to Europe from China captivated them, for their native ceramics were earthy, peasant pottery vessels made primarily for storage and the kitchen. This emphasis on the "ideal" qualities of Chinese porcelain, a dominant influence in the West for some time, accounts for the development of a stark white clay body in Europe. Böttger's original porcelain body developed at Meissen was considered imperfect because it had a yellowish cast.

The Qualities of Whiteness

Although the Europeans strove toward an austere white in their porcelain, variations still exist in both the tone and quality of the color white. Most people think of white as a neutral color or even as a non-color. On the contrary: as Winkelmann, the eighteenth-century art historian, pointed out, white is not the absence of color, but the blending of all colors of the spectrum. Furthermore, white can take on coolness or warmth, dullness or brightness, relative to its context.

White porcelain can have a great deal of subtle color, which it takes not only from its surroundings, but also from its constituents. The color of a particular porcelain is determined by the amount of iron or other minerals present in the clay and by the type of firing process to which it is subjected. Ball clay, added to porcelain to enhance workability, also alters its hue by introducing iron particles that give the clay a yellowish or tan cast. The atmosphere in oxidation firing (containing an ample supply of oxygen) is clean and clear. In most porcelain bodies it produces a color range from dead white to creamy warm white. On the other hand, the atmosphere in reduction firing (fossil fueled and therefore containing organic remnants) burns smokily and is charged with carbon. During firing, the kiln atmosphere reacts chemically with the iron particles in the clay body, producing whites in the cooler, bone-gray range. We are so accustomed to seeing commercially produced tableware and dead-white bathroom fixtures, from which virtually all impurities have been removed using magnets, that this uniform, antiseptic porcelain influences our perception of all white porcelain. To circumvent this kind of "toilet bowl" sterility in his work, Minnesota potter Warren MacKenzie adds a handful of yellow ocher or stoneware containing iron to his porcelain body. By warming up the color, he avoids coming too close to an industrial "perfection" in his simple, classic vessels. Even when a warmer white is desired, the physical purity of the porcelain clay body is important; in the potter's studio, cleanliness is a necessity if porcelain is not to be spoiled.

The kiln's atmosphere also can affect the color of a piece by producing what is known as "flashing." This occurs when elements or oxides—which vaporize during firing—settle on the surface to produce unexpected colorations. For example, wood firing produces fine ash that settles, making unpredictable, irregular surface marks—evidence of the firing process. The process of salt glazing produces intentional flashing. Unexpected color variation may also occur when the flames of a combustible fuel such as oil, wood, or gas are especially intense within certain areas of the kiln. At these locations, the "hot spots" will cause a scorched appearance on the ceramic surface. Extraordinary effects also occur when color transfers from one piece to another. Sometimes an oxide such as cobalt, copper, or chrome burns off a glazed pot in firing and its residues in the atmosphere migrate to a nearby piece—producing a soft blush of color in a white pot, for example, or a blaze of rich copper red in the glaze. By knowing and utilizing the kiln's natural smokiness and variations in temperature, the ceramist can open the way to endless opportunities for subtle nuances in surface variation. Paula Winokur, who works exclusively in porcelain, utilizes the subtle variations made possible by reduction firing to enrich her celadon and clear glazes. They softly gradate in hue within a single piece; a celadon may range from gray to green, and a clear glaze from blue-gray to pale pink or ocher.

Ceramics with such markings have legendarily exemplified the mystery of the firing process: in the realm of the kiln god, the works were thought to be out of the potter's control. These mysterious markings have traditionally enhanced a pot's value. Today, with a greater technological understanding of firing, ceramists have unraveled the enigma of flashing and can deliberately place pieces within the kiln to produce these "mysterious" marks where they want them.

Light and Shadow

Just as porcelain's whiteness captivated its initial imitators in Europe, it offers today's ceramist limitless possibilities for creating statements of pure form, as well as representational visions, untouched by the diversion of color.

White reflects light. A white surface also forms a background against which even the faintest shadows create stark contrast. Porcelain's whiteness is ideal as an empty stage for the interplay of light and shadow. Shadows provide clues to an object's surface, volume, and form; furthermore, as the rhythms of

Bowl by Warren MacKenzie, 3″ x 5″ (7.6 x 12.7 cm). MacKenzie prevents the whiteness of this wheel-thrown bowl from becoming sterile by adding color impurities to the clay. Photo: Jerry Mathiason.

Slave, Bennington Pottery, Bennington, Vermont, 10″ (25.4 cm) high. This cast parian ware sculpture was made after a marble statue by Hiram Powers. Courtesy Bennington Pottery, Inc.

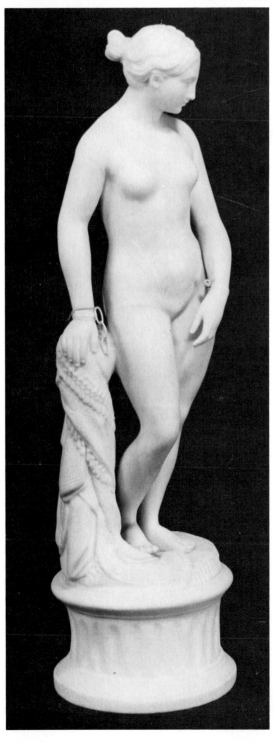

light and shadow change, movement is created within the work.

In the eighteenth and nineteenth centuries statues and busts of prominent statesmen and nobles became extremely popular. Many sculptors went to study in Italy, which was then considered the source of the greatest marble statuary. The sculpture of that day combined naturalism and classical idealism. Horatio Greenough's marble statue of George Washington, portrayed naturalistically but draped in the robes of Greek antiquity, set a stylistic precedent in America. Parian ware, named for Paros, the Greek island noted for its exceptional marble, was developed in Victorian England to reproduce miniature clay statuary in multiples. This clay body closely resembled both the color and surface of marble, and it was usually left unglazed. Highly detailed statues, pots, and jewelry were created from it.

Parian was first introduced in 1844 by the Copeland and Garrett partnership of the Spode factory, at Stoke-on-Trent. The material, easy to work and inexpensive, was hailed as a new sculptural medium. Parian figures became common as prizes for art leagues and other cultural societies popular in England at that time, as they were an attractive departure from the usual medals, lithographs, and engravings.

Parian was a type of porcelain to which frits made of pulverized bone china and feldspars had been added. Its uses and appearance are related to the French *biscuit,* a soft-paste, unglazed clay body like those used for modeling statuary by such prominent eighteenth-century sculptors as Étienne-Maurice Falconet. It contained a small amount of iron, which produced the desirable creamy color of marble when fired in an oxidation atmosphere. Colored slips were at times applied as a background for refined white carvings, but mostly the works were left uncolored to emphasize the carving itself. The unglazed surface of matte parian was sometimes combined and contrasted with other materials such as various metals. The clay body was employed by most of the major manufacturers in nineteenth-century England—Minton, Copeland, Coalport, Worcester; Belleek of Ireland; and Bennington Pottery in the United States. Parian vanished from popularity by the beginning of the twentieth century, aside from its present use by Belleek and Lenox (in the United States), which is known for the creamy color of its porcelain. Historically, parian was most valued for *pate sur pate,* a decorative technique of painting with parian slip on a darker ground color. Parian was never as highly valued as true porcelain. This, together with its extreme fragility, prevented parian's wide

Left
Parian Vase, Minton, Stoke-on-Trent, England, with pâte-sur-pâte decoration by Marc Louis Solon, 1875, 10¼'' (26 cm) high. Courtesy Victoria and Albert Museum, London.

Below left
Rape Quadrivial by Glenn Doell, 1978–79, 8'' x 21'' (20.3 x 53.3 cm). Doell leaves this wheel-thrown vessel unglazed so that the fine white surface appears soft and absorbent, and highlights and shadows can play over the carved areas. Photo: Eddie Owen.

Top right
Wall Piece by Ruth Duckworth, 1980, 16½'' x 50'' x 6'' (41.9 x 127 x 15.2 cm). This powerful slab-built mural allows shadows to play in the crevices, contrasting with the stark flatness of the outermost thick slabs. Courtesy Exhibit A, Chicago. Photo: Eddie Owen.

Right
Geteiltes # 16 by Gerda Spurey, 1979, 10½'' x 6'' x 4'' (26.7 x 15.2 x 10.2 cm). In this cast and altered form, abstract folds of clay convey ''vessel'' with a solidly anthropomorphic quality. Courtesy Florence Duhl.

Above
Frog with Umbrella by Frank Fleming, 1979, 17'' x 6'' x 6'' (43.1 x 15.2 x 15.2 cm). Although contemporary, this modeled sculpture resembles parian ware in its creamy whiteness and its unglazed surface.

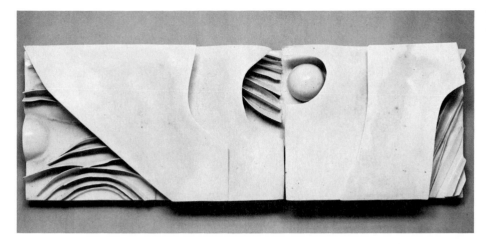

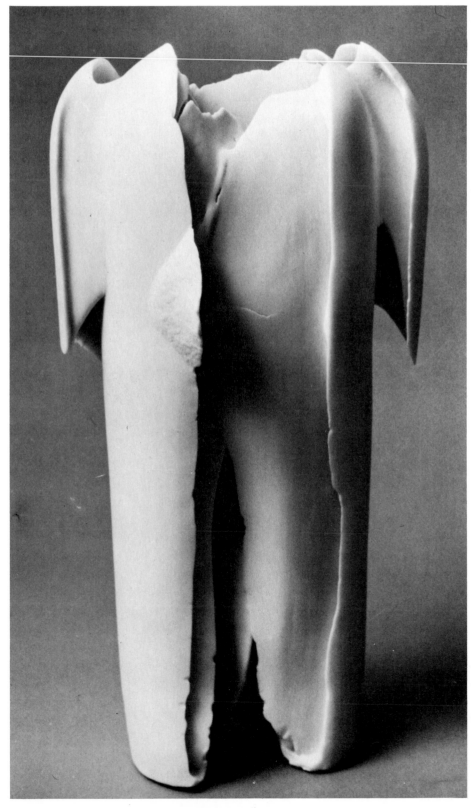

use, and when Victorian statuary was no longer fashionable, the material itself was no longer desirable.

The figures of Frank Fleming, a contemporary sculptor from Alabama, resemble parian in their creamy white color and unglazed surfaces, though his subjects spring from his imagination rather than classical antiquity. Fleming leaves his surfaces free of glaze because, as he says, "the glaze seems to put a wall between myself and the object." Glaze, which often adds a sense of life and sensuousness to porcelain would in this case conceal the refined detail of Fleming's part-human, part-mythical bestiary.

The effects of light on porcelain are influenced not only by the form of the piece but also the nature of the surface itself, which can either reflect or absorb light. Aside from the need to protect the clay surface with glaze, there are the aesthetic questions of whether or not to glaze and what characteristics are desirable in a porcelain glaze. The degree of reflectiveness, the color, and the intensity of shadows on a porcelain piece can all be altered by manipulating the matte or glossy character of the clay's surface or glaze. Unglazed or matte surfaces are more light-absorbent, whereas shiny surfaces are more reflective and cast harsher shadows.

Glenn Doell is another contemporary ceramist who chooses to leave his work unglazed to dramatize the effects of light. Doell reinterprets historical models like Wedgwood's Portland vase and the relief-carved Sèvres porcelains of the 1780s. He carves the collars of his vessels in heavy, friezelike borders, suggesting the reliefs on architectural pediments. The reclining posture of Doell's figures echoes that of classical figures conceived to fit within the triangular shape of Greek temple pediments. This horizontal position also aptly suits the contour of a pot. He purposely throws that area of his pots much thicker to accommodate carving up to one and a half inches in depth. In his work, a sense of movement is created by the flicker of highlights and shadows cast on the carving. The unglazed porcelain surface appears soft and absorbent, resembling the limestone and marble of classical friezes.

Light also dramatizes and energizes abstract works in porcelain. Ruth Duckworth is an influential ceramist who taught at the University of Chicago until her retirement in 1979. Her monumental wall murals emphasize the contrast between interior and exterior—concepts stemming from our ideas about containment that are so essential in a discussion of ceramics. With energetic gestures, Duckworth rolls out thick slabs of clay and skids them onto a flat surface in order to stretch and enlarge them. Repeating thin slabs at close intervals in the interior cavities of closed forms and attaching multiple slabs horizontally to the wall, she creates powerful relief murals. The viewer is drawn into the mysterious inner reaches of these forms, which express a private, feminine vision. The interplay of positive and negative space creates visual movement in these pieces. Duckworth disregards the notions of lightness and fragility and handles porcelain with strength and solidity.

Kurt Spurey's wall pieces share similar concerns of light and shadow. This Austrian ceramist pours slip the consistency of pancake batter onto plaster bats in wafer-thin sheets. The smooth slabs are then overlapped, creating light-catching crevices that express the rhythm of waves or of grass blowing in the wind.

White materials seem inherently fragile and insubstantial, particularly on a small scale. Using the scale and sometimes the shape of an egg, English ceramist Irene Sims makes objects having the delicacy we so often associate with porcelain. The forms are so fragile looking and tiny, one is hesitant to handle them. Made from bone china, they become translucent when fired, and their translucency is further enhanced by the varying thicknesses created by relief carving. Her surfaces are unglazed, smooth as ocean-polished beach stones, and receptive to shadows.

Wisconsin ceramist Dick Evans underfires his porcelain and uses low-fire glazes to achieve a dulled surface, which makes the work appear physically soft to the viewer. The forms are sliced into even segments. Movement is enhanced by the play of cast shadows between segments, and there is a push-pull relationship between shadows and form. This work has none of the historical connections usually associated with porcelain, for though Evan's circular works allude to containment through scale and form, they clearly are not functional containers.

Surrealism

The color white connotes purity, serenity, the eternal, and otherworldliness. What better use of white porcelain than to express a surreal vision? Its stark whiteness gives representational images an incorporeal quality and heightened drama, making it an ideal medium for juxtaposing incongruous images that straddle the line between waking and dreaming. In the stark forms of Lucian Octavius Pompili, the placement of various elements—human hand and shod foot, tiny leaves and tendrils, teapots and leafy cups—he allows us a glimpse into his unconscious. The pure whiteness of the material gives them the ghostly appearance of apparitions.

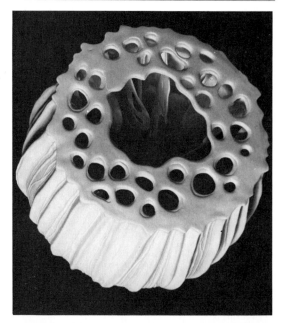

Left
Interior, Exterior by Gudrun Klix, 1977, 14″ x 10″ (35.6 x 25.4 cm). This cast and assembled structure plays the visible interior darkness against the undulating exterior whiteness.

Below
Carved Elliptical Form by Irene Sims, 4½″ x 6″ x 1½″ (11.4 x 15.2 x 3.8 cm). The delicacy and fragility of porcelain is apparent in this cast and carved bone china piece, left unglazed to absorb shadows. Collection Karen McCready. Photo: Michael McTwigan.

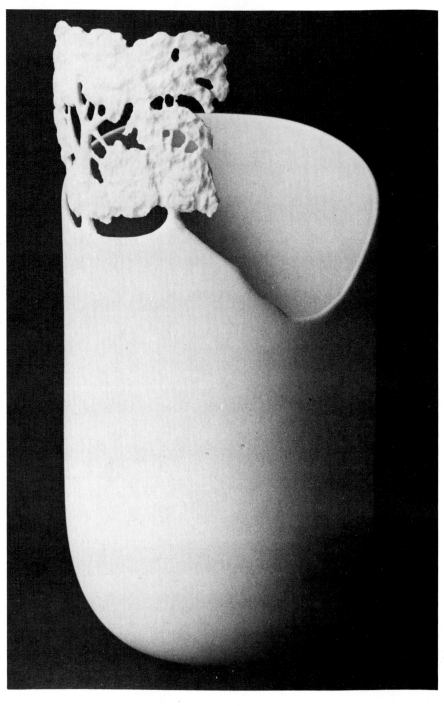

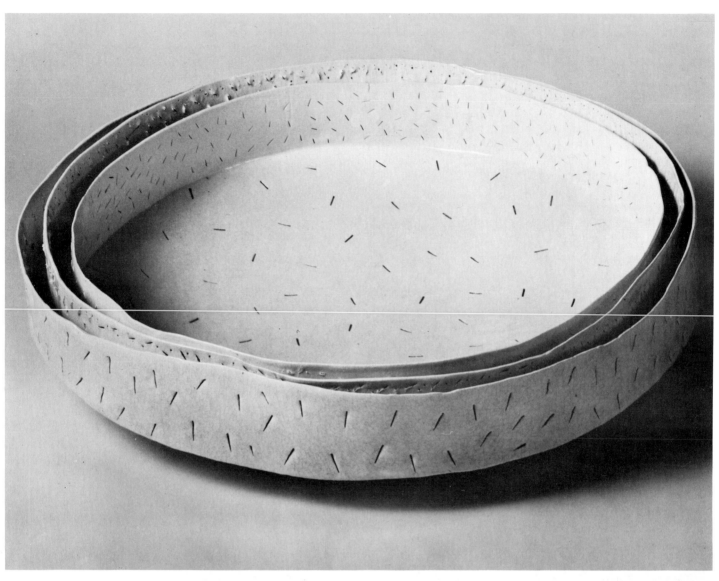

Above
Fragile Territory by Marge Levy,
1980, 6″ x 22″ (15 x 56 cm). Levy
strives to create forms that are
fragile and delicate, yet strong.
Photo: M. Lee Fatherree.

Right
Segments XXXII by Dick Evans,
1978, 10″ x 16″ (25.4 x 40.6 cm).
The soft appearance of this hand-
built structure is achieved by low-
fire glazing.

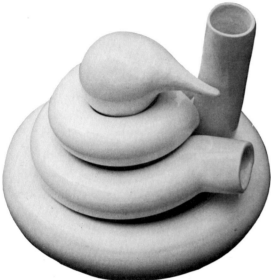

Above
Untitled by Bill Lau, 1970, wheel-thrown and hand-built. Courtesy Greenwich House Pottery, New York.

Above right and far right
The Room for C.A.—The Elsa Epilogue, Marrying the Hangman by Lucian Octavius Pompili, 1977, 22″ x 20½″ x 20½″ (55.9 x 52.1 x 52.1 cm). This surrealistic, mixed-media piece is made of porcelain, wood, gessoed cotton, wire, and rope. Both front and back views are shown here. Courtesy Theo Portnoy Gallery, New York.

Right
Untitled (limited edition) by Susan Beckman, 1980, 10″ x 46″ x 5¼″ (25.4 x 116.8 x 13.3 cm). Beckman explores various states of mind, using altered human forms to give tangible views of inner feelings as seen in this hand-built, press-molded porcelain and wood construction. Courtesy Helen Drutt Gallery, Philadelphia. Photo: Eddie Owen.

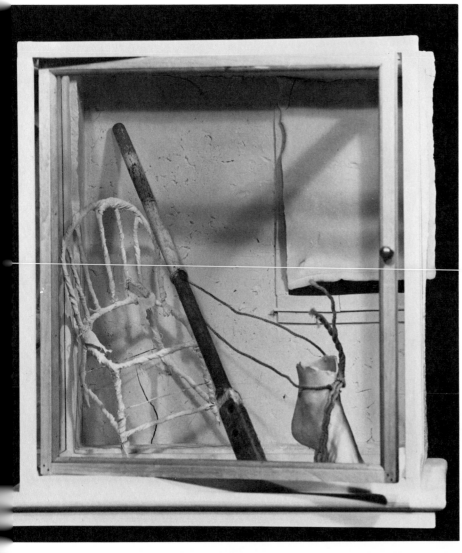

Although a purist in his definition of porcelain, he is not bound by ceramic materials. He has moved from small-scale, functionally rooted pieces to mixed-media sculptures combining porcelain, wood, rope, and other organic materials. These more recent works continue to delve into the unconscious, without the fragile delicacy of Pompili's earlier pieces. Now he uses porcelain in a paradoxical manner: whereas the material is usually thought to be thin and smooth, he fashions it into thick bricks laid with porcelain mortar; even cracks are accepted as part of the piece.

Sandra Shannonhouse's background in costume and stage design is evident in her work, which combines representational elements—hats, boots, gloves—with abstract forms resembling bodily organs. Strung together on a "vertebral column," they have a surreal quality. Shannonhouse makes the individual parts by layering porcelain slip over stuffed fabric forms, which results in a raw, uneven surface. The work is left unglazed, though common table salt is rubbed into the fired clay surface for a waxy, glimmering effect. The scale of the forms, installed in groups, belies the inherent fragility of their construction and the same quality in their subject matter.

Contrast of Color and Materials
Many ceramists use porcelain for its particular whiteness in relationship to other ceramic

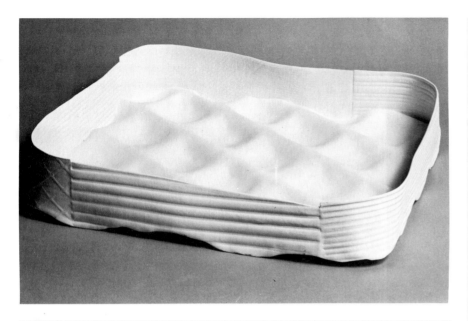

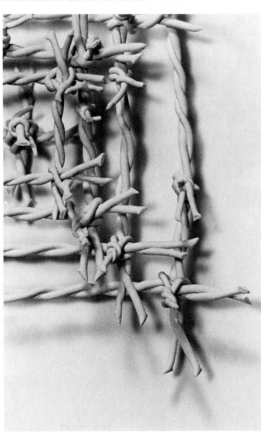

Top
Terrain Tray by Barbara Frey, 1980, 13″ x 14″ (33 x 35.6 cm). Press-molded and hand-built, this unglazed tray absorbs shadows that emphasize the undulating contours. Photo: Paul Pearce.

Above
Overboard by Tony Hepburn, 1976, 15″ x 20″ x 16″ (38.1 x 50.8 x 15.2 cm). Here Hepburn contrasts the surfaces, textures, and colors of porcelain, stoneware, wood, and leather. Photo: Eric Webster.

Right
Web (detail) by Jan Axel, 1979, 6″ x 6″ x 1″ (15.2 x 15.2 x 2.5 cm). This piece constructed of porcelain is mounted on canvas to capture the movement of shadows.

Far right
Hatted Figure VII by Sandra Shannonhouse, 1979, 68″ x 16″ x 16″ (172.7 x 40.6 x 40.6 cm). Using multiple parts to construct her larger-than-life figures, Shannonhouse is able to far exceed the scale traditionally associated with porcelain. Courtesy Quay Gallery, San Francisco. Photo: Colin C. McRae.

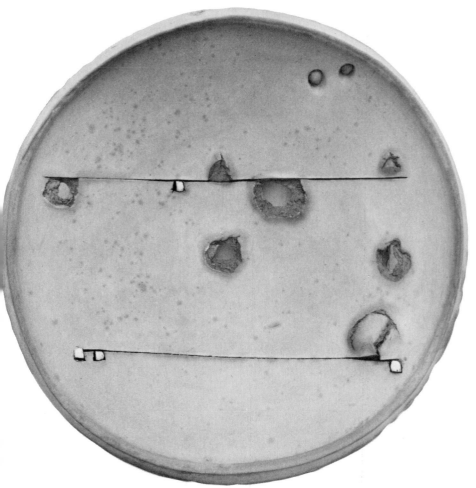

Top
#13 Ore Processor with Mine Shaft, Section 2 by Raymon Elozua, 1980, 24″ x 48″ x 14½″ (61 x 122 x 36.8 cm). This construction is primarily stoneware painted with acrylic. Only the abstract domes are porcelain. Collection Allan Chasanoff. Courtesy O.K. Harris Gallery, New York.

Above
Ceramic Drawing by Peter Voulkos, 1978, 24″ (61 cm) diam. The tiny bits of porcelain add bright contrast to the duller tone of the stoneware plate. Collection Central Iowa Art Association, Fisher Community Center. Photo courtesy Braunstein Gallery, San Francisco.

materials or even other media. It can be used very effectively to create contrast and emphasis. Juxtaposed with another clay, such as stoneware, porcelain differs strikingly in color, density, and texture.

Peter Voulkos is known for his vital, energetic stoneware works. In 1972 he began making stoneware plates which, through a process of pushing, pulling, pinching, and gouging, became three-dimensional expressionist "drawings." All were emphatically pierced, and sometimes Voulkos plugged up these "passthroughs" with bits of white porcelain, using its smoothness and density as dramatic highlights in the finished objects and giving them "another weight, another white, another light."[2]

New York artist Raymon Elozua creates carefully constructed landscapes that portray decaying water tanks, railroad trestles, coal tipples, and bunkers from American industrial mills and factory sites. Primarily made of stoneware, these landscapes are interspersed with abstract porcelain domes that play a role similar to that of the porcelain elements in Voulkos's plates. Elozua's process in creating these landscapes is unique. After building the stoneware sites with their inexplicable domes, he then systematically breaks down the images. Using water to soak and deteriorate the dry clay, texturing the surfaces, firing the structures, and finally directly painting them, he transforms and "weathers" the landscapes. Within the individual landscape stands the glaring, perplexing porcelain dome.

Tony Hepburn, an English artist now head of the ceramics department at Alfred University, also combines porcelain with various stonewares, and literal objects with abstractions. His work emphasizes the inherent nature of each clay body by contrasting several kinds of clay within a single work. He sometimes places a porcelain cup within his abstract landscapes, often balancing it on the edge of a stoneware plane. Perhaps these "cups" are metaphors for ceramics within the larger context of fine art. Whatever their associations for the viewer, Hepburn's ceramic sculptures reveal a loyalty to the inherent nature of his materials.

CHAPTER FIVE

TRANSLUCENCY

MANY OF US have shared a common childhood experience: a china teacup is held to the light and, magically, the hand's silhouette shows through the seemingly opaque material. The first Europeans to see a thin porcelain teacup also must have been amazed by this marriage of solid substance and light—for translucency is about light. They considered translucency so essential to porcelain that it became a motivating factor in their relentless search for the clay's formula. Johann Friedrich Böttger's journal entry on January 15, 1708, documenting the exact moment when he obtained a "white, translucent body," [1] demonstrates this.

Historically, translucency has been primarily a European preoccupation. Ch'ai wares of the Sung dynasty—so delicate they were termed "bodiless"—were thin as paper, resonant, and covered with a pale blue glaze, but little else is known about them aside from their resemblance to "the sky after rain." [2] Chinese porcelain makers, however, have never striven to embody translucency in particular; for the Chinese, porcelain always has been simply a resonant, vitreous clay, and translucency has been of secondary importance. In eighteenth-century Europe, fascination with translucency resulted in naive but understandable attempts to create it: because porcelain resembled glass, early attempts to formulate it incorporated a great deal of ground glass. Since alabaster and seashells are also naturally translucent, they too were added to clay—also without success.

Curiously, translucency—the most awe-inspiring characteristic of porcelain—is virtually unexplored. Despite its importance to both ceramists and those who appreciate porcelain, little has been written to explain why translucency exists.

Physical Facts of Translucency

Although porcelain is thought to be the purest ceramic material, it actually evolved quite naturally from stoneware, and there is no precise dividing line between the two types of clay. There is little chemical difference between porcelain and refined stoneware bodies, except for the presence or absence of impurities such as iron. Among clays, however, porcelain alone has the capacity to become translucent.

An examination of the physical properties that contribute to translucency will give a better understanding of both its aesthetic possibilities and technical limitations. Like all of porcelain's qualities, translucency is a progressive quality—that is, it exists to varying degrees within the broad range between transparency and opacity. Though all true porcelains have the potential to become translucent, this quality is only expressed when the clay is thinly formed (3/16 inch or less). This thinness is made possible partly by porcelain's fine particle size and creamy texture. Along with thinness, the degree of vitrification and amount of crystal formation that occur during firing contribute to the translucency of a given clay body.

Vitrification, the fusion of clay particles

Stardust Serenade by Curtis
Benzle, 1979, 7″ x 10″ (17.8 x
27.9 cm). As light floods the interior cavity of this hand-built vessel,
it illuminates patterns of inlaid colors
and translucent clay. Photo: Kent
Bowser.

into a glassy substance, occurs most commonly at a high temperature—at least 1300°C (2372°F)—when silica (glass), fluxed by the feldspar in the clay body, flows into the spaces between the clay particles. When this happens, the kaolin in the clay is also melted, and a glassy matrix is produced that welds the clay particles together. The clay most capable of becoming vitreous is porcelain. Hypothetically, if earthenware were to be brought to vitrification, it would simply become a puddle of glass, as its constituents are incapable of withstanding high temperatures.

Vitrification is the furthest stage to which a clay can be taken in firing without deformation. The greater the vitrification, the more glass is formed in the clay body, and therefore the more capable it is of transmitting light. Complete vitrification is not necessary for translucency to occur, however, and porcelain clays have a range within which vitrification can take place. In fact, in pursuit of complete vitrification the ceramist might over-fire the clay, at which point the porcelain would deform and become brittle and weak. Firing porcelain involves both timing and temperature. At the point of maturity the degree of porosity, opacity, and strength becomes permanently fixed; this bonding caused by the fluxing of the silica and kaolin results in a hard, dense clay body.

Though the final product is strong, porcelain is highly vulnerable during firing, when distortions such as slumping and warping can occur. This paradox is inherent in porcelain: extreme vitrification, and therefore strength, is achieved only at extremely high temperatures, when the clay is at its most tenuous, molten—and therefore vulnerable—state. Additional fluxing agents such as frit, lead, bone ash, and feldspar are sometimes added to the clay to reduce the temperature required for vitrification. This produces a glassy, light-receptive surface while simultaneously lessening the peril from heat. While such hybrid clays may compare aesthetically with those employing higher-firing feldspars, they are not as strong.

Bone china, while not a "true" porcelain, is a highly fluxed clay body that retains a good deal of porcelain's traits. Made from approximately one-half bone ash, it is given high bisque and low glaze firings; clay and glaze do not mature at the same temperature. Many of our perceptions of porcelain stem from our experience of bone china, which shares translucency and a common aesthetic with porcelain. Some traditionalists, however, feel the clay-glaze fusion is essential and therefore do not consider bone china to be porcelain at all.

Translucency also may be achieved at lower temperatures by maintaining a given temperature for a period of time at crucial points during firing. This process, called "soaking," gives silica more time to flux and form more cristobalite, which creates translucency. In China, firing temperatures were actually much lower than eighteenth-century Europeans considered necessary for porcelain. But the Chinese soaked their kilns for up to five days, producing highly translucent wares. This is extreme, of course, for even a short soak of thirty minutes at maximum temperature enhances translucency, and a combination of high temperatures and long soaks (of over an hour) can, in fact, over-vitrify the clay.

It is important to understand that although vitrification allows translucency, many works are highly vitreous and yet do not transmit light. Sometimes this is because of the clay's thickness and sometimes because of its actual chemical composition, as when a clay is high in kaolin, which opacifies. For example, a mortar and pestle made for use with chemicals are fully vitrified so they will be capable of retaining strong acids, yet are completely opaque.

Resonance, like translucency, is a consequence of vitrification. Like fine crystal, porcelain is resonant when lightly struck—a classic way of determining its quality. High, clear notes denote a thin, vitreous object; duller, more muffled sounds are produced by thicker, more heavily glazed, or more porous clays such as earthenware. In these clays less glass is present within the clay body and there are more air spaces between clay particles, preventing sound from traveling.

In China, resonance was the criterion used to distinguish one clay type from another. Resonant clay was called tz'u and included what we now term porcelain, as well as porcelaneous and vitrified stonewares.

A feature of resonance—and this is of particular relevance to collectors—is its usefulness in detecting hairline cracks not readily apparent to the eye. When an object is gently struck, cracks will either prevent the work from ringing or deaden its sound.

Whether or not translucency is desired in porcelain, vitrification results in a specific chemical structure. Porcelain has latticelike interstices between its particles that form a pattern known as a "crystal lattice," [3] which literally carries light through it. When light hits this lattice, it bounces from crystal to crystal, producing a glistening effect not unlike that of snow—which has, in fact, the same kind of crystal lattice. Porcelain and snow share more than a common crystalline structure, however; both also contain the mineral kaolinite, the pure mineral form of kaolin. This unexpected coincidence was

Bowl by Lucie Rie, 3½'' x 7'' (8.9 x 17.8 cm). The translucence of this wheel-thrown, pierced, and glazed bowl emphasizes contrasting areas of thick and thin clay. Collection Bryce Holcombe. Photo: Michael McTwigan.

Above
Molded Form by Jacqueline Poncelet, 1974, 4½'' (11.5 cm). The translucency and eggshell-like fragility of porcelain is obvious in this cast, unglazed vessel of bone china. Collection Daniel Jacobs.

Right
Triple Lamp of Translucent Calcite, Egyptian Dynasty XVIII, Thebes: Valley of the Kings, Tomb of Tut-Ankh-Amun. Light can be seen through translucent porcelian in the same way that it can be seen through the walls of these calcite lamps. Courtesy The Metropolitan Museum of Art. Photo: Harry Burton.

discovered by a team of Japanese scientists. Using an electron microscope to examine natural snow crystals, they found the particles at the center of snow crystals to be "predominantly of terrestrial origin, with clay minerals, especially kaolinite, being a major source."[4]

As with snow, when light hits unglazed porcelain it is carried by the crystal lattice from one particle to another, traveling into and through the porcelain wall. When porcelain is glazed, the interaction of clay and light is more complex. Clay and glaze mature, or vitrify, at the same temperature in high-fired porcelain; as a result the two fuse to create an intimate bond, or interface. Fusion results in a unique surface, lending the glaze visual depth by carrying the eye through it and on into the clay. Light's complex interaction with both clay and glaze is therefore of a dual nature, as it is simultaneously reflected and absorbed by both surface and body, making a solid substance appear diaphanous.

Translucency in both clay and glaze continues to be sought by contemporary ceramists. Don Pilcher, writing of the interaction of clay, glaze, and light, put it this way: "Glossy surfaces will identify their light sources and matte surfaces will modulate them. The phenomenon of light passing through a lightly colored glaze to a white reflecting surface, and then back through the glaze, is visually powerful."[5]

The integral relationship of fused clay and glaze is apparent in the work of Harris Deller. Deller has developed a unique signature for his work by exploiting the glaze's natural tendency to flow during firing. In *Animated Bowl*, 1979, he manipulates the glaze by carving and applying clay "troughs" or hollows to catch the glaze as it runs, forming icelike pools both inside and outside a form. The Chinese referred to pools like these as "tearstain" markings, as they were originally caused by excess glaze masses that simultaneously reflected and trapped the light, carrying it through to the clay body beneath. Deller effectively "controls" pools of glaze so that in their molten state they form ribbonlike sashes of extremely glossy, rich color.

The Paradox of Fragility
It is translucency more than any other quality that gives porcelain the appearance of great fragility. To achieve this most precious quality, the ceramist takes many risks, balancing on a tightrope between destruction and perfection of form. This is well illustrated in the work of Jacqueline Poncelet, an English artist who at one time worked in bone china. She confesses that when she opened the kiln door she never knew whether she would find puddles of glass or

the delicate bone china forms she was striving to create. Her cast vessels embody balance, both physically and visually. Their rounded bottoms are propped on tiny three-sided feet, their precarious stance enhanced by the clay's eggshell thinness. Of hand-held scale, some pieces are embroidered by patient scraping and piercing so that their surfaces will channel light through the vessel wall and create a delicate pattern. Their translucence and preciousness make this a difficult task, for Poncelet plays upon the material's fragile nature.

Despite its vulnerability during the firing process, porcelain's fragility is, in fact, a myth. Though light penetrating delicate porcelain walls creates the illusion of fragility and weightlessness, porcelain is the hardest, strongest, most dense of all clays. When fired to maturity it can withstand more abuse than any other type of ceramic material. The lower-fired earthenwares and stonewares—though their names imply rough textures, darker hues, and that they are as durable as earth and stone—are in fact more porous and breakable than porcelain.

Luminosity
Although no other clay body responds to light in the manner of porcelain, porcelain shares the quality of translucency with several other substances such as semiprecious stones, seashells, and paper.

Translucency sometimes occurs as a subtle, luminous glow within a clay wall. This is most readily observed in a vessel where the cavity of the form acts as a chamber to capture light. Such a vessel can give the viewer a sense of its inside and outside simultaneously. The glow of light seen through the walls of a thin porcelain vessel is not unlike that of the alabaster oil lamps made by Egyptian artisans during Tutankhamen's reign (1378–1360 B.C.). Carved to resemble lotus plants, they were filled with oil and ignited, and the viewer beheld light through the fine-textured white alabaster.

With translucent porcelain, we also can experience a sense of movement created by the flicker of images illuminated through solid walls. Light transmitted through porcelain is diffused, and our perception of distinct images is likewise blurred—just as it is when we view them through frosted glass. An internal glow carries elusive images through vessel walls. Rudolf Staffel, a leading ceramist from Philadelphia who has used porcelain for decades, calls them "ghost images," as they allude to something imagined in the mind's eye rather than to something solid or corporeal. The union of form and material in his vessels—"light gatherers," as he calls them—creates a foil for translucency.

Tree-Edged Bowl by Mary Rogers, 1977, 5″ (12.7 cm. This carved and pinched bowl has a gray crackle glaze. Photo: Eric Webster.

Spiralling Bowl by Mary Rogers, 1975, 4½″ (11.5 cm). The edges of this hand-modeled bowl are pinched to a paper-thin consistency, thus enhancing the translucency. The colors are inlaid oxides. Photo: Eric Webster.

Staffel balances his clay body on the edge between clay and glaze, manipulating the composition so that it best exercises its light-transmitting capacity. His forms are created with a combination of throwing and pinching techniques. At times he inadvertently pinches through a vessel wall. Where the wall tears, he applies a patch over the hole, thereby creating contrasting thick and thin areas of clay. This enhances the translucent effect of the vessels, which appear to summon light into their cavities. Occasionally Staffel adds a hint of cobalt, copper oxide, or water-soluble metallic salts (sulfates) to his vessels, creating a luminous glow of color through the sheer material.

Comparisons to seashells are especially frequent in contemporary ceramics, as shells appear to be "glazed" with delicate colors in patterns that seem to follow a meticulous master plan of design. Often a ceramist takes visual cues from nature. The English potter Mary Rogers, who has influenced many European ceramists, utilizes porcelain's capacity to be eased and pinched to near nothingness in order to capture the luminous potential of the paper-thin clay. Unfurling leaves and flowers, shells, pods, and agates are all the subjects of Rogers's work, though they are transformed into patterns.

The porcelain wall of Rogers's *Spiralling Bowl,* 1975, acts as a veil that dissolves the

Above right
Series 24 by Lea Embree, 1979, 3″ x 7″; 1.5″ x 4.5″ (7.6 x 17.8; 4.1 x 10.8 cm). The subtle variations of these similar hand-built forms emerge as they are assembled in a group. Courtesy Exhibit A, Chicago. Photo: Eddie Owen.

Right
Untitled # 66 / Fragment Series by Linda Grimm, 1980, 4½″ x 13″ x 14½″ (11.5 x 33 x 36.9 cm). The paperlike qualities of the box, together with shadows cast by the fragments suspended on monofilament wire, lend a sense of delicate movement to this hand-built form colored with oxides. Photo: Michael McTwigan.

Left
1,000 Sheets (detail) by Concetta Fenicchia, 1980, entire piece 75″ x 300″ (180.4 x 722 cm); each square 5″ x 5″ (12.7 x 12.7 cm). Fenicchia manipulates the clay here by folding, crumpling, and fluttering it, emphasizing its paper-like quality. The piece is unglazed, which gives subtlety to shadows cast by each sheet.

Below
Culindrus by Sherry Haxton, 1979, 50 separate units, each 8″ x 1″ x 2″ (20.3 x 2.5 x 5.1 cm). Photo: Paul Lawrence.

Bottom right
Metamorphosis by Sherry Haxton, 1979, 4″ x 16″ (10.2 x 40.6 cm). The layering of this slab-constructed piece creates a density in contrast to the thinness and delicacy of the individual sheets. Collection Jacques Gael Cressaty. Photo: Paul Lawrence.

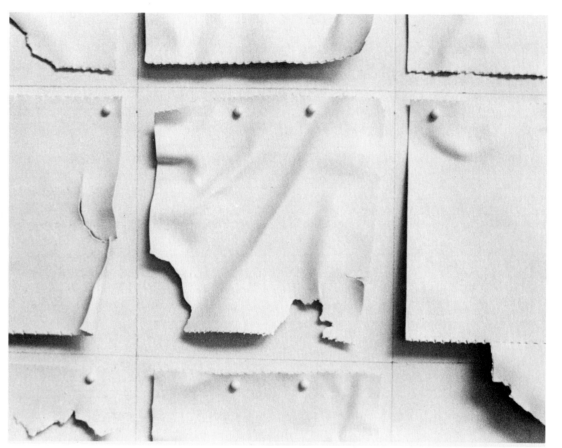

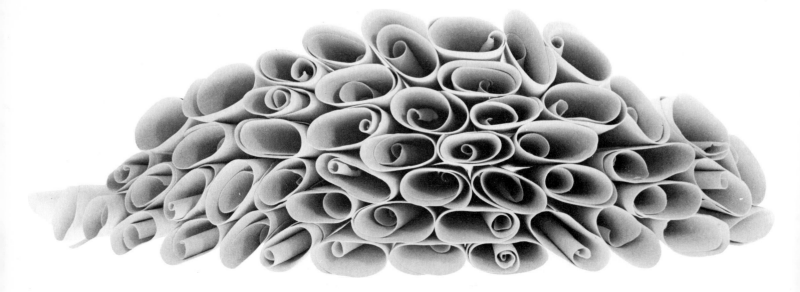

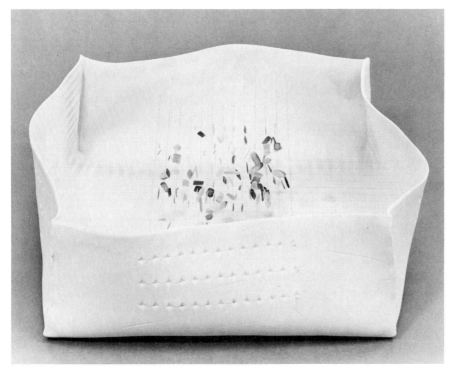

definitive pattern of its winding ribs of inlaid oxide dapples. By contrasting dark with light, she enhances the clay's translucency. Light passing through the solid wall also creates an awareness of the play between the interior and exterior surfaces of the vessel.[6]

Porcelain also can resemble paper, not only because it is translucent, but because it can be formed into a wall as thin and as smooth as paper. Both paper and porcelain are translucent when backlighted, though they lose their appearance of sheerness when illuminated from the front. Both California artist Sherry Haxton and New York ceramist Concetta Fenicchia make forms of very thin sheets of porcelain, playing with its plasticity while alluding to its paperlike quality.

Haxton stacks diplomalike tubes to make pyramidal forms such as *Culindrus*. She also places wafer-thin leaves of porcelain one upon another, forming layered bowls such as *Metamorphosis*. The depth of each tube allows for a dark interior cavity, as do the spaces between the rolls or concave sheets when stacked. This darkness sharply contrasts with the delicacy of the forms, heightening their austerity.

In a wall installation entitled *1000 Sheets*, Fenicchia assembled sheets of porcelain resembling water-soaked, rippling, bathroom tissue (complete with perforated edges). The undulating "torn" squares of these grid formations compose a fragile image in low relief.

Often one senses translucency only by contrast, experiencing thinness in relationship to thickness; an object's translucent quality may be visible only where its rim tapers to utmost thinness. The phenomenon of translucency holds porcelain's most explicit paradoxes: its fragility/strength, its translucency/opacity. And these very qualities continue to compel ceramist and viewer alike.

CHAPTER SIX

FLUIDITY

THE WORD *fluidity* calls to mind images of rounded contours and moving, liquid sensations—in effect, flow. The dictionary definition of fluidity—"the quality or state of having particles that easily move without a separation of mass. . . . The physical property of a substance that enables it to flow"[1]—helps us understand the nature of fluidity in clay. This general definition applies to all wet clays, which are by nature fluid. This quality in porcelain results from its unique texture and sensuousness, and it also can be expressed in the finished form. The essence of porcelain's smooth touch when wet is its texture, which is appreciated by all who use it. In describing the feel of porcelain, ceramists often compare it to cream cheese, butter, or putty. When emphasized in modeling, this smoothness also gives porcelain its unique capacity for conveying a sense of softness, fluidity, and movement. Some ceramists like to make the most of this play between actual and visual reality, expressing their aesthetic ideas in their work by manipulating the physical nature of the material itself, turning process into product.

Fluidity and Plasticity

The buttery smoothness of porcelain might lead us to conclude that it is a very malleable material, yet this same characteristic actually *reduces* plasticity. Surprisingly, porcelain is one of the least plastic clays. Its *seeming* plasticity is due to its overall small particle size and its smooth texture. Ordinarily the smaller the *clay* particles within a clay body—as opposed to other materials such as feldspar and silica—the more plastic that clay body is. Because kaolin, the clay within porcelain, is actually of larger particle size than those clays used in earthenware and stoneware, porcelain is less plastic than one would anticipate. Furthermore, the accompanying materials of porcelain—feldspar, silicá, ball clay, and bentonite, for example—are generally of fine particle size, which means that porcelain is a homogeneous substance in contrast to stonewares that contain grog for strength. Because all its particles are of relatively similar size, porcelain has little innate friction. The result is a slippery clay that is difficult to grip. In other words, porcelain holds a paradox in its texture, or lack of it: its smoothness makes it difficult to work while at the same time fooling our senses into equating smoothness with plasticity.

Porcelain's water content is also crucial. Because the liquid surrounding the clay particles acts as a lubricant, allowing them to slide on one another, the flat surfaces of the clay particles cling together and create a strong bond. If the clay contains too little water, it will be stiff and "short," but if it is too wet it also will lose its workability: the particles will slide back on themselves and "sit down," creating a tendency to collapse during the forming process. A test of the workability of any new clay is rolling a bit of it into a coil and bending it. When the clay is nonplastic, as porcelains generally are, it may crack and will be difficult to work; if it

Vase by James Makins, 1977, 10″ (25.4 cm). Makins emphasizes the rhythmic fluidity of the clay by leaving throwing marks.

Trophy by Coille Hooven, 1975, 22″ x 13″ x 7″ (55.9 x 33 x 17.8 cm). The attenuated, ribbony handles, exaggerated in scale, give this wheel-thrown and hand-built vessel a fragile and fluid appearance. Photo: M. Lee Fatherree.

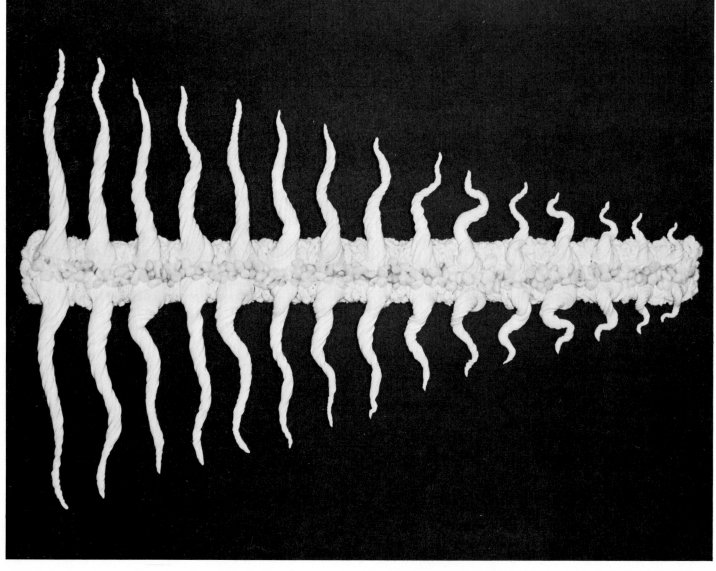

can be bent and twisted, yet still holds together as a coil, it is plastic and workable.

Porcelain formulas can be manipulated to gain workability, but other characteristics are likely to be sacrificed. Adding plasticizers and grog to "open" the clay body, or give it extra texture, enhances workability, but color purity and fineness of texture are diminished correspondingly. Nonceramic substances such as urine, vinegar, beer, or cola can be added to the clay body to advance bacterial growth, thereby promoting plasticity while preserving porcelain's valued color and texture.

Aging the Clay to Enhance Plasticity

Any clay becomes more workable when it is aged, giving water time to penetrate between clay particles. This is not a modern notion where porcelain preparation is concerned. According to Marco Polo:

> The Chinese collect a certain kind of earth, as it were from a mine, and laying it in a great heap, suffer it to be exposed to the wind, the rain, and the sun, for thirty or forty years, during which time it is never disturbed. By this it becomes refined and fit for being wrought into the vessels above mentioned (cups, bowls, dishes).[2]

Guido Pancirollus, a famous antiquarian of Padua, wrote in the year 1612:

> In former ages porcelains were never seen. Now they are a certain mass composed of gypsum, bruified eggs (ovo trito), the shell of marine locust, and other substances, and this, being well tempered and thickened, is hidden under ground in a secret place which the father points out to his children; for, as respects others, he does not wish them to know it. And there it remains hidden for eighty years; at the end of which time the children or grandchildren dig it out, and when it has been again reduced to a fluid state, and made fit for working up, they form of it precious vessels, very beautiful to look at, quite transparent, and wrought of any form or colour which those workmen think proper.[3]

These early descriptions of porcelain reflect certain beliefs—among them porcelain's great value as evidenced by the need to hide the clay—that still persist today. They also illustrate the hoary conceit that it is necessary to store porcelain for many years before it is usable. Every potter knows that while aging does promote plasticity, the clay is fairly workable after only a few days (though some let it stand for several months). It is the initial aging process, which allows each particle within the clay to be surrounded evenly by

water, that is especially important. Reconditioned clay that has been previously worked is even more plastic than newly made clay.

Fluidity and Process

When the art of porcelain-making was in its infancy in Europe, the medium was not considered plastic enough for use on the wheel; hence, such industrial techniques as slip casting and press molding developed. The idea that porcelain presents difficulties in modeling produced a great deal of apprehension in the minds of potters, and there are still some ceramists who hesitate to work with it.

Porcelain's extreme fluidity, however, can act as a vehicle for the artist's ideas and may even become the idea itself, as in the work of Carol Jeanne Abraham. She exploits the very qualities in porcelain that other ceramists often fear—its tendency to sag and collapse during the forming process. As if she were pulling taffy, Abraham drapes, folds, and pulls the clay over molds while it is in a semi-fluid state, as she has done in *Annelid*, 1977. She uses large quantities of lithium, potassium, or sodium to alter the equilibrium of the clay body, making it thixotropic. Thixotropy, the property of becoming fluid when shaken or stirred, is caused by the presence of an excess of these deflocculating, or liquefying, elements. When undisturbed or compressed, the clay is dull and hard; a slight shaking motion triggers a chemical reaction, bringing the clay to a shiny, elastic, fluid state—the most fluid form that clay can take without actually being liquid.

Thixotropy is also a necessary quality, though to a lesser degree, in casting slips, for it allows the slip to set in the mold without distortion. Minute quantities of sodium silicate and soda ash are used to deflocculate casting slips so they will pour easily but still maintain a high density. In other words, the slip need only contain a proportionately small amount of water to be fluid enough to pour. Deflocculants reverse the usual behavior of close clay particles, causing them to repel each other when lubricated rather than to form a suction.

Some ceramists particularly relish the rhythmic movement of modeling porcelain on the potter's wheel and the way in which clay forms seem to spring to life on the wheel, as if appearing magically from nowhere. The wheel's sensuous motion offers a satisfying experience, and though a fluid gesture may not be visible in the final form, it exists for the ceramist at the time of creation. Bernard Leach once commented: "The wheel upon which a potter moulds his hollow forms is one of the most peculiar and intimate devices which human beings have invented. There is

Bowl by Colin Pearson, 1980, 5" x 9" (13 x 23 cm). The sensuousness and fluidity of porcelain is readily seen in this wheel-thrown vase with combed handles. The metallic color is achieved with copper and manganese glazes. Photo: Christopher Hurst.

Annelid by Carol Jeanne Abraham, 1977, 28" x 42" x 3" (71.1 x 106.6 x 7.6 cm). This unusual piece made of thixotropic porcelain, cotton, wool, and wood exemplifies porcelain's capacity to be draped, folded, pulled like taffy, and molded into organic forms.

nothing quite like throwing in any other craft."[4]

Rhythm and the potter's wheel are inextricable. The subtle experience of rhythm and change derived from the wheel is not unlike that of musical rhythm. As with music, making pottery on a wheel is not accomplished in a single motion, but in repeated movements and the intervals between them.

In Japan the sense of rhythm that exists between the potter and the wheel is used to train the mind—to bring it in contact with the Zen Buddhist idea of the ultimate. This is one of the significant features of the practical arts in Japan, which are intended not only for the creation of objects, whether utilitarian or aesthetic, but also as a means of achieving "oneness." The potter's process, form, and life are unified. The apprentice trains with a master for several years, throwing two or three hundred cups a day, only to destroy them; through the repeated motion of throwing a single form over and over again, the potter learns to create pieces unselfconsciously, almost without thinking. Only then are they worth keeping. The Japanese potter's aesthetic sensibility and concern with process—the antithesis of the commonly held Western concepts of productivity and product—have influenced many contemporary Western potters.

In Jim Makins's work, the rhythm of throwing is expressed through what he describes as the "intimate choreography that happens with finger gestures." Makins controls these gestures—wide, intentional throwing marks left in the clay—to achieve a loose, fluid quality in his bare-bones, functional forms.

Though throwing marks have existed as long as the wheel itself, historically they have been anathema to industrial producers of porcelain wares as well as to many studio ceramists. As early as the Sung dynasty, they were removed by Chinese potters to make way for decorative carving and painting, which were felt to be more suitable for porcelain's clear, smooth surface. Finger marks and other evidence of the forming process, however, are among the chief ways in which we can experience the clay's softness and fluidity—even in its fired, hardened state. They are also one of the oldest forms of decoration. While throwing marks may signify an unfinished state to many ceramists and connoisseurs, Makins accepts and manipulates them, as evidence of the process and as decorative element.

Makins's forms seem to grow inevitably from the nature of clay and the process of throwing, but they are not accidental. The sort of "accident" that produces a spontaneous masterpiece certainly can occur, but

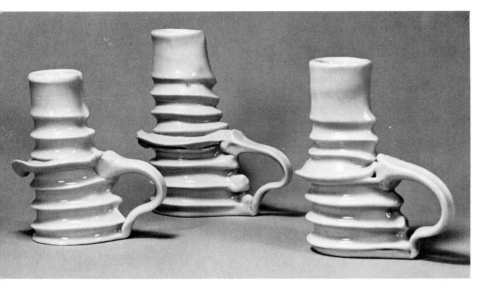

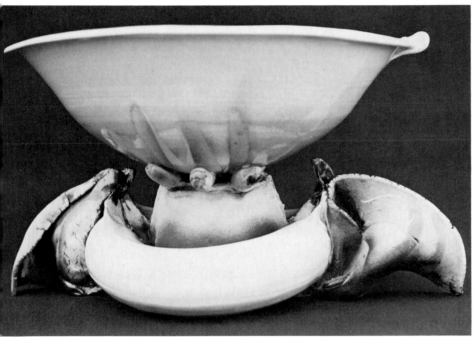

Above left
Two Bowls and Cup by Tom Coleman, 1980, 3″ x 7″; 5″ x 5½″; 3″ x 3½″ (7.6 x 17.8 cm; 12.7 x 14 cm; 7.6 x 8.9 cm). The sensuous forms of the wheel-thrown and altered cup and bowls reflect both the action of the wheel and the hand's touch. Photo: Rick Paulson.

Left
Ritual Vessel by Jerry Rothman, 1980, 26″ (66 cm). Solidity and weight characterize this wheel-thrown and hand-built vessel, but the luminosity of porcelain is still apparent even under the dark glaze.

Top
Three Cups by Kit Yen Tien Snyder, 1974, 6″ (15.2 cm). The deep ridges and the movement of these forms are another example of the sensuousness possible because of the fluidity of the clay. Collection Robert L. Pfannebecker. Photo: Axel and McCready.

Above
Donut-Footed Bowl by Susanne Stephenson, 1978, 8″ x 13″ x 15″ (20.3 x 33 x 38.1 cm). In this wheel-thrown and hand-built bowl, a sense of movement and contrast is expressed through juxtaposition of forms, glazed and unglazed surface textures, and colors.

this does not happen very often with a demanding material like porcelain, where mistakes due to inexperience or lack of control tend to look like just that. Makins's forms exhibit sureness and control while playing upon the inherent fluidity of porcelain. His technical competence and understanding of the limits of the wheel permit him the freedom to explore both material and tool, seemingly without restraint.

Fluidity and Form
Though all clays are soft and pliable before firing, none have the ability to permanently embody soft, voluptuous, flowing forms—in effect, to give permanence to fluidity— in the same manner as porcelain. It is the ultimate ceramic material in its ability to respond to actual movement during the forming process and to visually capture a sense of movement in its finished form. No matter how fluidity is expressed, the firing process freezes it in time the way a photograph permanently captures a passing moment. When this characteristic is utilized toward aesthetic ends, porcelain can create an appearance of billowy softness that belies its actual hardness and density when fired.

No art style illustrates organic form and line better than Art Nouveau, which dominated England and Western Europe from 1880 to 1910. Art Nouveau porcelain, specifically, marked a break with the neoclassical and other past movements. Henry Van de Velde, an influential Belgian artist, designer, and architect, became the major exponent of the new style in porcelain. Van de Velde made models for the Meissen factory, concentrating on fluid, functional forms in the Art Nouveau style. Believing that line has power, he strove to unify form and decoration rather than apply decoration as a secondary element. His flowing, linear motifs were applied to streamlined forms expressive of the new functionalism then beginning to develop (and which later evolved into the Bauhaus aesthetic).

The work of Paula Winokur exhibits the same affinity for flowing line and organic volume. One source of inspiration for Winokur is the rural Pennsylvania landscape where she lives. She transforms the elements of this environment, such as its rolling hills, into intimate personal images. Not only do Winokur's images parallel nature, but her forms also seem to evolve naturally from the physical character of the clay.

Imaginary landscapes portrayed on box lids exemplify the fluid potential of porcelain, where voluptuous surfaces, rich with gestural modeling, draw the eye over, around, and into the undulating folds of clay. Winokur provokes the desire to touch her

Eggshell Vase by Rozenburg factory, The Hague, Netherlands, 1900. This vase exemplifies the fluidity of both form and decoration typical during the Art Nouveau period of design in Europe at the turn of the century. ©Sotheby Parke-Bernet. Agent: Editorial Photocolor Archives.

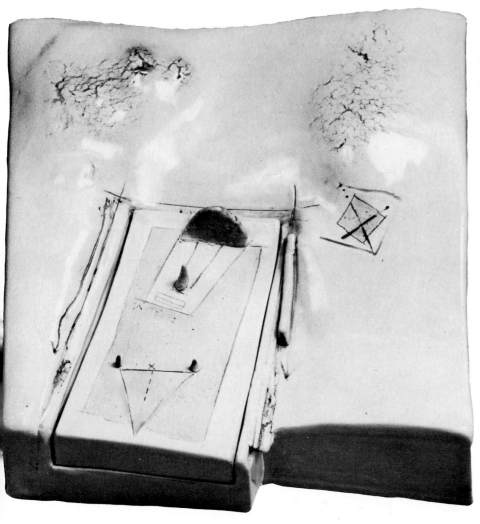

Above
Cylinder by Molly Cowgill, 1978, 12″ (30.5 cm) high. Although monochromatic, and very contemporary, this wheel-thrown and carved vase also has the swirling lines and lyrical contour typical of Art Nouveau.

Above left
Dreambox by Paula Winokur, 1974, 7″ x 11″ x 10½″ (17.8 x 27.9 x 26.7 cm). The celadon glaze, sulfates, and lusters with which Winokur has decorated this hand-built box help create the tactile, voluptuous surface.

Left
Aerial View: Hill by Paula Winokur, 1980, 28″ x 16½″ x 10″ (71 x 42 x 25 cm). Here, as in *Dreambox*, Winokur uses the box form to elevate and frame the tableau on top. The hand-built structure is decorated with a clear glaze, sulfates, and stains. Courtesy Helen Drutt Gallery, Philadelphia.

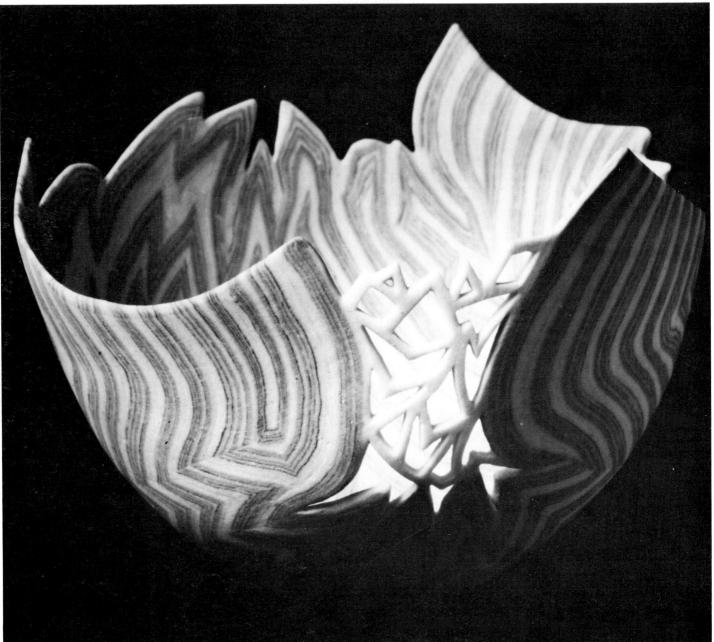

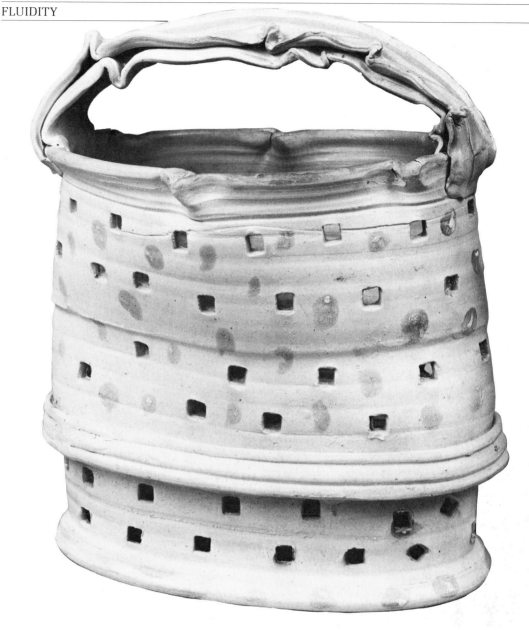

Top left
Bowl by Elsa Rady, 1979, 5½" x 14" (23 x 35.6 cm). The wide walls and angular rim of this wheel-thrown bowl project the form into space. The black matte glaze helps to anchor the form. Photo: Bob Lopez.

Left
Untitled by Dorothy Feibleman, 1980, 3½" (8.9 cm) high. Pierced. This form is made of inlaid turquoise, green, yellow, and white clays.

Right
Basket By Betty Woodman, 1979, 15" (38.1 cm). This wheel-thrown, salt-glazed basket has been altered, pierced, pulled, and distorted to create a visual weight not usually associated with porcelain. Photo: George Woodman.

pieces, for the tactile qualities of porcelain are an important aspect of her work. The imagery, which often incorporates sleeping faces, conveys the sense of being both the pillow on which one dreams and the dream itself, as in *Dreambox*, 1974. The angularity of her boxlike forms serves to heighten, by contrast, the feminine imagery on the lids. In her more recent boxes Winokur develops abstract images that resemble topographical views, combining these with three-dimensional protrusions and linear drawings that move from the exterior of a box to its interior cavity.

Another form of fluid "motion" is evident in Elsa Rady's bowls, which create a visual sensation of flight. The fluid line of the rim is enhanced by the widely flared walls, which grow from a tenuously balanced foot to lead the eye along the form and out into space. Sometimes Rady carves the rim of a piece with freehand curves, producing a scalloped effect and a pattern of rhythmic movement. The expectation of movement and flight, together with appreciation for Rady's great

skill, increases when one lifts a bowl to find it so light that it almost "takes off" from one's hands.

While most ceramists treat porcelain with extreme care and sensitivity, Betty Woodman speaks to the clay in a different language—and it listens. Her method of manipulating the wet clay is unique, as are her results. Using the wheel as a starting point, she makes thick discs which she aggressively pulls, cuts, and pushes, making them sag loosely. She actively distorts the symmetry of wheel-thrown forms into lively new postures, self-confidently capturing this gestural movement in her finished pieces. Woodman subverts the notions of preciousness and delicacy so often associated with porcelain forms.

The fluidity of porcelain can be expressed visually in many ways—from pristine, classical lines to forms that ooze with sensuality. Once fired, porcelain, above all other clays, conveys a sense of permanent fluidity—motion suspended in time—with unparalleled distinction.

CHAPTER SEVEN

THE SURFACE

A GOOD DEAL of porcelain's reputation as the "accompaniment of splendor and magnificence"[1] is due to the beauty of its surface, which not only embodies porcelain's essence but also serves as a blank canvas for embellishment. Pure white and glassy smooth, porcelain's surface offers the artist a multitude of possibilities for decorative treatments—from the simple clear glaze used during China's Sung dynasty to today's methods incorporating glazes, stains, slips, enamels, overglazes, decals, and carving. Although early Chinese and European decoration often consisted of simply a glazed surface embellished with a family or clan emblem, the contemporary ceramist is more inclined to use it as a means of personal expression.

Taken literally, a surface is a skin, an outer layer. Where clay and glaze are fused by extreme heat, however, as in high-fired porcelain, the surface is not superficial. Indeed, porcelain is porcelain through and through: all its qualities—whiteness, density, glassiness, and creamy texture—coalesce in its surface.

The edge of a broken shard of glazed porcelain would reveal, upon close examination, an almost imperceptible line separating clay from glaze. This intermediate layer is the interface where clay and glaze join. For many traditionalists this interface serves to define true porcelain, as clay and glaze mature at the same temperature and fuse completely. By this definition, bone china does not qualify as porcelain—regardless of some similarities and a shared aesthetic—because of its high bisque- and low glaze-firing temperatures. Likewise, in low-fired white earthenware there is minimal fusion of clay with the glaze, which rests on the surface as a coating.

Decoration

Before the issue of decoration can be discussed, it is important to clarify some misused terms surrounding it. There are two types of ornamentation: structural and applied.[2] A subtle example of structural decoration alone is the finger marks left by the potter's hands while throwing a form on the wheel. These marks are both the physical trace of the forming process and decorative horizontal bands that give the piece a sense of vitality. Structural ornamentation also can evolve from the nature of the material itself. For example, glaze provides both physical strength and an impermeable finish, but it also lends a piece color and texture, which are decorative characteristics—and these are consciously applied. There are other examples of decorative elements that are both structural and applied. The handle of a cup exists primarily so that the cup can be held. Why then, given such a simple function, are there so many varieties of handles? Because the handle also must be visually integrated with the form of the cup itself. Applied decoration alone is pure embellishment—such as painting, carving, incising, and plastic additions—that is not structurally part of the form.

Left
Vase by Carolyn Chester, 1980, 10½″ (26.7 cm) high. Manganese pink glazes fuse at the top of this vase and visually soften this area of the form. Photo: Harvey Ferdschneider.

Right
Aesthetic Craze by Louis Marak, 1978, 18½″ x 11½″ (47 x 29.2 cm). This slab-built, standing box form is finished with underglazes, underglaze pencils, and china paint. Photo: Eddie Owen.

A deeply rooted semantic confusion about the words *decorative* and *decoration* has led to further misunderstandings concerning the decorative arts. The term *decorative* too often refers to any forms made of traditional craft materials, regardless of their intention or use. The term *decorative arts* originated during the eighteenth century, when the French made an arbitrary distinction between painting and sculpture on the one hand, and the making of utilitarian objects such as ceramics, furniture, and woven tapestries, on the other.[3] Before this time, no distinction had been made between the so-called fine and decorative arts. Herbert Read says of the issue, "A form in itself may be 'decorative,' but that usually implies the relation of an object to its setting."[4] He is suggesting that things intended to function in the kitchen should not be categorized with highly embellished objects intended to decorate the parlor. This distinction between the fine and decorative arts is beginning to fade, as materials usually associated with the decorative arts, such as clay, glass, and fiber, are now being used to create works that are expressive rather than functional. In time, the merits of all works of art will be contingent, not on their materials, but on the level of their aesthetic rewards.

The decorative arts are a playground for ornamentation. The phenomenon known as *horror vaccui*—an intolerance of empty space—perhaps explains the common need of all human beings to fill spaces and the reason we often experience bare environments as uncomfortably sterile. Another explanation for ornamentation is, of course, the simple human need to create and be surrounded by beauty. Perhaps out of striving to emulate nature's creative powers, artists persist in their efforts to beautify. All civilizations exhibit decorative tendencies, and even the simplest tribal societies show strong impulses to embellish homes, tools, weapons, utensils, and even the human body, disproving the notion that art and decoration are only of secondary importance to humankind.

A present-day example of the need for ornament may be found in the recent reaction against the cerebral content of Minimal Art. Finding so little visual nourishment in Minimalism, many artists have turned to pattern painting and other styles incorporating the vocabulary of decoration—color, rhythm, pattern, harmony, and balance. Some people judge decorative expression as trivial and its motives as suspect. "There are those who think that decorative art exists not so much to bind up the wounds of the nation," wrote *New York Times* critic John Russell, "as to smother it in confectioners' sugar."[5]

Vase by Edward O'Reilly, 1980, 26" (66 cm) high. The fusion of overlapping, multiple glazes creates depth and brilliance in this wheel-thrown vase. Photo: John Littleton.

Faceted Jar by Stephen Fabrico, 1980, 12" x 5" (30.5 x 14 cm). Fabrico designs forms specifically to be used with glazes that break into brilliant colors as one glaze flows through another, as shown in this wheel-thrown and carved jar. Photo: Robert E. Barrett.

The complex relationships between material, surface, form, and function rest on a delicate balance. Even those who regard decoration as ancillary to form must admit that a form's identity is affected by it. The idea that "ornament should be appropriate to the form of the object it decorates,"[6] in Herbert Read's words, is reasonable if form is primary; but "appropriateness" is always subject to the moods of current fashion. During the rococo period, decoration took power over form, which served as a background for elaborate ornamentation. The Bauhaus school, on the other hand, held that form and decoration should be synonymous: their tenet that "form follows function" leaves little room for extraneous additions.

Often the success of decoration reflects the initial intentions of the artist. If decoration has been used to cover a mediocre form or is added as an afterthought, this is usually obvious in the finished piece. When considered from the start, however, decoration can enhance and harmonize with the form.

A modern artist who attempts to unify form and decoration is Louis Marak. In *Mug with Boxed Balls*, 1972, he paints and draws with underglaze, building up relief with repeated, sketchy lines. Porcelain's smooth white surface accepts Marak's detailed two-dimensional drawings, which become three-dimensional and hence part of the form itself. He juxtaposes drawings with thin folds of porcelain, adding festoons and draperies around his "cups." Modeled ribbons and illusionistic drawing make the forms appear to be draped in the manner of classical statuary. To some of these forms he adds wings (vestigial handles), which give them a trophylike presence.

Intimate scale is important in these early works by Marak, for the viewer can enter the space of the object. In his recent larger-scale work, Marak has gone on a decorative escapade, creating elaborately patterned, abstract drawings that visually jump forward from tall, standing box forms. At the top of the form, as he has done with *Aesthetic Craze*, he places rodlike three-dimensional appendages that recall the earlier vestigial handles on his cups.

Glaze

In fourteenth-century China, the simultaneous development of a refined clay body, feldspathic glazes, and sophisticated firing techniques affected surface treatments as well. The most fundamental of these was glazing, which still endures as a valued surface treatment because it not only makes the clay body stronger and impervious to liquids, but also because it is beautiful. Early Ch'ai wares earned such a reputation that "fragments of it were said to dazzle the eyes, and when worn on armour to turn aside missiles in battle."[7] Glazes were thought to be capable of detecting poisoned foods as well. In China and also in medieval Europe, it was thought that if foods containing poison were placed in celadon dishes, the glaze would turn black—a useful indication to royalty fearful of assassination.

The following Chinese legend indicates how highly prized certain glazes were. While a potter was closing up his kiln, a chicken managed to enter it unnoticed and was trapped inside. When the firing was finished and the pots emerged covered in a beautiful, never before seen, copper-red glaze, the potter and his whole village were astonished. So, too, was the emperor, who was so impressed he made him a royal potter and promptly ordered hundreds more copper-red pots. The potter set to work, diligently trying to duplicate the red glaze. The tale continues as told by Rona Murray:

Despite years of effort, [he] was not able to achieve the glorious red glaze that his Emperor wanted. Poor man, no matter how he mixed his formulas, how he controlled the atmosphere, to what temperature he fired, his dream collapsed every time he opened his kiln. Finally, one day in despair over losing face so continuously, he had his assistant brick him into the kiln before starting the roaring fires. After the cooling period, when his horrified friends were able to approach the dead ashes, they found no trace of his body, which had been totally consumed. However, his pots were the glowing, immortal red of blood, known as copper red and famous throughout the world to this day.[8]

Partly due to their technical difficulty and partly to their sheer beauty, copper-red glazes have always been fervently sought by potters. Nonetheless, even simple, clear glazes capture the glassy brilliance that has so captivated potters throughout history. To porcelain especially, glaze imparts a shimmering vibrancy that is caused by the fusion of body and glaze. Whether a viscous Chinese Sung glaze, a fatty Korean glaze, or a fiery copper red, the brilliant chromatic depths possible in glazed porcelain are very different from the appearance of a superficial glaze coating on earthenware. Glaze surfaces can range from clear and shiny to dry and matte, from transparent to opaque.

Along with clay and glaze composition, the kiln's atmosphere during firing plays a crucial part in determining the character of a glaze. Oxidation firing allows for a greater range of colors that are pure and bright, but these generally lack the depth and richness of glazes fired in a reduction atmosphere.

Copper reds and celadons, especially treasured for their resemblance to rubies and
jade, can be achieved only in reduction firing. This is because in an oxidation atmosphere copper becomes green, not red. Likewise, the small amount of iron used to create
the turquoise, green, and gray hues of celadon glazes in the reduction kiln would, in an
oxidation kiln, produce tan and brown. (It is
interesting to note that Chinese celadons varied from region to region; the native feldspars largely determined their quality and
tone.)

Salt or sodium vapors introduced into a reduction atmosphere volatize and create a
glaze by combining chemically with the clay.
This self-glazing technique produces a beautiful pebbly surface often likened to that of
an orange peel. Another firing technique produces crystalline glazes, created by slowly
cooling the work in an oxidation atmosphere.
Although this method causes the glaze to become almost perilously fluid, it allows crystalline patterns resembling flowers and star-
bursts to form on the surface. A crackle glaze,
characterized by a network of cracks that
gives the surface a kind of spider-web effect,
is caused by a glaze that doesn't perfectly
"fit" the clay. Though it can be considered
a flaw (referred to as crazing, because it
lacks the strength of a well-fitting glaze), the
crackle is also decorative. The Chinese often
rubbed tea, colored dyes, or even metallic
lusters into the cracks of these wares to emphasize the web pattern.

Contemporary ceramist Harris Deller
glazes his work with rich copper reds and
celadons because, as he says, porcelain's
"brilliance and purity, fused with a fluid and
luminous glaze, bring forth abstract qualities."[9] Glaze allows light to play on the surface, but its complete fusion with the clay
also brings the whiteness beneath closer to
the eye and simultaneously carries the eye
deep into the clay itself.

Many modern ceramists, no less than their
ancient forerunners, are avid experimenters,
always searching for the "ultimate" glaze.
Some strive to equal Chinese achievements,
while others use the past as a starting point
for new effects. Laura Andreson and Al King,
both Californians, have been developing
new clays and glazes since the 1930s. Andreson established the ceramics department
at the University of California at Los Angeles
in 1933 and remained there until her retirement in 1970. In the early fifties, Andreson
was inspired to work in porcelain by the
work of Al King, who has devoted himself to
developing iridescent and opalescent colors
for porcelain, "soaking" his pots for days in
the Chinese manner to achieve a more vivid
appearance.

Left
Covered Jar, Sung dynasty (960-1280), 10″ (25.4 cm) high. This jar is a piece of porcelaneous Lung Ch'uan ware with a celadon glaze. Collection The Metropolitan Museum of Art, Fletcher Fund, 1934.

Right
The Firmament by Norman Schulman, 1979. The pebbly surface on this wheel-thrown, slip-trailed jar is the result of salt firing. Photo: Eddie Owen.

Far right
Crab Vase by Adelaide Alsop Robineau, 1908, 7½″ (19.1 cm) high. Incised with a crab form for decoration, this wheel-thrown vase is finished with brown and tan flowing matte glazes and aqua, blue, and orange crystalline glazes. Collection Everson Museum of Art, Syracuse, New York. Photo: Jane Courtney Frisse.

Three Pots by Harlan House, 3″ x 11″ (7.6 x 27.9 cm); 7″ (17.8 cm); 9″ (22.9 cm). These pots are finished with a crackle glaze.

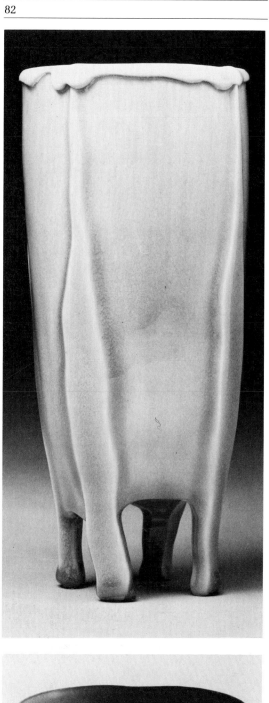

Andreson's forms follow clean, simplified lines and are made to fulfill a particular function, such as holding flowers. She takes pride in creating a glaze to suit each individual form. Some treatments include adding cobalt nitrate to the body and covering it with white glaze to produce a mustard green or yellow color. Through the years Andreson experimented with such things as shellac and moth balls (until it was learned they produce a deadly nerve gas) during reduction firing. This gave the glaze a slightly runny but lustrous metallic finish with occasional crystalline spots.

The Surface as Canvas

Whether it is seen as a flat surface or a rounded form, porcelain is an alluring foil for color. But using color on porcelain presents a specific challenge the artist who paints on canvas does not experience—that of an indirect method that sometimes yields surprising results. Whether it is poured, dripped, dipped, or sprayed, liquid glaze applied to a piece leaves much to the ceramist's imagination, since the unfired metallic oxides are not the same colors they will be once the firing process has changed them chemically. If multiple glazes are used, they react with one another and chemically unite during firing, and their combined color effects may differ markedly from their appearance when used individually.

Toshiko Takaezu, an influential teacher and artist, and Eva Kwong, a ceramist from Pennsylvania, are among the large number of ceramists who treat glaze in a painterly way. They are interested in exploring the depth and beauty of glaze; for them, white porcelain serves as a ground upon which abstractions appear in a high-fired palette of colors. Glaze is handled as paint might be, in built-up layers.

Eva Kwong's work, in particular, evinces an affinity with painting canvas. She applies glaze directly to dry clay in thicknesses varying from a thin film to low relief. Using brush and spray techniques, she builds up numerous layers of different glazes, at times scratching through them to the clay. *Warm Currents*, 1978, is an example in which images from nature—mountains, water, and air—are transformed into a sea of soft, dreamlike color, creating three-dimensional landscapes on a two-dimensional surface.

Geoffrey Swindell grew up within the environs of Stoke-on-Trent, England. Though surrounded by ceramics manufacturers such as Wedgwood and Coalport, he was not interested in designing for industry. He found commercial ceramic forms too predictable and limited to repeating historical patterns, and so he chose to work as a studio ceramist,

Left
Vase by Al King, 14″ (35.6 cm) high. This wheel-thrown vessel has a flambé crystal glaze. Photo: Herman V. Wall.

Far left, top
Cylinder by Harris Deller, 1980, 9″ x 4″ (22.9 x 10 cm). The glaze on this cylinder adds to the abstract quality of the form, creating an appearance of depressions and mounds in the clay. Courtesy Helen Drutt Gallery, Philadelphia.

Far left, bottom
Vase by Laura Andreson, 1979, 9″ x 6″ (22.9 x 15.2 cm). A rust crystal glaze completes this vase, which was wheel-thrown and then altered. Photo: Mark Schwartz.

Top right
Bowl by Barbara Tiso, 1976, 8½″ (21.6 cm) diam. This bowl is finished with an oxide glaze applied in an abstract, painterly way. Photo: Michael McTwigan.

Bottom right
Untitled by Toshiko Takaezu, 1977, 10″ x 6″ (25.4 x 12.2 cm). The glaze on this form is treated in a particularly painterly way. Collection Ruth and Edward Tanenhouse. Photo: Michael McTwigan.

creating individual pieces. Swindell says he is seeking a blend between organic and manufactured forms, which is evinced by his interest in seashells and toys.

> The ideas for my work come from the objects and images I collect. The influences on my current work include: shells and other sea creatures; tin-plate toys; science fiction landscapes; bad illustrations of space hardware; bad illustrations of natural forms; molded plastic artifacts; juke boxes; early industrial pottery like Elers, Whieldon, and Wedgwood.[10]

Though of a miniature scale (from three to four inches), Swindell's forms have a monumental presence. A typical vessel swells from a tiny foot to a bulbous belly and culminates in a small mouth. The various elements of the pot are sharply articulated, emphasizing and defining the sections. These areas act as boundaries for layers of built-up glaze that give modulated color effects. Swindell's mastery of glaze techniques is apparent in his blending of graduated colors and textures to render a surface that is best described as elegant.

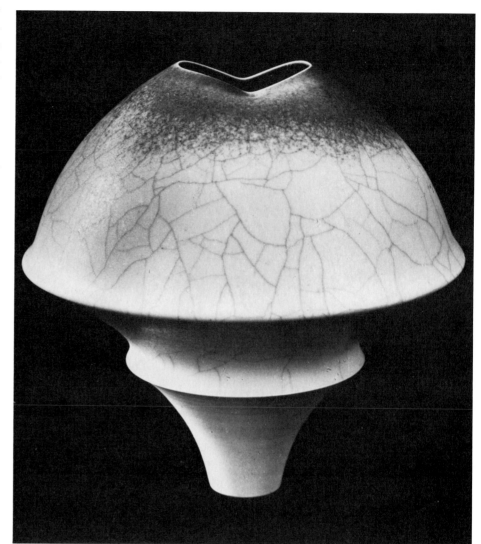

Berkeley, California, ceramist Juta Savage treats utilitarian forms as blank two- and three-dimensional canvases; when they are leather hard (still damp, yet dry enough to handle without their losing shape), she applies colored slips to them. She overlays wet strips of newspaper on the clay's surface to form a resist and then paints the slips over the entire surface. When the paper is removed, irregular areas of slip remain where the clay had been exposed. She and Ann Christenson, with whom she has shared a studio, both use this technique. While Savage tends to utilize porcelain's smooth, clear surface as a base for complex patterns, Christenson's painting on porcelain is expressionistic. Spontaneous, loose splashes create festive surfaces on baskets, teapots, and cups. She uses the clay very thickly and facets the outer surfaces of forms. The decorative painting may seem unintegrated with the forms, but on close examination it exhibits a cohesive boldness.

Porcelain's surface has been compared to vellum, and some artists use it just as they would a blank sheet of paper. Jim Rothrock, who lives in Los Angeles, begins by casting voluptuous forms intended to capture porcelain's sensuous potential. Irregularly shaped, some are lidded containers and others are spherical forms with recessed cavities. He paints their silky surfaces with watery patterns, lines, and marks to "punctuate the movement, sometimes harmoniously and at other times in discord."[11] The colorations of these marks have the softness of watercolor paints soaking into paper, with calligraphic

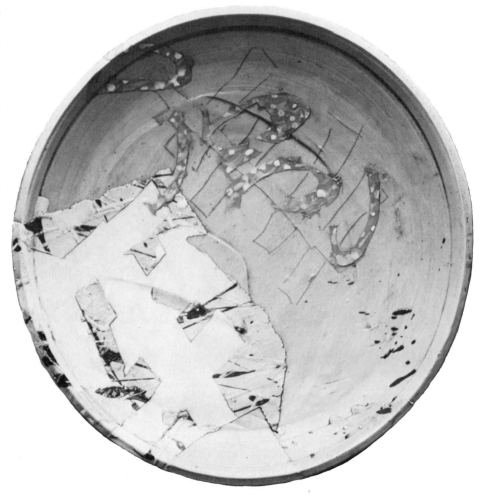

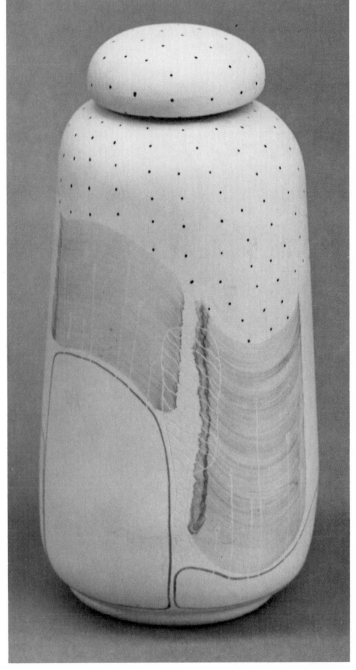

Top left
Pot by Geoffrey Swindell, 1977, 4'' (10.2 cm) high. Modulated colors and textures create surface elegance on this glazed wheel-thrown pot.

Left
Plate by Juta Savage, 1978, 13'' (33 cm) diam. This wheel-thrown plate is done with resist design, underglaze, and glaze. Photo: Charlie Frizzel.

Top
Cups With Saucers by Juta Savage, 1980, 3'' x 5'' (7.6 x 12.7 cm) each. Loose splashes of color create a spontaneous effect on these wheel-thrown, hand-trimmed, colored cups and saucers finished with an underglaze and a glaze. Photo: Eddie Owen.

Above
Large Bowl with Round Hole by James Rothrock, 1979, 7'' x 11'' (17.8 x 27.9 cm). Typical of the way Rothrock works, this bowl was cast and assembled and then oxide-decorated and partially glazed. Photo: Eddie Owen.

Right
Untitled by James Rothrock, 1976, 12'' x 5'' (30.5 x 12.7 cm). This lidded container was cast, decorated with oxide, and partially glazed. Collection Michele DeAngelus.

inflections disrupting the surface and at the same time carrying the eye over the form. Other pieces are tied with string and stained when they are bisqued, producing in the finished form the effect of once having been bound and wrapped. Rothrock emphasizes porcelain's creamy, tactile quality by applying colorants to unglazed clay so that both the quality and color of the surface become more visually accessible.

Colored Clays

Porcelain's purity and texture provide an ideal base to which to add color, thereby introducing color into the structure of the form itself rather than merely applying it to the surface. This is done by blending pigments into either dry or plastic clays. English ceramist Mary Rogers has pointed out the similarity between colored clays and rocks such as granite, sandstone, and slate.[12] By coloring the clay itself, the ceramist achieves detailed patterns and textures without additional surface painting. The tonal range of these clays is affected by firing temperature, for high heat causes bright colors to burn out somewhat, producing a more muted spectrum.

As early as A.D. 600, clays were partially blended to produce a variegated, marbleized body. Marbled clays were popular in Europe during the eighteenth century, but they reached the height of sophistication in nineteenth-century Japan. Emulating *millefiore* glass techniques, ceramists worked various colors into the clay which they then formed into rolls resembling refrigerator cookie dough. Sliced into multiple *pastilles* or lozenges, they were used as mosaic sections and pressed into a mold to build the form. The particular beauty of these wares lies in their intricate, ordered detail.

Thomas Hoadley, Curtis Benzle, and Jane Peiser are contemporary ceramists who use these techniques. Hoadley incorporates both marbleizing and mosaics into his classical, stonelike forms. Benzle's visually weightless bowls, which appear to stretch toward the light, are made by combining colored, translucent patterns. Jane Peiser, a resident artist at Penland School of Crafts in North Carolina, uses a complex variation of *millefiore*, incorporating numerous sections—people, animals, and abstract patterns—made of colored clays into each piece. After the structure is complete, it is salt-glazed and china-painted. Her whimsical imagery celebrating texture and bright colors is a unique blend of decorative methods akin to folk art from around the world.

Carving and Incising

Throughout porcelain's history, carving and incising have been especially effective

Top left
Piedmont by Marge Levy, 1980, 7″ x 22″ (17.8 x 55.9 cm). This unusual combination of circular and geometric forms was hand-built and then underglazed and overglazed. Photo: M. Lee Fatherree.

Left
Untitled by Irene Sims, 1979, 4½″ (11.5 cm) high. The bird images are painted in black and gray slip on this unglazed jar. Photo: F. Thurston.

Above
You May Be Luckier than You Think by Alexa Grace, 1979, 7″ x 11″ (17.8 x 27.9 cm). This illustrative porcelain piece has the same sensibility as Grace's illustrations for *The New York Times, New Yorker* magazine, and various books.

Right
Covered Jar by William Wilhelmi, 1979, 8″ (20.3 cm) high. The artist created the design on this jar with wax resist, underglaze, and glaze.

Left
Tall Vase by Jane Peiser, 1976, 13" x 8" (33 x 20.3 cm). This fanciful creation is made with colored clays, china paints, decals, luster, and a salt glaze. Collection Ruth and Edward Tanenhaus. Photo: Michael McTwigan.

Right
Scarab Vase (The Apotheosis of the Toiler) by Adelaide Alsop Robineau, 1910, 16½" (41.9 cm) high. The intricate beetle decoration on this vase is created by incising and piercing the clay. The glazes are copper green. Collection Everson Museum of Art, Syracuse, New York. Photo: Jane Courtney Frisse.

Below
Marie by Curtis Benzle, 1979, 6" x 10" (15.2 x 25.4 cm). Photo: Kent Bowser. This delicate, translucent bowl is patterned with colored clays using a millefiore technique.

Bottom
Striped Jar by Thomas Hoadley, 1980, 8" (20.3 cm) high. Here color is added to the clay itself. Hoadley feels that marbleizing effects and inlay are like frozen slices of soft clays interacting with each other.

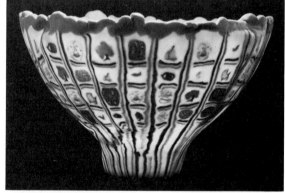

modes of surface decoration, largely due to the fact that relief decoration stands out so clearly on porcelain's smooth white surface. The apogee of carving was achieved by Adelaide Alsop Robineau, whose *Scarab Vase* of 1910 required over one thousand hours to create. An obsessive tour-de-force, the entire surface is covered with tiny beetles.

Molly Cowgill is a modern ceramist who adheres to this mode of delicately embellished, monochromatic decoration, following; the Chinese tradition of carving natural subjects and abstract patterns. Cowgill's gentle, low-relief carving is straightforward, but subtle color variations occur where celadon glaze collects in and around crevices. Her images have no direct symbolic meaning; rather, they are a synthesis of decoration and form that is more abstract than representational.

Symbolic Decoration

Ceramic materials have almost always served as carriers of symbolic language. Whether expressed graphically or sculpturally, "the emblems have a genuine meaning in relation to life," writes Philip Rawson.[12] As we know from studies of ancient cultures (including earlier stages of our own), people believe these symbols have the power to affect their environment. Emblems on primitive pottery have associations with food and water, ceremony and superstition, life and death. On Chinese ceramics, the ubiquitous dragon represents kingly power and natural forces such as thunder, floods, and the stirring of springtime. The phoenix, unicorn, and fish exemplify virtue, readiness to fight, and good luck, respectively. Flowers, too, have possessed "magical and honorific power."[13] Appearing first on architecture, they later inspired ceramic decoration. The rose, queen of flowers, is a prevalent symbol for constant renewal, long life, and eternal spring. The lotus, from the time of ancient Egypt and Greece, has represented the spirit's passage between the physical and metaphysical worlds. While metaphysical and superstitious emblems may hold little importance in industrialized Western society, artists continue to borrow from past sources, keeping the tradition and techniques of embellishment vital. Pat Probst Gilman's dragons certainly differ from those menacingly sober ones found on Chinese vessels, for beyond the formality of her classically carved and embellished urns is a humorous side. Gilman's breed lazily sprawl around otherwise severe forms, yet her work is obviously linked to the Chinese in the way she blends form with incised floral meanders and graphic motifs.

Many contemporary ceramists continue to

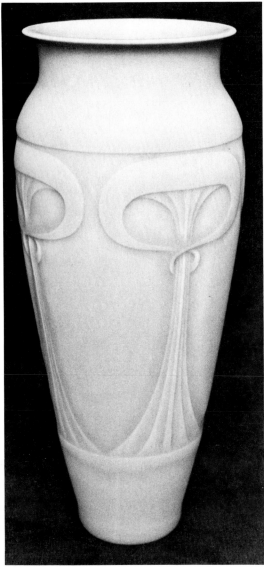

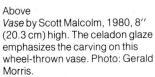

Above
Vase by Scott Malcolm, 1980, 8''
(20.3 cm) high. The celadon glaze
emphasizes the carving on this
wheel-thrown vase. Photo: Gerald
Morris.

Top right
Bowl by Molly Cowgill, 1978, 3'' x
6'' (7.6 x 15.2 cm). The monochromatic decoration is carved into this
wheel-thrown bowl finished with a
celadon glaze.

Right
Dragon-Covered Urn by Pat
Probst Gilman, 1978, 16'' (40.6
cm) high. This clear-glazed urn
with incised design was wheel-
thrown and then assembled with
pulled and hand-built handles.

Opposite page
Untitled by Regis Brodie, 1980,
20'' (50.8 cm) high. Brodie creates
the intricate pattern on this salt-
glazed vessel with inlaid clay and
black slip.

interpret life through symbolism, but their symbols tend to have personal rather than universal meanings. Deborah Horrell, Frank Fleming, and Jack Earl are intrigued by animal imagery, but the connection appears to be deeper than mere fascination with animals. For example, Horrell uses the duck as a vehicle for both sculptural forms and graphic images resembling those seen in Japanese Ukiyo-e prints. Her delightful exploration of the geisha's identity (and undoubtedly her own) as personified in the duck is humorous, yet serious. In her piece entitled *Courtship à la Utamaro,* 1979, she places a slate, bearing the image of a duck, against a nest made of white, unglazed porcelain bones. Although the viewer first experiences the piece as ambiguous stacked forms, its shrinelike presence soon makes itself felt. *It's a Question of Identity,* 1979, is a piece that is half skeleton, half duck; anatomical drawings on the duck's "skin" make visible the hidden bones. Both works by Horrell reveal a vulnerability usually protected from view by outer layers of skin.

Under and Over the Glaze

Underglaze, glaze, overglaze—each of these ceramic processes produces a variety of effects. Underglazes are oxides that are used as washes or slips and are fired to high temperatures along with the glaze. Brushwork is softened by the fusing of the substance with the glaze itself. Great skill is required to brush on underglaze, for "painting on the absorbent surface is irrevocable and so requires a particularly sure touch."[14]

Especially renowned for the beauty of their underglaze painting are the blue-and-white Ming wares from China. Intricate designs incorporating three-clawed dragons, floral and fruit sprays, folk tales, and emblems were painted on the clay in cobalt blue. Then they were covered by a transparent glaze that blurred the fine lines during the molten stage in firing. The Japanese also developed refined painting techniques and styles. Prevalent among styles using underglaze imagery was Nabeshima ware, which employed painted decorative motifs of pine, bamboo, and peonies, among others. The final development of this style was polychrome Nabeshima, which combined underglaze blue outlines of the decorative subject with overglaze enamels.

Overglaze enameling (or china painting) was fully developed in China by the fifteenth century and has taken various forms as it has traveled from Asia through Europe to the United States. Hard-edge china painting is applied over the fired glaze and then fired at a lower temperature. China paints do not actually fuse with the glaze but adhere to the

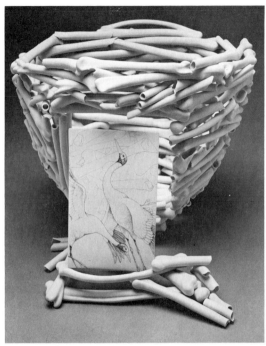

Above
Courtship à la Utamaro by Deborah Horrell, 1979, 18'' x 13'' x 14''
(45.7 x 33 x 35.6 cm). Horrell equates the white unglazed bones with life, seeing them as the essence of structure and the foundation of existence. The duck image on the slate is created with graphite. Photo: Steven Young.

Right
It's a Question of Identity by Deborah Horrell, 1979, 25'' x 36'' x 5½''
(61 x 91.4 x 14 cm). Here Horrell creates this half skeleton, half duck from modeled and cast porcelain with graphite and basswood.
Photo: Steven Young.

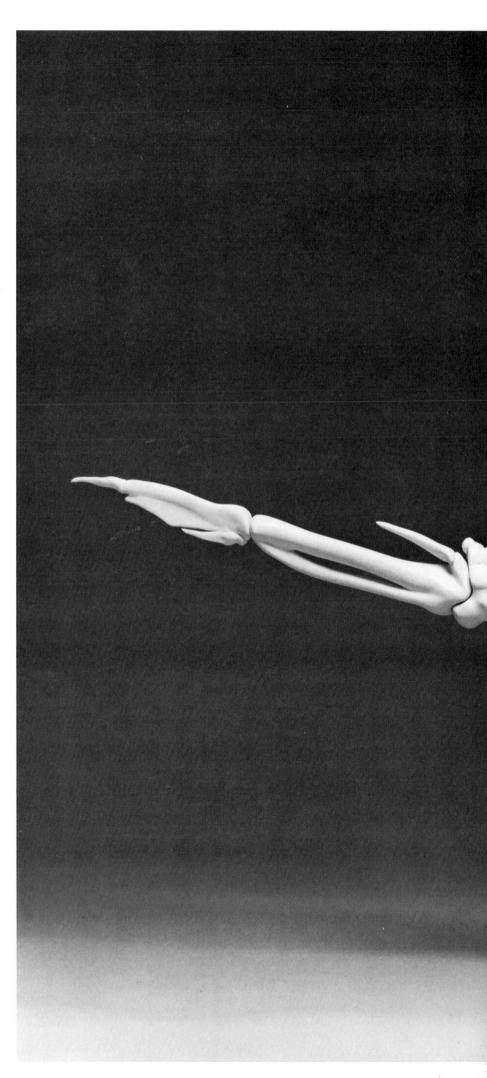

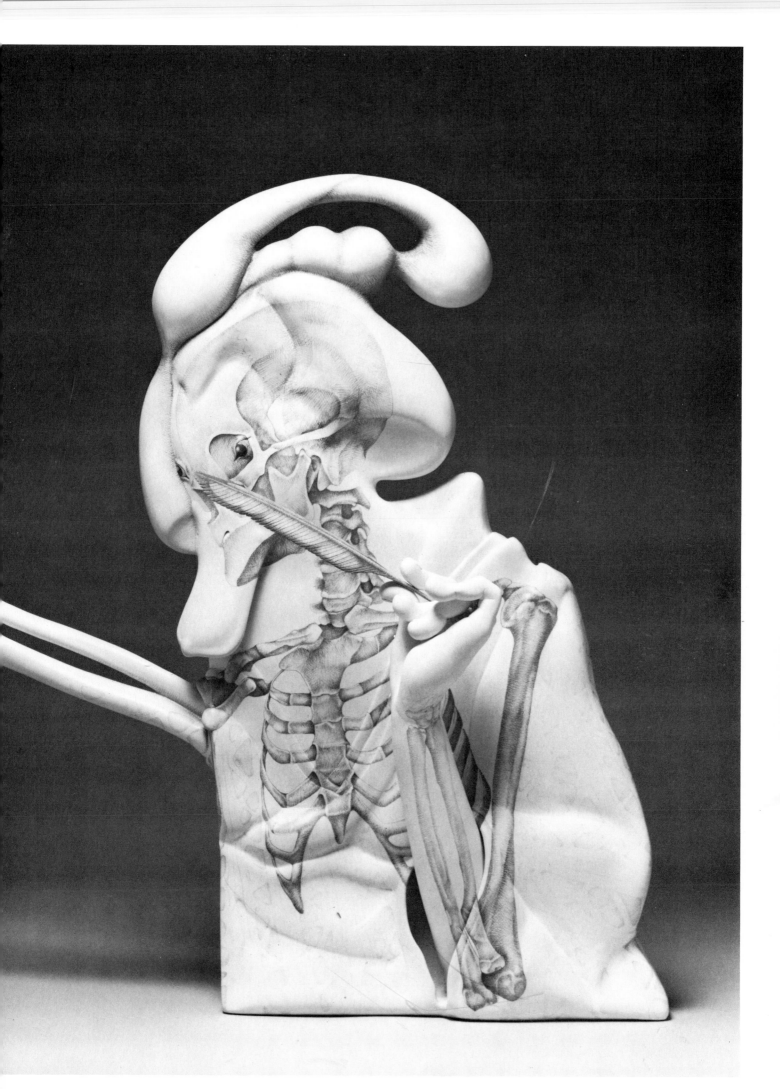

surface as if they were an outer skin. They are therefore not as durable as glazes.

In France, by the third quarter of the eighteenth century, Sèvres had developed an extreme form of overglaze imagery in which gilt and polychromatic decoration obliterated the clay surface. The baroque style prevalent at that time reflected people's taste for ornate decoration—"the more the better" seems to have been their aesthetic credo. While such surface decoration was certainly ambitious, the Sèvres porcelain makers seem to have lost sight of the unique qualities of porcelain itself.

The styles exemplified by both Chinese and European attention to detail and the expressiveness of the Japanese brushstroke have influenced many of today's ceramists. Richard Hensley uses underglaze in a fashion directly reflecting historical brushwork treatments. Tom Spleth brushes undulating ribbons of color on his cast forms and, by scratching through the oxide and glaze, reveals the clay's surface below. This creates a crisp line within the bold brushstroke of color.

Ralph Bacerra is a well-known California ceramist who paints with a sumi brush or French quill, employing traditional overglaze and underglaze brush techniques. His patterns and colors are a direct reflection of his passion for Asian ceramics, especially the colorful Imari ware of Japan. Bacerra's stacked and lidded forms are his true strength. He selects specific areas to serve as backgrounds for his designs, which are at their best when the softened underglaze colors, fused with the glaze, are highlighted by areas of crisp overglaze enamels. Some areas of clay are left uncovered to juxtapose patterns over and under the glaze; hence, porcelain's lustrous surface potential and depth are brought out fully.

In nineteenth-century America, the work of china painting was considered suitable only for women. In midwestern and southern cities—Cincinnati, St. Louis, New Orleans—prominent women then had a large, if undervalued, role in the decorative arts. Society's attitude at the time was: "Let men construct and women decorate."[15] As decorators, women fulfilled this restricted role until the late 1870s. Then a few women began to both form and decorate their wares, much to the dismay of those who could not believe that socially prominent ladies would choose to "dirty" themselves with wet clay. China painting flourished in America until the 1920s, when it declined due to a lack of materials during World War I and to a change in taste—for by then earthy, gestural painting in the Japanese manner had displaced the calculated aesthetic of china painting.

Above
Untitled by Jenny Lind, 1979, 18″ (45.7 cm) high. This form is both wheel-thrown and assembled, the surface accomplished by applications of underglaze, glaze, and black luster. Photo: R. Faller.

Left
Vessel by Tom Spleth, 1979, 21″ x 8″ (53.3 x 20.3 cm). Spleth paints bold, undulating color onto this cast, oxide-decorated, glazed form. Courtesy Helen Drutt Gallery, Philadelphia. Photo: Eddie Owen.

Opposite page, top
Plate by Richard Hensley, 1979, 18″ (45.7 cm) diam. Hensley's intricate brushwork is evident here on this wheel-thrown plate with oxide decoration and glaze.

Opposite page, bottom
Plate by Mineo Mizuno, 1971, 20″ (50.8 cm) diam. Cobalt underglazes and transparent glaze help create the hard-edged design on this wheel-thrown plate. Collection Fred Marer.

Left
Sappho Plate from *The Dinner Party* by Judy Chicago, 1979, 14″ (35.6 cm) diam. This porcelain plate is jiggered, glazed, and painted with china paint. © Judy Chicago. Photo: Mary McNally.

Below
The Dinner Party by Judy Chicago, 1979, 46½′ (11.8 m) each side. This mixed-media project is a combination of china-painted porcelain and neddlework. © Judy Chicago. Photo: Mary McNally.

Right
Figure of the Virgin, Fulda factory, Germany, about 1780, 14½″ (37 cm) high. This hard-paste porcelain figure is finished with enamels and gilding. Courtesy Cooper-Hewitt Museum, Smithsonian Institution.

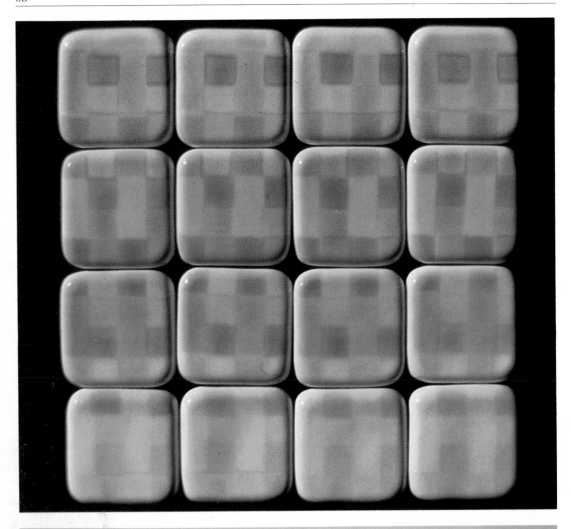

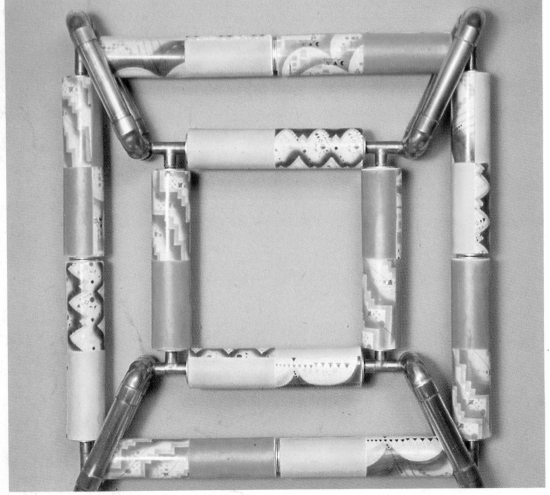

Wall Piece by Joseph Detwiler, 25″ x 25″ x 2″ (63.5 x 63.5 x 5.1 cm). Detwiler casts the forms and patterns of the modules that form this grid.

Clip by Robert Milnes, 1979, 33″ x 35″ x 7″ (83.8 x 88.9 x 17.8 cm). This construction is cast porcelain with airbrushed underglazes, transparent and opaque glazes, and copper tubing. Courtesy Theo Portnoy Gallery, New York. Photo: Eddie Owen.

Right
Mochian Memories by Joe Bova, 1979. Bova models his forms and then applies china paints directly to the unglazed surface to get a waxy, somewhat dull finish.

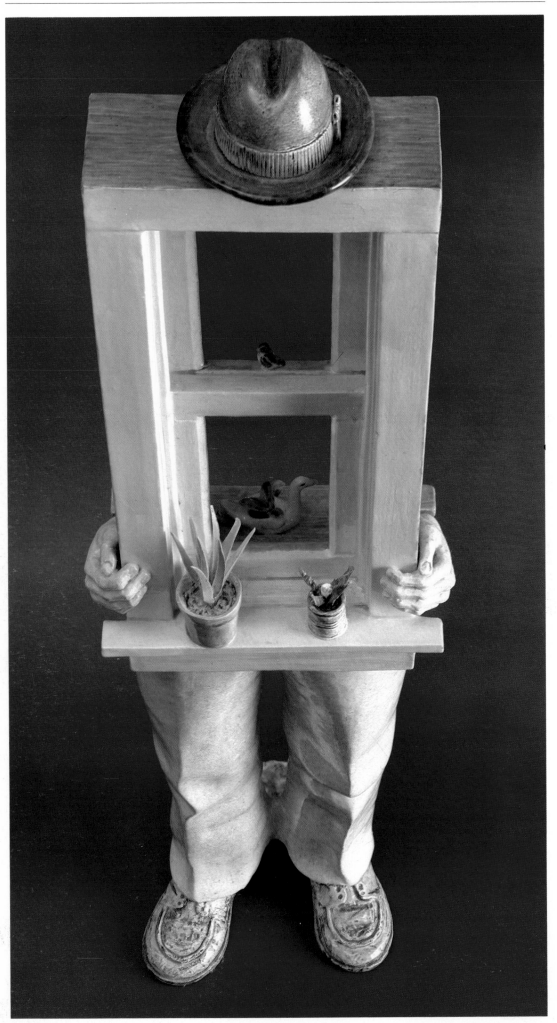

Left
Springtime in Ohio by Jack Earl,
1978, 20″ (50.8 cm) high. Earl
decorates this modeled piece with
underglazes. Collection Malcolm
and Sue Knapp. Photo: Malcolm
Knapp.

Right
House of Cards #3 by Richard
Shaw, 1979, 18″ (45.7 cm) high.
Each piece in this construction
was cast, assembled, and finished
with glaze and decals. Collection
the Oakland Museum of Art. Courtesy Braunstein Gallery, San Francisco.

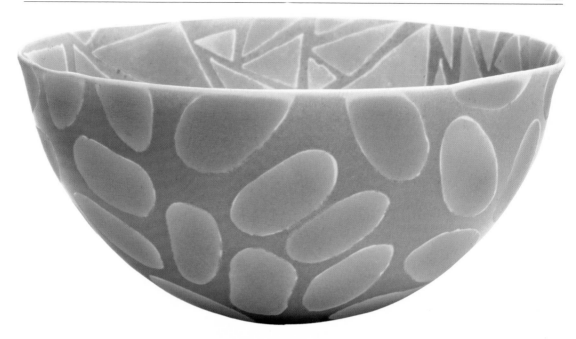

Left
Animated Bowl by Harris Deller,
1979, 9″ x 7″ (22.9 x 17.8 cm).
This wheel-thrown bowl with copper-red markings is celadon
glazed.

Above right
Bowl by Phillip Maberry, 1980, 10″
(25.4 cm) diam. This cast bowl is
decorated with stenciled glazes.
Courtesy Hadler / Rodriguez Galleries, New York.

Right
Vase by Laura Andreson, 1979, 9″
x 8″ (22.9 x 20.3). Andreson uses
a lemon ash glaze on this wheel-
thrown and altered vase. Photo:
Eddie Owen.

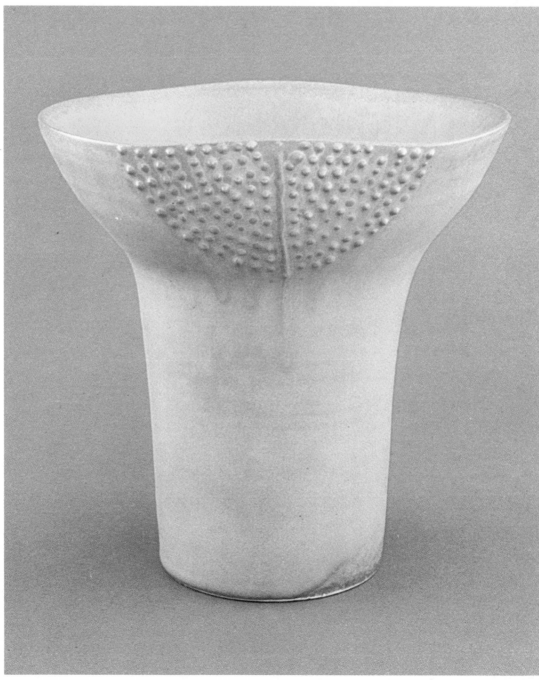

Above
Polar Bear, Portland, Oregon by
Chris Unterseher, 1979, 5″ x 8″ x
½″ (12.7 x 20.3 x 1.3 cm). Unterseher underglazes this hand-
built and modeled construction.
Courtesy Quay Gallery, San Francisco.

Opposite page
Untitled Covered Jar with Base by
· Adrian Saxe, 1978, 26″ x 7½″ (66
x 19.1 cm). The geometry of this
hand-built jar is typical of Saxe's
work.

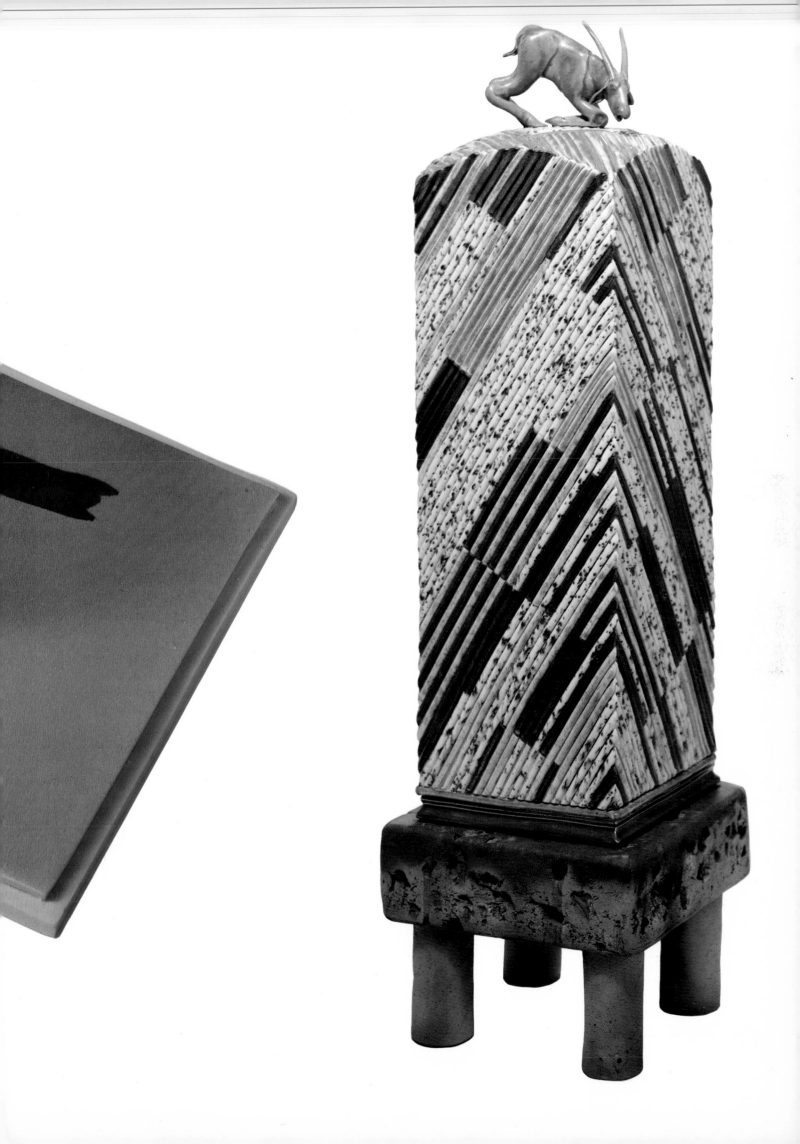

Virginia Woolf Plate by Judy Chicago, 1979, 14" (35.5 cm) diam. This three-dimensional plate decorated wtih china paint is a piece from *The Dinner Party.* © Judy Chicago. Photo: Don Miller.

Two Vessels by Karl Scheid, 1979, 4⅔" (12 cm), 6⅔" (17 cm) high. A white glaze covered wtih albany slip decorates these slab-built and relief-carved vessels.

Right
Three Trumpet III by Elena Karina, 10" x 15" (25.4 x 38.1 cm). This unusual piece of molded, carved, and textured porcelain is decorated with glazes and lusters. Photo: Bill Scott.

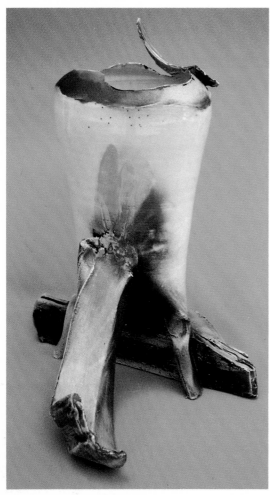

Above
Sled Vase by Susanne Stephenson, 1978, 16" x 14" x 12" (40.6 x 35.6 x 30.5 cm). Airbrushed stains and slips enhance this unusual wheel-thrown, altered, and hand-built vase.

Above right
Low Bowl by Adelaide Alsop Robineau, 1905, 9½" (24.2 cm) diam. This wheel-thrown bowl has incised decoration, a titanium and crystalline matte glaze, and zinc and copper glazes. Courtesy Everson Museum of Art of Syracuse and Onondaga County, Museum Purchase, 1916, from the artist. Photo: Jane Courtney Frisse.

Right
Pot by Geoffrey Swindell, 1978, 3½" (8.9 cm) high. Swindell applies mottled glazes to this wheel-thrown pot.

Opposite page
Vase by Lori Gottlieb, 1980, 12" (30.4 cm) high. Gottlieb's translucent cast form is inlaid with colored porcelain. Photo: Jim Kiernan.

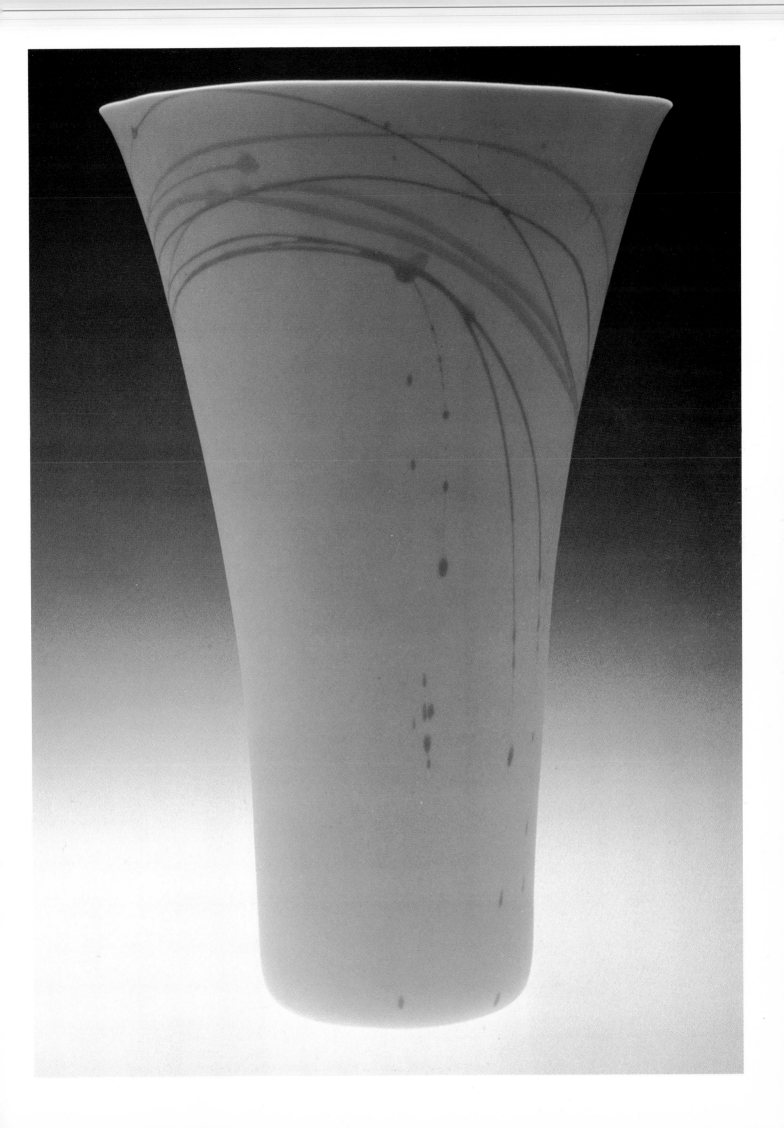

Flask and Cups by Lynn Turner, 1979, flask, 7½'' x 4½'' (19.1 x 11.4 cm). These pieces are cast in molds taken from eggplant and bamboo and then partially glazed. Photo: Colin C. McRae.

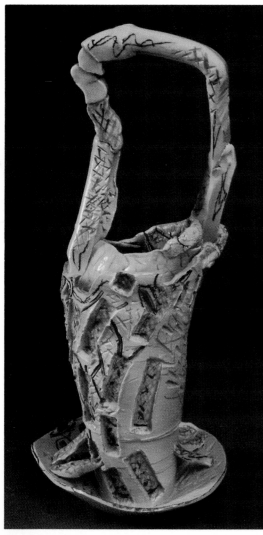

Above
Basket by Ann Christenson, 1978,
19″ x 8″ (48.3 x 20.3 cm). Underglaze stains and glaze decorate
this asymmetrical wheel-thrown,
hand-built, carved, and altered
basket.

Right
Butterflies and DNA by Jane Osborn-Smith, 1978, 5½″ (14 cm)
high. Molded in a conical form with
a scalloped edge, this vessel is
decorated with underglazes and
china paints.

Opposite page, top
Bowl by Ralph Bacerra, 1980, 5½″
x 15½″ (14 x 39.1 cm). Depth and
surface are revealed here as Bacerra plays off heavily patterned
areas against the undecorated
sections. Collection Daniel Jacobs. Photo: Artography.

Opposite page, bottom
Untitled by James Kvapil, 1979,
16″ (40.6 cm) high. Kvapil uses
laminated porcelain colored with
oxides for this wheel-thrown, slab-
built vessel.

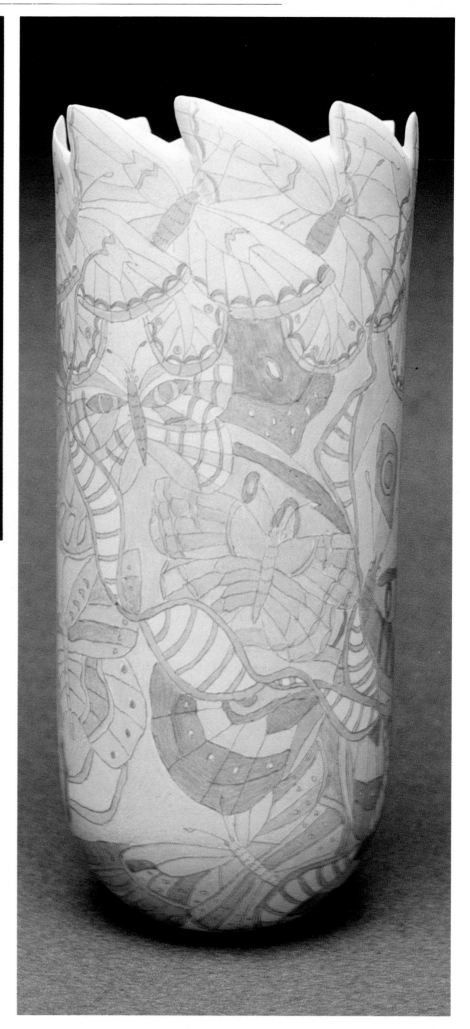

Above
Mug with Boxed Balls by Louis Marak, 1972, 6″ (15.2 cm) high. This was wheel-thrown, slab-built and assembled, and decorated with underglazes, underglaze pencils, china paints, and glaze. Collection Judy and Richard Gottehrer.

Right
Gothic Basket by Kaete Brittin Shaw, 1979, 13″ x 12″ (33 x 30.5 cm). Graduated color emphasizes the movement of this wheel-thrown, hand-built basket.

Two Bowls by Jacqueline Ponce-let, 1975, 3″ (7.6 cm) diam. These cast bone china bowls have been carved and pierced to reveal their fragile, translucent quality.

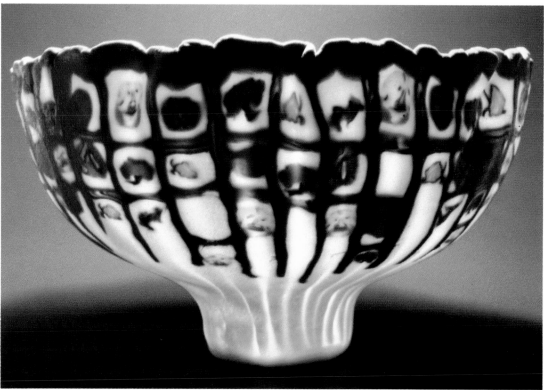

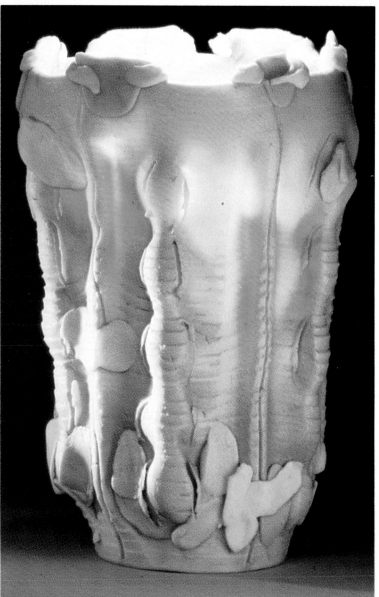

Above
Ain't Misbehavin' by Curtis Benzle,
1979, 7'' x 11'' (17.9 x 27.9 cm).
This hand-built bowl is inlaid with
colored clays.

Left
Light Gatherer by Rudolf Staffel,
1976, 9'' x 5'' (22.9 x 12.7 cm).
The translucency of porcelain is
dramatically exemplified in this
vase. Courtesy Helen Drutt Gallery, Philadelphia.

Far left
Tall Bowl by Elsa Rady, 1978, 7⅔''
x 9½'' (19.8 x 24.1 cm). Rady
completes this wheel-thrown bowl
with a carved rim and copper-red
glaze.

Left
Portrait of a Modern Artist by Tom Rippon, 1978, 20″ x 11″ (50.8 x 27.9 cm).

Top right
Look Alikes Plate by Howard Kottler, 1971, 10½″ (26.7 cm) diam. The artist has applied luster and a commercial ceramic decal of Grant Wood's *American Gothic* to a blank porcelain plate.

Right
Colonial Rockettes Plate by Howard Kottler, 1967, 10½″ (26.7 cm) diam. Kottler uses commercial decals and luster on blank plate. Photo: William Eng.

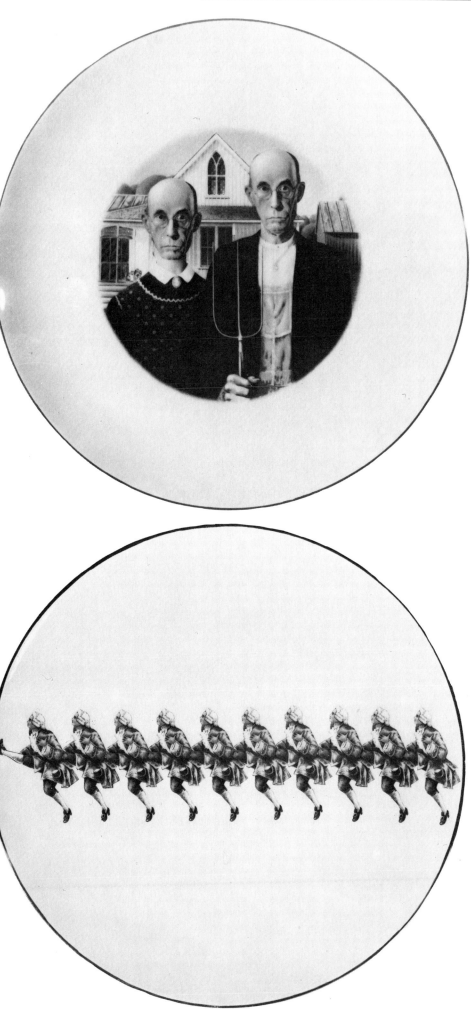

In the 1940s, interest in china painting renewed and continued to grow among hobbyists, who used commercial blanks as surfaces for painting. Until the 1960s, however, china painting, use of decals, and other overglaze techniques remained at this level (aside from industrial applications, of course) and were not taken seriously by studio ceramists. Studio ceramists trained in fine-art schools and universities looked upon this subculture of china painters and hobbyists with disdain. Those who simply painted porcelain surfaces were no more respected than the European and American "decorators" of the eighteenth and nineteenth centuries. Art-school graduates at that time were unaware of the complex, sophisticated world of the china painter. Apart from those who were strictly amateurs, there were and still are thousands of china painters all over the world who are truly accomplished. Well organized, they continue to hold classes, expositions, and seminars, and mount exhibitions, and publish magazines.

Very few university-trained ceramists knew about overglaze techniques, but in the early 1960s artists in Southern California began turning toward a new aesthetic that embraced clean lines and pure colors. For a few, this kindled a fascination with hobby shops, commercially prepared materials, and the use of low-fired whiteware. Contrasted with high-fired ceramic materials, whiteware was predictable and rendered a reliable range of colors with ease. Lower firing temperatures allowed a wide variety of bright, candy colors. At a time when the Abstract Expressionism of Peter Voulkos and his followers was the prevailing ceramic style, the carefully constructed forms and slick surfaces of work by artists such as Kenneth Price and Ron Nagle was considered "precious" and insignificant. By the mid-1970s, however, the influence of china painting on contemporary ceramics could be seen everywhere.

Judy Chicago's mixed-media project, *The Dinner Party*, is a cooperatively executed installation piece produced over a period of six years. This awesome exploration of the history of women in Western civilization celebrates craft as craft—using china paint, porcelain, and needlework to express feminine images. To make her extensive statement about women, Chicago created a triangular table, measuring 46½ feet (11.8 m) on each side, and set it for a ceremonial banquet with thirty-nine porcelain plates. Each plate honors a particular woman, either mythical or real, beginning with the goddesses of prehistory and extending into the twentieth century with notables such as Georgia O'Keeffe.

In the process of creating *The Dinner Party*, Chicago extensively researched the history of china painting, learned techniques from its aficionados, and experienced their world firsthand. Using powerful feminine images of varying aesthetic quality, Chicago has taken a form of porcelain decoration considered outside the mainstream of American art and craft and has brought it to broad public attention, leaving herself open to criticism from both fine artists and craftspeople.

Storytelling on ceramics has been common since ancient Greece, and contemporary English ceramist Jane Osborn-Smith illustrates characters and situations on bone china vessels by applying china paints directly to the clay's surface, rather than over a glaze in the usual manner. Each story unfolds on the vessel's continuous surface as the cylinder is turned in the hand. Osborn-Smith depicts characters beseiged by insects and imaginary beasts, in soft pastel pigments she grinds herself. A little like candy-coated medicine, her childlike illustrations are not the "pretty pictures" the sweet colors lead us to expect at first glance.

Transfer Printing

Decals have been a popular form of decoration for studio ceramists since the 1960s. The method was developed in Staffordshire, England, in 1756 as a mechanical way of transferring engravings onto ceramics. Decals are china paints that have been silk-screened onto a film-coated paper in monochromatic or multicolor patterns. When the paper is soaked in water, the film slides from the paper onto a glazed surface. (Decals can also be applied under the glaze, but these are used primarily by industry.) It is noteworthy that an industrial technique, which played a major role in robbing ceramics of its artistry when first introduced, is today used by ceramists as a means of individual artistic expression.

Perhaps the ultimate expressive use of transfer images is found in Howard Kottler's "palace pottery." An avowed decalomaniac— "one who suffers an irresistible and insatiable craving to work with decals"[16]—he culls images from commercially made decals intended for the hobbyist and applies them to porcelain blanks after cutting and reassembling them. Familiar historical pictures such as Grant Wood's *American Gothic* and Gainsborough's *Blue Boy* undergo subtle, irreverent transformations in Kottler's statements. Without altering its form, he transforms a commercially made functional object such as a porcelain plate into an aesthetic vehicle that resembles the commemorative plates produced by large manufacturers in "limited" editions.

While the handcraft aspects of ceramics are not present at all in Kottler's pieces, he

Left
Artist Walking with Palette by Richard Shaw, 1980, 36" x 21½" x 19" (91 x 55 x 48 cm). The fine, elegant surface of porcelain is here counterpointed with mundane objects such as pencils and brushes in a studied randomness to form a most unusual construction. Courtesy Braunstein Gallery, San Francisco.

Right
Turtle Soup Tureen with Bird by Lizbeth Stewart, 1976, 10½" x 20" x 15½" (26.7 x 50.8 x 39.4 cm). Lusters are used as the overglaze on this exotic hand-built turtle. Collection Campbell Museum. Photo courtesy Helen Drutt Gallery, Philadelphia.

Below right
American Vase: The West by Erik Gronborg, 1978, 19" x 16" (48.2 x 40.6 cm). Gronborg here uses photo decals and lusters to decorate this hand-built, lidded vase. Photo: Eddie Owen.

puts a great deal of old-fashioned craftsmanship into making elaborate cases to house them. These are reminiscent of the elaborate traveling cases outfitted with tea services that were popular among the European aristocracy during the eighteenth century.

Richard Shaw's trompe l'oeil constructions might not appear to require porcelain; but porcelain's potential for color, the fine detail its smooth surface will accept, and the added strength of high-fired clay make it the most viable medium for his work. Shaw prefers porcelain for what he terms its "tongue-in-cheek" preciousness. His interest in surface treatment and the need to produce multiple images led him to develop a four-color silkscreen process for transferring photographic images onto a clay surface. Like any mechanical technique, transfer printing requires restraint and resolute aesthetic content to avoid being craft for craft's sake.

Shaw's work recalls Sèvres porcelain in that its decoration often totally obscures the surface. An admitted junk collector, Shaw takes incongruous elements—scraps of paper, tin cans, antique books—from his environment and assimilates them into cohesive forms. *Artist Walking with Palette*, 1980, is an example in which substance and surface visually merge. Shaw's images are varied; at times they have the haphazard, casual feeling of the accumulated remains of daily life, at other times they are stacked high in a kind of balancing act, as in *House of Cards #3*, 1979. Though Shaw's trompe l'oeil tableaux may appear random, their meticulous execution is anything but incidental.

Erik Gronborg's handbuilt, highly embellished forms are closely linked to historical precedents found in Persian lusters and Japanese Oribe ware, but they are also very much a statement of what might be called twentieth-century baroque. This California artist's repertoire includes lusters, drawing, and photo decals—images accumulated from contemporary newspapers, magazines, and other printed sources—which he uses to obscure the surfaces of his forms.

Lusters, another form of overglaze, lend silver, gold, or iridescent hues to porcelain's finish. Luster overglaze is thought to have been developed in pre-Muslim Egypt (the late ninth to early tenth centuries) and traveled through the Islamic world to Spain as early as A.D. 1303 in the form of Hispano-Moresque luster wares, which represented the beginning of Spain's golden age of ceramics. Metallic lusters were painted in a thin film on already fired tin glazes. They became widely used in Europe during the eighteenth and nineteenth centuries. Before that time, gilding with leaf was a more common way to achieve a gold surface on ceramics. Lusters

Above
Covered Jar by Andra Ellis, 1980, 12″ x 5½″ (30.5 x 14 cm). The pale peach and pink hues of this wheel-thrown and hand-built lidded jar are the result of sprayed matte glazes.

Left
Untitled by Adrian Saxe, 1980, 18½″ (47 cm) high. Saxe here reveals a contemporary combination of humor and opulence in this hand-built and carved celadon- and barium-glazed piece. Photo: Eddie Owen.

Right
Rhinoceros Vase, Rockingham, England, about 1830, 38½″ (98 cm) high. Painted by Edwin Steel for Rockingham, this vase is a wonderful example of opulent decoration. Crown Copyright. Victoria and Albert Museum.

were used to mimic precious metals, and pearl luster was used over white, tin-glazed earthenware to emulate porcelain. Lusters today are primarily used on glazed surfaces for their pearly effect, although Tom Rippon uses them on unglazed porcelain. In this case, the luster soaks into the clay itself, rather than coating the surface, and the metallic residue leaves a dulled but slightly glimmering color.

Philadelphia artist Lizbeth Stewart adds lusters to her figurative forms. Exotic monkeys, turtles, and others are reminiscent of some of the great modeled animals one would expect to find in Augustus the Strong's Japanese Palace. On each work, Stewart uses many different lusters, which require multiple firings and expertise with materials. Though multi-firing presents the risk of cracking, porcelain is the appropriate clay for her work: it is strong when fired yet its texture allows for manipulation of fragile and delicate forms, and the high-fired surface serves as a rich foil for lusters.

Adrian Saxe's work is a mini-retrospective of porcelain-decorating methods from colored clay to modeling, carving, coloring, and glazing—often all in the same piece. Not unlike centerpieces for state occasions and royal banquet tables, his work seems to exist for decoration. Saxe has consciously set limitations on the scale and format of his pieces and has intentionally maintained a connection with function no matter how fully the work becomes a vehicle for decoration. He "courts disastrous lapses of taste by use of visual derivations from overstated, pretentious, fussy historical examples,"[17] such as the "rhinoceros vase" made in 1830 at Rockingham, an early-nineteenth-century English manufactory. They share a sense of humor and overworked opulence, yet Saxe's work does remain within the realm of "good taste." It exemplifies the way in which porcelain can maintain a conscious connection with history while allowing the most contemporary ideas to be expressed.

Porcelain Environments— The Ultimate Surface

Applications of porcelain on an architectural scale date as far back as the fifteenth century in China. In 1421, in Nanking, a tower measuring 80 meters (265 feet) in height was erected and hung with porcelain slabs. (Unfortunately it was destroyed by revolution in 1862.)

In Europe, entire rooms were made of porcelain. One, at the palace at Portici, Italy, was made by the Capodimonti factory (1757–59). Porcelain sections make up the walls, ceilings, and fixtures. The room represents a technical tour de force and creates a visually

Above
Bowl and Cones by Phillip Maberry, 1980, 6½″ x 12″; 4″ x 4″; 3″ x 4″ (13.5 x 30.5 cm; 2 x 10.2 cm; 6 x 10.2 cm). These cast and hand-built pieces are stencil-glazed. Photo: Michael McTwigan.

Left
Porcelain Room made by the Capodimonte factory for the Royal Villa at Portici, Italy, 1757–59. This room, made entirely of porcelain, represents the obsession of some eighteenth-century European monarchs for porcelain. Courtesy Museo di Capodimonte, Naples.

Right
Porcelain tower of Nanking, China.

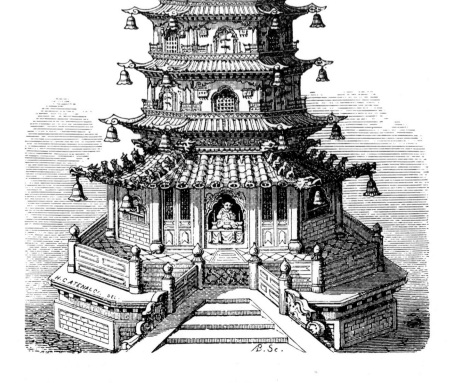

consuming environment of elaborate fantasy. Such rooms exemplify the extent to which European monarchs sought to possess porcelain. Their obsession with completely encrusting their environment with the material was to the eighteenth century what the work of environmental designers and some "decorative" painters is to the late twentieth century (such as Joyce Kozloff's rooms of ceramic tiles painted with designs or Cynthia Carlson's pattern-painted walls).

Phillip Maberry is creating an environment very much in the spirit of late twentieth-century culture. Accumulating parts made of various materials, he constructed a portable environment complete with floor, walls, and functional ceramics. His patterned decorative concerns overlap with those of contemporary painters like Robert Kushner and Kim MacConnel. Like them, he spent time at the Fabric Workshop in Philadelphia, where he designed and silk-screened stretch fabrics displaying splatters of color to make table and chair covers for his environment.

Maberry's ceramic forms are simple, delicate, slip-cast bowls. They warp when fired, assuming an irregular shape like that of a crisp potato chip. He decorates by dripping, spraying, and applying designs using multiple layers of rubber latex resist. Each multicolored bowl is fired up to five times to achieve the desired layers of color and pattern. His style and color sense—lapis lazuli and flamingo pink are favorites—have caused some people to designate Maberry a "punk" potter. This style extends to flat tiles installed as walls and even to drip-painted linoleum flooring.

Modular Wall Panel (detail) by
Joseph Detwiler, 1978, 19'' x 32'' x
4'' (48.2 x 81.3 x 10.2 cm), cast and
glazed porcelain.

CHAPTER EIGHT

THE EVOLVING VESSEL

PORCELAIN'S POTENTIAL for expression is seemingly limitless, whether in the form of elegant vessels or abstract objects. An abstract, heavy-looking porcelain art object is as truly porcelain as the proverbial thin white porcelain teacup that is durable, yet highly translucent. The almost baffling variety of works being created today with porcelain amply demonstrates not only the breadth and diversity of the material's uses, but its adaptability to new and innovative expressions. The medium will perform any role, assume any guise, that the artist wishes. The vessel, or container, is one of the oldest and most widespread of porcelain traditions.

The Anatomy of the Vessel

Since ancient times the parts of the vessel have been described in anthropomorphic terms: lip, neck, shoulder, waist, belly, and foot. The lip and foot—the top and bottom—establish the boundaries of the vessel. A pot with a flimsy rim may appear amateurish and weak, though when thinness is handled successfully, even a rim tapering to translucent nothingness can add elegance to a form.

In Asian ceramics, traditionally the foot was said to reveal the "signature" or unique character of the potter and the virtue of the pot. Though the foot is often hidden, it can determine whether a pot works visually as a complete entity or is unresolved; the form rests on it, both literally and figuratively. A narrow base lifts the form, creating a visually lighter work than one with a broad base. The foot so affects the visual weight, proportions, and silhouette of the pot that simply manipulating it can radically alter the rest of the form. Unfortunately, the foot is often incidental to a pot, having been impatiently created by the ceramist as an afterthought.

Between the extremities of lip and foot are the pot's belly, waist, shoulder and neck. The variety of combinations and proportions of these parts is infinite, and they coalesce to give a form its particular shape and "presence."

How a pot looks only provides half the sensory information required to judge a piece; visual expectations must be met by physical realities. A glazed white porcelain teacup resembling a delicate eggshell should be feather-light when lifted as well. It follows that a massive stoneware form need not be light, for its color and texture create the expectation of weight. With functional ware, the weight and feel of a form also determine how a piece handles when used.

Porcelain's qualities generally create expectations of lightness and delicacy—expectations fulfilled with exceptional ability by the Chinese during the Ming dynasty and again in the eighteenth century. Their so-called eggshell porcelains were trimmed to absolute thinness, both inside and out. In factt Imperial porcelains not only were potted thinly, they also were left to dry for a year and then turned on a lathe.

Contemporary potter Elsa Rady employs this Chinese method, though using a rib instead of a lathe, when she feels trimming is

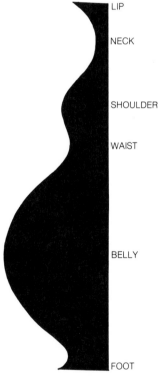

Above
Anatomy of a Vessel

Right
Tall Covered Jar by Tom Turner, 1980, 19" (48.3 cm) high. Turner's combination of incised lines and salt firing creates a heavily textured surface.

called for in perfecting the shape of her bowls. She concentrates on bowls, influenced by the simple elegance of Sung and Ming dynasty wares. At the same time her striking forms have an assertive character—geometric in stance. Rady's bowls are light as air and balance on a single point like a fulcrum. Simultaneously pushing upward and outward, they seem driven by centrifugal force. By carving their rims in hard-edge or curvilinear lines, Rady gives these forms an unusual sense of movement. The rim's broken line carries our eye around, instead of out from, its circumference. Rich monochromatic glazes, from glossy copper red and peach blossom to sober matte black, further enhance their strength and clarity of form.

Don Pilcher also makes forms that are clean and pure. Primarily employing traditional celadon or clear glazes, the surfaces of his spherical, lidded containers and soft, voluptuous cylinders are interrupted by gestural slip drawings in relief. On others he spontaneously, though sparsely, splatters and dashes the surface with a second color, activating the form's surface.

The Traditional Vessel Today

> I am for an art that is political-erotical-mystical, that does something other than sit on its ass in a museum. I am for an art that grows up not knowing it is art at all ... I am for an art that embroils itself with the everyday crap & still comes out on top.[1]

Claes Oldenburg did not make this statement with reference to pots, but it accurately describes the ambition of functional potters in the days before their vessels were termed "curios" or relegated to a cabinet shelf behind glass doors. Nonetheless, the vessel's heritage—conditioned by everyday use and arrived at through centuries of tradition—remains vitally important today despite its changed circumstances.

Although in past times all utilitarian items were handmade, in a technological society most day-to-day needs can be met more easily and efficiently by mass-produced wares. A machine-made plastic bowl serves its purpose as well as any other, and so when an individual chooses a handmade porcelain bowl, he or she does so to fulfill aesthetic, ceremonial, or spiritual needs, not utilitarian ones. Therefore, functional porcelain now assumes more limited roles that include not only manufactured dinnerware but also dental, electrical, plumbing, and chemical applications. The handmade porcelain vessel is thereby freed to function in a spiritual and artistic mode, as it has always done in Chinese and Japanese cultures.

Contemporary ceramists of both East and West look to their forerunners for wisdom and guidance. Chinese wares of the Sung dynasty in particular have always been esteemed for their harmonious union of material and form, of tactile and visual qualities. Even today they are often the standard against which pots are judged.

Warren MacKenzie, David Leach, and Kenneth Ferguson are among the contemporary Western ceramists who employ the unpretentious pot as a means of human expression. They are traditionalists who believe a humble object can possess all the vitality and spirit of the exalted—an attitude reflected in the Japanese concept of *shibui*, which means simple and unassuming beauty created out of humility. The result of such belief is an art of restrained elegance and quietness that might seem out of keeping with the high ambitions of modern art. MacKenzie, Leach, and Ferguson work within the tradition of the anonymous potter, embracing "the ideal of impersonal perfection of form and glaze, rather than an artist striving to express the pecularities of his personal vision."[2] Theirs is not sterile perfection, however; accidents and flaws are incorporated as part of the spontaneity of the handmade object.

The monochromatic austerity of Robert Turner's cylindrical forms is ameliorated by their sense of contained force pushing out from within. Although they are not traditional vessels, Turner's iconographic forms exhibit sureness, a lack of self-consciousness, and an understanding of form that evolves through repetition—qualities that are also found in the finest traditional Asian pots. Turner is also among a group of vessel makers who follow some of the approbations set forth by William Morris:

> First. Your vessel must be of a convenient shape for its purpose. Second. Its shape must show to the greatest advantage the plastic and easily-worked nature of clay; the lines of its contour must flow easily; but you must be on the lookout to check the weakness and languidness that comes from striving for over-elegance. Third. All the surface must show the hand of the potter, and not be finished with a baser tool ...[3]

The Hybrid Vessel

From the tradition of the potter making functional forms and the individual artist expressing his or her own imagination, there has arisen a hybrid form—the functionless vessel—which has come to represent an individual artist's signature the way style does for a painter. While such vessels often incorporate traditional notions of ceramic scale and substance, their primary raison

---

Far left
Kumme by Ursula Scheid, 1975, 3½″ x 4¼″ (9.4 x 11.7 cm). This simple glazed form, with three streaked iron-oxide slips under white feldspathic glaze, demonstrates the elegance that can be achieved through traditional methods. Photo: Beatrice Frehn.

Left
Vase by Karl Scheid, 1980, 5⅝″ x 5¾″ (14.5 x 15 cm). Graceful relief-carved lines accentuate the thrown form while acting as troughs for accumulating glaze. Photo: Bernd Peter Göbbels.

Far left
White Porcelain Feelie by Rose Cabat, 1976, 7″ x 4½″ (17.8 x 11.4 cm). Cabat individualizes a simple bottle by giving it a gourd-like stance and delicate neck. Surface interest comes from her use of a rich matte crystalline glaze. Photo: Eddie Owen.

Left
Covered Jar with Waist by Peter Shrope, 1980, 8½″ x 7″ (21.8 x 17.8 cm). The wheel-thrown form covered with celadon glaze is enhanced by calligraphic brushwork.

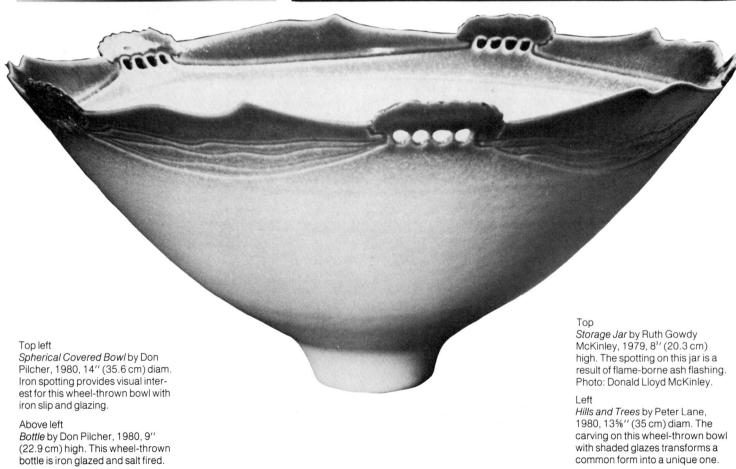

Top left
Spherical Covered Bowl by Don Pilcher, 1980, 14″ (35.6 cm) diam. Iron spotting provides visual interest for this wheel-thrown bowl with iron slip and glazing.

Above left
Bottle by Don Pilcher, 1980, 9″ (22.9 cm) high. This wheel-thrown bottle is iron glazed and salt fired.

Top
Storage Jar by Ruth Gowdy McKinley, 1979, 8″ (20.3 cm) high. The spotting on this jar is a result of flame-borne ash flashing. Photo: Donald Lloyd McKinley.

Left
Hills and Trees by Peter Lane, 1980, 13⅝″ (35 cm) diam. The carving on this wheel-thrown bowl with shaded glazes transforms a common form into a unique one.

Above
Footed Vase with Flared Rim by
Lucie Rie, 1976, 8¼″ x 4″ (21 x
10.1 cm). Characterized by Rie's
opulent use of a pebbly glaze with
incised lines, both form and decoration reveal a steady hand. Collection Bryce Holcombe. Photo:
Michael McTwigan.

Above left
Wine Set by Ruth Gowdy
McKinley, 1979, 11″ (27.9 cm)
high. The exquisitely thrown, refined forms are enhanced by the
mottled, wood-fired azurite glaze.
Photo: Donald Lloyd McKinley.

Left
Faceted Covered Box by Warren
MacKenzie, 5½″ (14 cm) high.
The unpretentious elegance of this
simple box is a hallmark of Mac-
Kenzie's work.

Far left
Bowl By David Leach, 5¾'' x 5½''
(14.6 x 14 cm). This wheel-thrown,
fluted, incised, and celadon-
glazed bowl acknowledges the
positive force of its thousand-year-
old Asian ancestry. Collection
Bryce Holcome. Photo: Michael
McTwigan.

Left
Unomi by Nancy d'Estang, about
1980, 3¼'' x 3'' (8.3 x 7.6 cm).
This traditional teabowl acquires
its surface interest from subtle,
controlled, peach-colored flashing
achieved by salt firing in a saggar.

Left
Covered Jar by Ken Ferguson,
1980, 14'' (35.6 cm) high. The sta-
bility and unassuming simplicity of
Ferguson's works are exemplified
in this salt-glazed jar. Photo: Gary
Sulton.

Right
Untitled by Robert Turner, 1979,
9½'' x 8½'' (24.1 x 21.6 cm). This
vessel is wheel-thrown and altered, glazed, and sandblasted.
Courtesy Hadler/Rodriguez Galleries, New York. Photo: Michael
McTwigan.

Bottom right
Vessel by James Kvapil, 1979, 17''
x 14'' (43.1 x 35.5 cm). This vessel
is wheel-thrown, slab-built, and
decorated with laminated colored
porcelain. Photo: Eddie Owen.

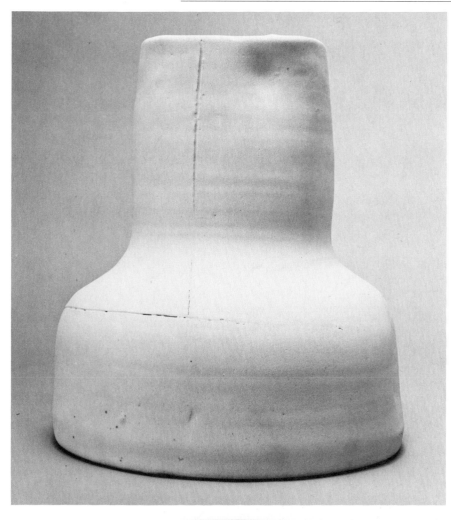

d'être is as the expressive vehicle of the individual, and so they break with the long tradition of anonymous pottery. Helen Drutt said the 1930s saw a return to the "enlarged vessel"—enlarged more in content than in scale—which acts as a catalyst for ideas while becoming the framework for the vessel's celebration.

Elena Karina and James Kvapil are but two of many ceramists who transform the pot into an exalted object, an expressive canvas, unconcerned with function. In Karina's "tide pools," the vessel's concern with volumetric space is somewhat camouflaged by the intricacy of form and color. The many thinly tapered layers of fluted sheets and textured segments resemble barnacles and coral as seen through ocean water. The delicate forms thrust sharply upward from an encrusted base, their entangled fold calls up the mystery of the sea—at once alluring and foreboding. Modulated with soft opalescent greens, mauves, and ivories, the interiors glow from beneath a skin of pearly luster.

James Kvapil laminates layers of colored clay to form surprisingly voluminous standing vessels. He utilizes a broad range of colors, from delicate pastels to reds and blues, recalling the richness of the Rococo. The fact that these are containers is superfluous, as they are unglazed and often pierced to channel light from inside the cavity. The pressure required to seal the layers of clay during the forming process creates colored patterns, different inside and out. The pliable quality of the clay, manipulated when wet, stretches and activates the image; as a result the decorative motifs appear to be moving in slow motion across the surface of the form. The slightly off-center, asymmetrical shape of the form itself reinforces the sense of movement.

Far left
Small-Footed Pot by Pat Schilston, 6'' x 4'' (15.2 x 10.2 cm). This cast form balancing on a tiny, tapered foot is painted with a polychrome enamel landscape. Collection Malcolm and Sue Knapp. Photo: Malcolm Knapp.

Left
Ivory Pod by Sandra Byers, 1980, 2⅞'' x 2¼'' (7.3 x 6.4 cm). This piece is constructed of four lobes colored ivory, brown, and pink. Using natural forms—egg, pod, floral bud—as an inspiration for her work, Byers explores the delicacy and fragility of porcelain and considers the blush of her glazes the gift of the kiln.

Left
Porcelain Basket by Ann Christenson, 1978, 14'' x 14'' (35.6 x 35.6 cm). The subtle watercolor effect achieved with slips and underglaze pencils sharply contrasts with Christenson's dramatic form built of torn porcelain slabs.

Above right
Folding Screen Pot by Louis Marak, 1973, 10'' (25.4 cm) high. Marak's drawing with underglazes, underglaze pencils, and china paint creates a complex visual entity from a pot of relatively modest scale.

Right
Flattened Bowls by Val Barry, 1979, 13''; 8½''; 6'' (33; 21.7; 15.2 cm). Granular iron particles mixed into the glaze provide a straightforward decorative treatment for these sleek, hand-built forms. Collection Daniel Jacobs. Photo: Artography.

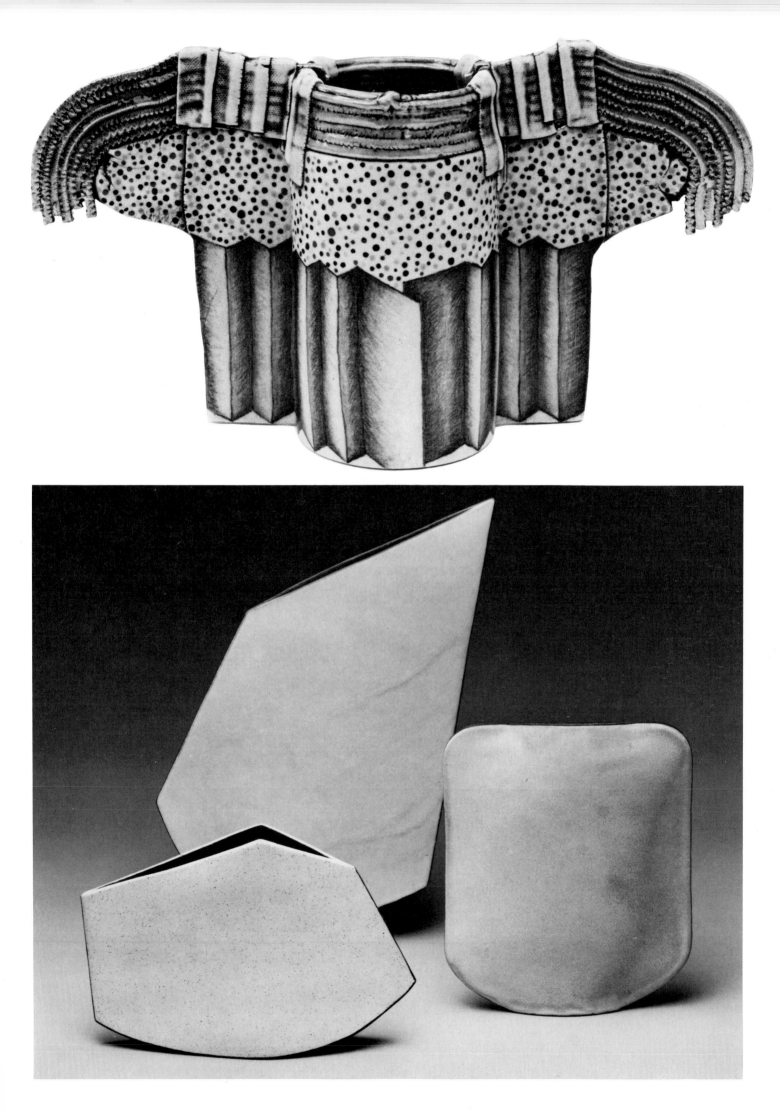

CHAPTER NINE

TEA AND CEREMONY

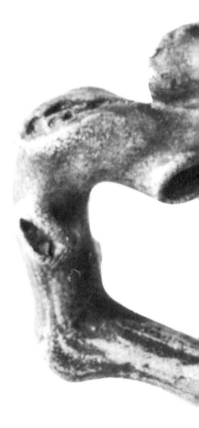

MANY OF US BEGIN and end the day with a porcelain cup in hand, and the custom of tea drinking has had worldwide influence on trade, lifeways, and religious customs. Tea drinking was an outgrowth of Zen, for the Japanese monks who brought tea from China in the twelfth century drank it as a stimulant to enable them to stay awake during long hours of meditation. The medicinal benefits of tea were written of, and the Emperor, upper classes, and samurai soon made the "way of tea" an integral part of their lives. But it wasn't until the fifteenth century that the tea ceremony, "an aesthetic manifestation of Zen,"[1] was established throughout the land. Such aesthetic principles as austerity, simplicity, reserve, asymmetry, and naturalness were thought to be necessary in all things of life. The way of tea grew so wide as "to be an excuse for the worship of purity and refine-

ment."[2] Laden with rules and ritual, the tea ceremony became both a means of disciplining the mind and a vehicle for bringing together all people, regardless of class. Tea bowls, which had to embody the same characteristics as Zen, were required to have a distinctive form: to be "perfectly suited to the hands;"[3] not be too thin, for they would become too hot; not be too thick, for they would be too heavy. The tea masters dictated taste not only in tea and the tea ceremony, but in all art; everything was designed to reflect Zen doctrines.

When Marco Polo brought tea (along with coffee, spices, silk, and porcelain) from China in the fourteenth century, Europeans developed their own interpretation of tea drinking. But tea remained a rarity in the West until around 1700, when it was imported in quantity by the Dutch East Indies Company. Europeans, the British especially, were fasci-

Far left
Cup Stand, Chinese, Sung dynasty (960–1280). This piece with a creamy glaze is Pai Ting Yao porcelaneous ware. Courtesy The Metropolitan Museum of Art, Gift of Mrs. Samuel T. Peters, 1926.

Left
Cup and Saucer, Saint-Cloud factory, France, about 1712–1730. these are soft paste with blue underglaze. The Saint-Cloud factory was one of the earliest successful producers of soft-paste or "artificial" porcelain in Europe. Courtesy Cooper-Hewitt Museum, Smithsonian Institution.

Magnolia Cup by Ch'en Ming-yuan, China, seventeenth to eighteenth century, 2¼'' x 3'' (5.7 x 7.9 cm). The cup is made of modeled stoneware with darker slip. Collection I. M. Pei. Courtesy China Institute in America. Photo: Carl Nardiello.

nated by this new herb, and though its consumption began as an upper-class pastime, it soon filtered into all classes (much to the dismay of the nobility, who would have preferred that tea remain their privilege).

The Teacup

Costly teas imported during the eighteenth century were suited to be served in only the finest porcelain teacups. Porcelain, in fact, served to best retain the liquid's heat. A major difference between the Asian teabowls and the European teacup is the addition of a handle. Although this innovation is to be found as early as about 1700 on Saint-Cloud cups of France, English specimens of handleless teabowls may be found as late as 1820. Traditionally, European drinking and serving vessels for liquids were fashioned of silver and gold, and because metals conduct heat, making the container too hot to hold, handles were common to Western cups. It was natural, therefore, that when porcelain wares were first made in Europe, they were modeled after the styles of gold and silver services, which meant that cups bore handles, regardless of the substance from which they were made. As in Japan, the serving of tea became a ritual, with its own aesthetic principles.

From the very simple to the highly decorative, cups are a pleasure to hold and drink from—a hand-held accoutrement of a participatory event. Even though cups follow traditional forms in a general way, they are often so elaborate, so physically unwieldy, that their actual use would never enter the mind of either their creators or their viewers. Such is the case with Kaete Shaw's winged cups, meant to be paired like the folding halves of butterfly wings, or Louis Marak's highly embellished forms, draped and festooned like prizes.

But cups are also sometimes employed purely as symbols, as in the work of Tony Hepburn, Richard Shaw, and Lucian Octavius Pompili. While Hepburn's *Spring Cup*, 1976, and Shaw's *Cardboard Teaset*, 1976, employ offbeat yet traditional associations of the cup's form and scale, Pompili's assume a symbolic role within the stage settings of his surreal assemblages. In *The Lamps and Carpets of My Vigil*, 1977, a leafy cup is held within a massive, carved-out teapot masked in a porcelain drape. Along with the artist's secrets, dreams, and memories, the cup holds the sustenance for his vigil. Under the cup, Pompili places twigs for the fire to transform the teapot into a metaphorical lamp. This piece exemplifies his preoccupation with containment—teacup within teapot, container within container—a theme evident throughout Pompili's work.

Opposite page, top
Cup by Concetta Fenicchia, 1979,
3½″ x 5½″ (8.9 x 14 cm). These
cast and wheel-thrown elements
are assembled into cup forms and
finished with an opaque black
glaze.

Opposite page, center
Spring Cup by Tony Hepburn,
1976, 7″ (17.8 cm) high. The swirling, marbleized porcelain bowl and
lever-type handle create a sense of
movement and balance.

Opposite page, bottom
Ceremonial Cup by Frank Fleming,
1977, 20″ x 21″ (50.6 x 53.3 cm).
Fleming's complex cup form
evokes a mythic ceremony.

Right
The Lamps and Carpets of My Vigil
by Lucian Octavius Pompili, 1977,
12″ x 10″ x 6″ (30.5 x 25.4 x 15.3
cm). This piece was hand-built,
modeled, and cast. Collection Karen McCready. Photo: Michael
McTwigan.

Below
Winged Cup by Kaete Brittin
Shaw, about 1978, 4″ x 6½″
(10.2 x 16.5 cm). In Shaw's hand-
built form, function is sacrificed to
a strong visual statement that suggests flight and dynamic movement.

Alligator Cup by Ann Adair, 1968,
4″ x 8.5″ (10.2 x 11.6 cm). The
elongated alligator handle, made
with a simple pinching technique,
has a humorous air. Courtesy
Quay Gallery, San Francisco.
Photo: Roger Gass.

The Teapot

Teapot forms run the gamut from those clearly intended for brewing everyday tea to those in which the form acts as a format for exploring far-flung fantasies. The precedent for the European teapot (from which some contemporary ceramists take their examples) is sixteenth-century Chinese I-hsing ware (made of fine, unglazed stoneware), which combines trompe l'oeil configurations of bamboo, nuts, snails, and foliage, around what we have come to know as the classical teapot form.

I-hsing ware teapots and cups, first brought to Europe by Dutch traders during the seventeenth century, served as models for teapots made by Delft, by J. P. Elers in England, and by Böttger at Meissen. In fact, Böttger's first productions were of a dense brown stoneware very similar to that of the I-hsing wares. The I-hsing teapot indicates the difference between the tea ceremony of Japan and that of China: in Japan tea is made without a teapot; hot water is poured directly on the powdered herb in a teabowl instead. Fortuitously, China's I-hsing teapot, which became the model for all the world (they are still made today), not only was a highly practical shape, but also embodied inordinate grace. It is interesting to note that *porcelain* teapots were never made by the Chinese for their own use, but rather for European taste alone.

Teapots gather together several components—the pot's volume, spout, lid, and handle—into a whole. A teapot is a complex assemblage of specific functional requirements: it must handle comfortably, balance properly even when full of liquid, and pour the beverage smoothly and without dripping. Seemingly a clear-cut challenge, the integration of form and function truly tests the ceramist's mind and eye. The difficulty of this challenge is affirmed by J. J. Kändler's remark upon entering the Meissen factory in 1732: the factory's new *modellmeister* commented that "there was not a handle which fit a pot."[4]

Elevated from the realm of mere function, the vitality of the teapot form is evidenced by the broad scope of wares being made. Ann Christenson begins to make her teapots by throwing very thick forms, which she then carves to create faceted surfaces on all parts of the pot: body, handle, spout, and lid. Her apparent casualness in handling the clay is, in fact, quite deliberate. Expressionistic gesturing animates the forms; pierced latticework bases, which sag a bit during the forming and firing processes, add to the "Mad Hatter's Tea Party" spirit of her work.

Coille Hooven's fluid, modeled forms have an unctuous, almost edible appearance. Where the edges taper to extreme thinness,

Military Series Thinware Teapot by Philip Cornelius, 1978, 8″ x 7″ x 7″ (20.3 x 17.8 x 17.8 cm). Assembled with thinly rolled slabs of marbled clays, these extremely fragile finished forms mimic early American tinwares.

Teapot by Ann Christenson, 1977, 8¾″ x 10¼″ x 6¼″ (22.2 x 26 x 15.8 cm). This wheel-thrown, hand-built and altered pot is decorated with underglaze pencils, stains, and decals. Collection Joan Weiss. Photo: Eddie Owen.

Teapot by Betty Woodman, 1974, 10″ (25.4 cm) high. Oxide droplets and glaze decorate this wheel-thrown and altered pot. Photo: George Woodman.

Above
Mermaid's Cottage by Coille Hoo-ven, 1975, 13'' (33 cm) high. Private collection. Photo: James Medley.

Below
Small Herd of Teapots by Jill Crowley, about 1976, from 2'' to 4'' (5 to 10.1 cm) high. These teapots are all hand-built. Collection Karen McCready. Photo: Michael McTwigan.

Top right
Teapot by Steven Ladin, 1980, 6½'' x 8½'' x 7½'' (16.6 x 21.6 x 19.1 cm). This cast pot has a celadon glaze. Collection Malcolm and Sue Knapp. Photo: Malcolm Knapp.

Right
Teapot by Sandra Simon, 1978, 10'' x 8'' x 6'' (25.4 x 20.3 x 15.3 cm). This simple, elegant piece is wheel-thrown and glazed.

the material has a milky, translucent glow. On her teapots, Hooven depicts childlike visions of fantastic animals and mermaids perched on shells. The applied decoration is most successful when left uncolored (recalling *blanc de chine*), allowing visual movement between form and decoration.

Philip Cornelius makes teapots of paper-thin sheets of marbled porcelain that are so thin, in fact, that he compares his working method to that of a surgeon. Cornelius constructs his delicate teapots as if he were a tinsmith, leaving seams clearly exposed. While the forms suggest teapots, they do not suggest function. Only a few inches in height, fragile and unglazed, they are obviously unusable as containers for liquid.

Jill Crowley utilizes both porcelain and stoneware clays, which she glazes and fires in a variety of techniques to create "herds" of teapots resembling little pigtailed animals. Some perch on their legs, alert, while others sit contentedly within the flock. Though a single pot may only measure one and one-half inches tall, it is modeled with a full-fledged spout, lid (stopper), and handle (tail), which give it an individual countenance that defies its size. Functional? Yes. When the right herd of gnomes appears, tea will be served—all by way of illustrating Crowley's active fantasies.

CHAPTER TEN

THE LANDSCAPE OF THE TABLE

SOCIAL CUSTOMS centering around food vary from society to society. Among certain castes in India, food vessels are smashed after meals, in accordance with Hindu laws regarding caste purity. When this is the case, there is very little incentive for potters to develop elaborately styled dishes. In Western Europe, on the other hand, high social status and position obliged members of the aristocracy to host opulent banquets. Enormous sums of money and energy were expended in developing appropriately fantastic food services that included not only serving dishes but numerous tureens, centerpieces, figurines, and ornamental extravaganzas. The European attitude toward porcelain dishes, though ostentatious by today's standards, was in keeping with the value the Chinese placed on their own wares. Indeed, the servant who broke a precious dish was likely to be flogged in China.

Our contemporary eating rituals reflect both extremes: the disposable ceramics of India and the precious ones of China and Europe. On the one hand, modern life often relies on the convenience of disposable paper or plastic dishes and utensils. On the other, we still engage in ritual eating occasions that require formal table settings and haute cuisine. At weddings and other rites of passage, the "good dishes" are still taken from their display cases and put into service. For all the reverence associated with porcelain dishes and the fear of breaking them, they still perform limited functional tasks

and symbolize a special kind of human exchange. While reaching a wider audience than in times gone by (when porcelain tableware was attainable primarily by the nobility or crowned heads of state), porcelain continues to figure as a household's emblem of a special occasion.

In addition to perpetuating formal styles of porcelain ware, the sumptuous banquets of rococo and baroque style in Europe engendered a new art form. *Garde manger* is the art of the table—one of presentation and culinary performance. Platters of food were sculpted and arranged in intricate, detailed patterns to adorn the banquet table. *Garde manger* developed in eighteenth-century France as a showcase for edibles to equal the elaborate porcelain services, and persists to the present day.

One renowned example of such a porcelain service is the Swan Service modeled at Meissen by J. J. Kändler in 1738 using *rocaille* forms and marine mythology. Its name derives from the swans and storks in relief among bullrushes and shells in the center of each plate. Count von Brühl, Augustus the Strong's minister in charge of the factory and its greatest patron after Augustus himself, commissioned the elaborate table service. But the Swan Service represented more than unsurpassed artistic achievement on the part of Kändler and the Meissen factory; it demonstrated Count von Brühl's political and financial superiority over everyone at court. His particular target was Count Graf Sulkowski, who rose from being a page at the Sa-

Four Forms by Marek Cecula, 1978, 4″ to 11″ (10.2 to 27.9 cm) high. Cecula utilizes the aesthetic advantages of mechanical processes in these colored clay forms, to which he has applied oxide wash and glaze.

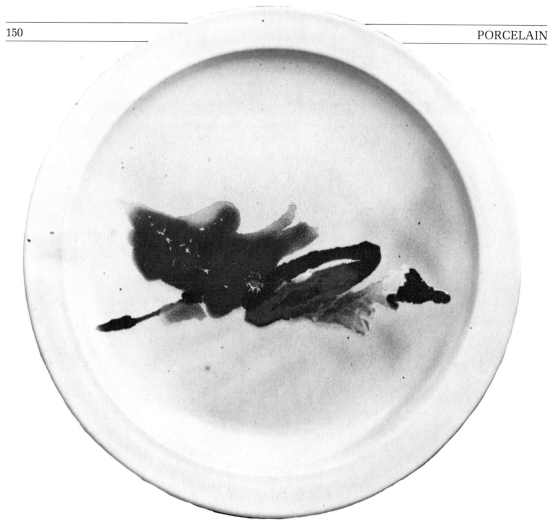

xon Court to Prime Minister of Saxony. Like von Bruhl, he too owned a baroque service modeled by Kändler. Aristocratic rivalries like this were commonly acted out using porcelain services as their battlements. Whatever the services did to foster their owners' social status, the influence of banquet-styled tablewares has been lasting.

By the nineteenth century, with the Industrial Age firmly entrenched, other materials had come to rival porcelain at the dinner table. Bone china and creamware were chief among these, as they were comparatively inexpensive. Eventually, large factories produced styles of dinnerware for all classes.

Handmade Dinnerware Today
Dinnerware is also being handmade by contemporary ceramists. Not intending to compete with mass production, these ceramists create individualized works for a discerning audience.

Jim Makins produces contemporary stateware—somewhat neoclassical and formal in feeling, yet true to the handmade spirit of the craft aesthetic. Working with colored clays—white, gray, and black—he creates forms that are straightforward yet sensuous in their undulating surfaces. Makins follows the tradition of Japanese pottery as exemplified by Leach and Hamada. Repeating the same form numerous times, he keeps only those that meet his strict criteria.

Confetti, the dinnerware of Dorothy Hafner, celebrates the ritual of dining—with or without the food or guests. The multicolored plates, cups, and bowls are clearly enjoying themselves regardless of any accompaniment. They are at once reminiscent of Sèvres porcelains and majolica earthenwares, as the surfaces are often completely obscured by brightly colored, whimsical patterning. Although they are the result of careful study, the doodlelike patterns have a childlike quality which also calls to mind printed cotton textiles.

Unlike Makins's delicate, somewhat precious forms and Hafner's graphically decorated dinnerware, Catherine Hiersoux's forms are sturdy. Strongly rimmed blue plates and hefty cups are expressively splashed with purple, recalling thirteenth-century Chinese Chun ware. The abstract patterning gives each piece an individual, spontaneous quality. The depth and lustrous quality of brilliant reds, blues, and yellows fused with the white ground exemplify porcelain's traditional elegance.

Multiples
Ceramics-related industries have emerged as a logical transition from the production of the unique, one-of-a-kind object, which, for many ceramists, is no longer an economically viable way to earn a living. A growing number of ceramists now combine their personal

Left
Plate by Catherine Hiersoux, 1979, 16" (40.6 ¢m) diam. The red-and-black design with sprayed amber luster lends spontaneity to the simple, satin matte white glaze. Photo: Leonard Joseph.

Above right
Confetti by Dorothy Hafner, 1980, dinner plate 10" (25.4 cm) square. The underglaze decoration is hand-painted on these press-molded forms. Photo: Malcolm Varon.

Right
Dinnerware by James Makins, 1980, dinner plate 10" (26.4 cm) diam. These wheel-thrown and glazed pieces combine formality and sensuousness. Photo: Joshua Schreier.

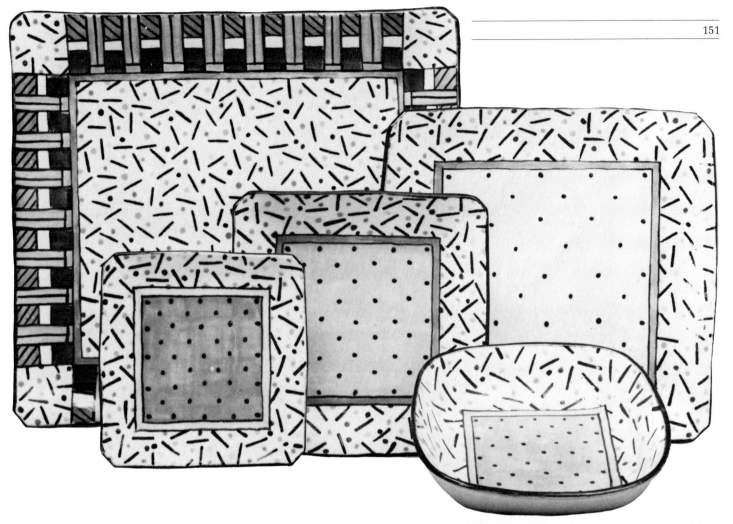

Cabaret (11 pieces), Sèvres factory, France, nineteenth century. Each piece of this opulent hardpaste tea set is decorated with openwork in gilt and rose. Courtesy The Metropolitan Museum of Art, Gift of Helen Boehm, 1969.

craft with industrial methods. Their goal is to produce multiples of expressive, functional objects. By mixing hand and machine processes, they can produce wares that would probably not be attempted by commercial factories due to complexity of design and high production costs. Limiting the scale of production enables these ceramists to maintain their individuality and autonomy.

Charles Nalle, James Rothrock, Lori Gottlieb, and Marek Cecula are among this emerging group of ceramists who design and produce objects in multiples. Ranging from functional to decorative, their work combines the economy of industrial processes such as casting with the individual character of their own designs. Striving to create a variety of wares with the highest standards of excellence, these ceramists may eventually influence commercial design.

Occasionally an artist learns production methods in an industrial setting and then establishes a separate factory. After designing for Franciscan (Interpace) for three years, Jerry Rothman formed a company with Janette Rothman in Los Angeles called Rothwoman. Since 1970 they have mass-produced forms combining industrial methods with hand-painted decoration. Although initially each piece was made by hand, the Rothmans eventually adopted the rampress, a sophisticated industrial machine that forms by high pressure. They are now also casting and, with the assistance of seven employees, distribute their dinnerware to major stores throughout the United States.

The Rothmans, who have adopted and incorporated industrial methods for their own purposes, represent one aspect of the relationship between the contemporary ceramist and industry—industry's contribution to the individual artist.

Above
Nalle Ceramic Dinnerware by Charles Nalle, 1980, 4½″ x 11‴; 2″ x 7″ (10.8 x 27.9; 6.4 x 17.8 cm). These bowls from a series of multiples are cast and celadon glazed. Photo: Eddie Owen.

Unfinished work in the studio of Charles Nalle.

CHAPTER ELEVEN

THE FIGURINE TRADITION

DUST TO DUST" is the familiar adage explaining humankind's origin and destiny. It is appropriate then that human beings have fashioned representations of the human form with wet dust—clay—even longer than they have made containing forms. Clay figures ranging from a few inches to life-size date back to the prehistoric periods of most cultures. A well-known example is the early representation of the female form (in Turkey from 5500 B.C., for example), modeled with bulbous breasts and thighs; such overt sexuality suggesting its use in religious fertility rituals.

In Middle Kingdom Egypt, secular activities such as brewing beer and making pottery were modeled in miniature also. These clay figurines were placed in the tomb of the deceased as representations of daily life to be taken on the journey to the afterlife. Today they remain as a visual record of domestic culture in ancient Egypt.

In the Far East, tomb figures modeled to resemble the dead and their entire retinue were buried in tombs during the Chinese Han (260 B.C.–A.D. 220) and Six Dynasties (A.D. 265–589) periods, though the figures of this genre known best to us were made during the T'ang dynasty (A.D. 618–906). Their beauty, solemnity, and composure still captivate us today. Japanese Haniwa figures of the fifth and sixth centuries A.D. (mounted on cylinders and placed around the tomb site), became surrogates for animals, servants, and even the spouse of the deceased, who previously were slaughtered as part of the burial ritual.

The ability of the figure in ceramic art to transcend reality and function on an elevated, spiritual plane is best exemplified by Te'hua (*blanc de chine*) figures, which often represent Taoist or Buddhist sages and deities. As discussed in "Whiteness," they exhibit the most exquisite modeling and exemplify porcelain's pure, fine-grained, and unctuous character. Used to adorn the desk or table, Te'hua figures draw the viewer into an imaginary space in a manner that would later be translated by eighteenth-century European modelers into imaginary landscapes on the dining table.

This imaginary landscape included not only dinnerware, serving dishes, and candelabra, but intricately detailed porcelain figurines. Developed to imitate grandly embellished table confections made of sugar or wax, figurines continued in three dimensions the fantasies begun in genre painting on porcelain wares. They depicted chinoiserie characters, aristocratic manners, commedia dell'arte actors, and pastoral scenes of peasant life. The figurine became a luxury art form patronized by kings and princes, and the spiritual and magical powers formerly ascribed to the ritual figure were transformed into fanciful imaginings drawn from dramatic literature, ancient mythology, and Christian religion.

Though the early eighteenth-century figurines of Meissen and other German factories were hand-painted for the most part, later examples from France, Italy, and England were covered only with a clear glaze or

Punchinello from Germany, 1748, 6¼" (15.9) cm) high. Like so many figurines of the period, this hardpaste clown is modeled after a character from an Italian comedy. The animated posture and dramatic coloring give stature to what is a miniature work of art. Courtesy The Metropolitan Museum of Art, Gift of Irwin Untermeyer, 1964.

Right
Untitled by Jack Earl, 1975, 6½" x 7" x 7½" (16.5 x 17.8 x 8.9 cm). This modeled and glazed piece is typical of Earl's work. Collection Robert L. Pfannebecker. Photo: Axel and McCready.

Left
Josiah Wedgwood Built His City out of Clay and Many People Have Visited His City and Those Who Visited There and Left to Build Their Own Cities Couldn't Help Thinking of Josiah's by Jack Earl, 1979, 10½″ x 11½″ x 8¼″ (27 x 29 x 21 cm). This dual scene is modeled and then colored with oil paint. Courtesy Helen Drutt Gallery, Philadelphia.

Below
Clues by Lizbeth Stewart, 1980, 7½″ x 43½″ x 27″ (19 x 59.9 x 68.6 cm). Stewart creates all these hand-built objects of porcelain and low-fire clay and then treats them with glazes, lusters, and paint. Courtesy Helen Drutt Gallery, Philadelphia.

left unglazed entirely. French bisquit porcelain and English parian ware, made to resemble marble carvings, are examples of the latter.

The sentimental treatment and rendering of many of these objects continues to the present day, as witnessed by the proliferation of figurine art in the marketplace at all price levels. Found in dimestores and the most elegant gift departments, figurine prices range from one dollar to the thousands. Their saccharine treatment of form, however, robs them of the imaginative spark and artistic quality possessed by their eighteenth-century models. The mythological, theatrical, and even grotesque themes of the originals are also more powerful than those of their sterile imitators.

Techniques of Figurine Making

Primitive cultures used no tools, but rather pressed, pinched, and pulled bits of clay from a mass to enact their figurative visions. Modeling in clay at a very masterly level was also practiced by Renaissance, Mannerist, and Baroque sculptors, who often made early sketches of their sculptures in terracotta. These studies, known as *bozzetti*, were formed using hardened knobs of clay to rough out the major volumes of the sculpture.[1] *Bozzetti* possess a vitality and spontaneity the finished works often do not capture. For this reason, in the late seventeenth century they began to be valued as much as the finished works and collected by connoisseurs of sculpture.

Porcelain altered the figurine tradition, both aesthetically and technically. Its fine texture allowed the modeler to capture details never before possible. The double-valve molds used to produce Te'hua figures were transformed by European modelmakers into highly complex molds for many-parted figurines. Those made at Meissen and Nymphenburg were so complex that much of the efficacy of the finished form was contingent on the work of the "repairer," whose job it was to assemble all the parts. This was a delicate task, for the slightest variation in the tilt of the head or sweep of the hand could change the overall effect of the figure's posture. Deviation from the modeler's original form, even a subtle change in nuance, could distort the original mood created by the modelmaker.

Contemporary Figurine Makers

Foremost among modern artists to embrace and revitalize the figurine tradition in recent times is Jack Earl, who began by making entire worlds of fanciful penguins. Like the Meissen figurines, Earl's first works were narrative in nature—romanticized records of everyday minutiae from his rural Ohio life. The precise, table-top surroundings are often accompanied by lengthy, stream-of-consciousness titles, sing-songy, conversational, and attentive to details. An example: "If the coffee's hot, the music's off and there's no flys, there is a dog standing on the bar. This place is set up so nothing works out nice."

Recently Earl's scenes comprise dual images, and double interpretations, of a given theme, such as the piece made to commemorate Josiah Wedgwood's 250th anniversary. On one side he painted a simple shed, simultaneously reflecting his own rural landscape and the memory of pre-industrial England. The opposite side depicts Wedgwood's eighteenth-century city of "progress"; gone is any trace of the shed or natural landscape, which are replaced by a garbage-strewn, deteriorating environment. Industry's gift amounts to refuse and by-products, Earl seems to be saying.[2]

Lizbeth Stewart, Frank Fleming, and Joe Bova are other contemporary modelers who utilize porcelain's surface for its fine white texture. Lizbeth Stewart's range of images is diverse and perplexing, though all are related by their technical virtuosity and realistic rendering. Free-standing monkey and turtle forms, measuring about three feet (91.4 cm) across, are almost beyond the realm of figurine scale, though their spirit is very much in keeping with historical models. The choice of exotic animals also recalls eighteenth-century Europe's fascination with distant Asia as expressed in chinoiseries—many of which depicted scenes that included monkeys on chains as household pets. Stewart's choice of these forms may, indeed, follow naturally from her selection of porcelain itself, thereby incorporating some of the material's historical thunder.

But she uses her skill not only in creating animal forms, but also in modeled human parts treated with lusters or acrylic paints. Stewart does not limit her creations to porcelain alone—she sometimes combines clay with other media such as fabric appliqué and wood.

Unglazed and uncolored, Frank Fleming's *Goat Man*, 1971, is phantasmagorically vivid. Shadows articulate its haunting, convincing character. For though the creature is imaginary, this half human–half goat is somehow identifiable. Fleming's mythical creatures are reminiscent of Greek figures, but derive from his need for nonverbal communication. Due to a serious speech impediment as a child, he simply stopped talking for eleven years. "I began to feel little need for verbal communications. I was more at ease with nature and animals than with people; I lived within myself. I didn't use words to describe the things

Left
Shop with Figures of a Man and Woman, Ludwigsburg factory, Germany, 1776, 6″ x 5½″ (15.2 x 13.9 cm). This vignette is typical of those made in Europe in the eighteenth century. Courtesy The Metropolitan Museum of Art, Gift of R. Thornton Wilson, 1950.

Right
Untitled by Frank Fleming, 1977, 44″ x 17″ x 19″ (41.3 x 32.4 x 15.6 cm). This mythical half-man, half-goat creature is modeled and left unglazed.

Below
Masta Gator by Joe Bova, 1978. This naturalistic porcelain piece was modeled and then painted with china paints.

I saw, and I'm sure that because I didn't use words I tended to think in images."[3] The child of Alabama tenant farmers, Fleming recalls that superstition played a prominent role in his home. "This kind of mystery, this obedience to primitive laws," as he states, "gets into your bones, and it's had a big influence on me."[4] The ambiguity of Fleming's figures lies between fantasy and reality, and it is unclear where the goat ends and the man begins, where the unconscious ends and the conscious mind begins.

Joe Bova's *Masta Gator*, 1978, is a direct descendant of German Baroque objects. Naturalistically painted animals and vegetables in the form of tureens and other objects were then favored to decorate sideboards and banquet tables. Unlike the glossy surfaces of the Baroque forms, however, Bova's are painted with matte underglazes and left unglazed. He also makes free-standing male heads, resting directly on their chins. Alluding to pre-Colombian Peruvian portrait heads, they have rounded, primitive bone structures and piercing expressions. Bova alleviates their solemnity with tiny, brilliantly colored birds that grow straight from their heads—reminders of a time when humans and nature were one.

Porcelain Tableaux

Contemporary tableaux are like stages with props, waiting for the characters of a drama to materialize. Their intimate scale acts as a magnet, drawing the viewer into its enclave. Chris Unterseher's postcard-size studies compel close examination. His subjects are nostalgic representations of the recent past—Art Deco diners and Boy Scout mythology among them. Sparse, rectangular slates are the setting for his distilled subjects. Unterseher's miniature scale intensifies and directs one's experience of the invented landscape or situation. The melancholy mood captured by his tableaux is reminiscent of that found in the paintings of Edward Hopper. In *Polar Bear, Portland, Oregon*, 1979, Unterseher turns an elongated cast shadow into an abstract element in his spare setting. He isolates his subject, in this case a polar bear, dramatizing it by permanently capturing the light of the late-day sun.

Richard Notkin packs each of his vignettes with astonishingly detailed objects—a broom, chair, and table holding a skull, for example—to create trompe l'oeil totems. The viewer is convinced of their reality by the meticulously accurate replication, yet astounded by their thumbnail scale. Aside from free-standing pieces, Notkin creates flat, hanging slabs resembling subterranean concrete walls with occasional bricks and stonework of porcelain. Cordons of bricks

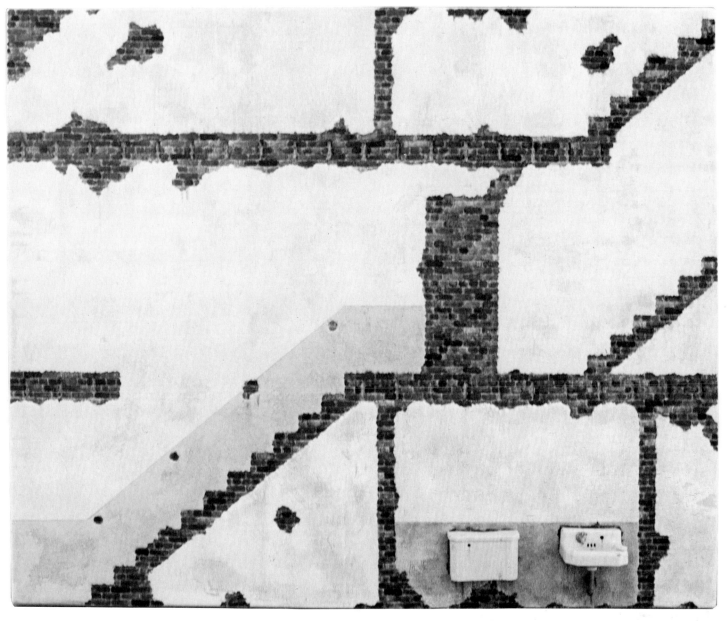

Above
Wall # 4 by Richard Notkin, 1976–1978, 20½" x 24½" (52 x 62.1 cm). This piece made of cast and carved industrial porcelain was created during a residence at the Kohler Company.

Left
Endangered Species # 2 by Richard Notkin, 1978, 11" x 6¼" (27.9 x 15.8 cm). Each item of this free-standing totem is modeled, under-glazed, and overglazed.

form grids on the flat slabs, which are interspersed with areas of modulated color, texture, and pattern. The overall effect approximates the pattern left when a building once standing adjacent to another is razed. Even when he tucks tiny bathroom fixtures into a corner against the background, they retain an abstract ambiguity, which is their strength.

Dolls

Eighteenth-century porcelain dolls were elaborately dressed, pristine fancies for the children of Europe's upper classes. Unlike these, the dolls of Gundi Dietz (Austria), Jane Osborn-Smith (England), and Augusta Talbot (United States) fuse the mobility of puppets with the soul-searching honesty of portraits.

Those of Gundi Dietz have exposed joints, loosely held together by metal pins. Scantily dressed, they are close to the precious sort one would find in antique shops. Osborn-Smith's sad-eyed harlequin sits upon his throne, which is actually his chest of tricks. Though modeled separately, figure and trunk

fuse into a single entity, visually held together by a wash of softly colored patterns.

Where Dietz and Osborn-Smith model youthful figures, Augusta Talbot's are aged women whose exquisitely detailed porcelain hands and faces clearly show the effects of time. Constructed on armatures of wire, wood, and cloth like antique dolls, some are free standing, others are strung like Indonesian puppets capable of animated movement. Costumes for the figures are often made of paper. Seemingly inspired by Italian Renaissance court dress and commedia dell'arte costume, headdresses and robes are built upon the figurative armature, then patterned and painted in ink and gouache.

In *Night Visit*, 1980, Talbot places individual punchinello figures within a box construction made of wood, clay, and paper, lighted from within. The mannerisms of the figures present a perplexing image. Talbot views her mixed-media assemblages as a more complete context in which to view the figures' surreal, dreamlike nature.

Five Dolls by Gundi Dietz, 1977, 3½'' to 4½'' (8.9 to 11.4 cm) high. Dietz's antique-looking dolls are made of moveable porcelain parts wired and hinged together. Courtesy Helga Orthofer. Photo: Michael McTwigan.

Three Spoons by Laura Wilensky, 9½'' x 2¾'' x 1½'' (24.8 x 6.3 x 3.8 cm). The spoons are hand-built and decorated with underglaze, overglaze, and decals. Left and center, collection Susan Wechsler; right, collection Jan Axel. Photo: Michael McTwigan.

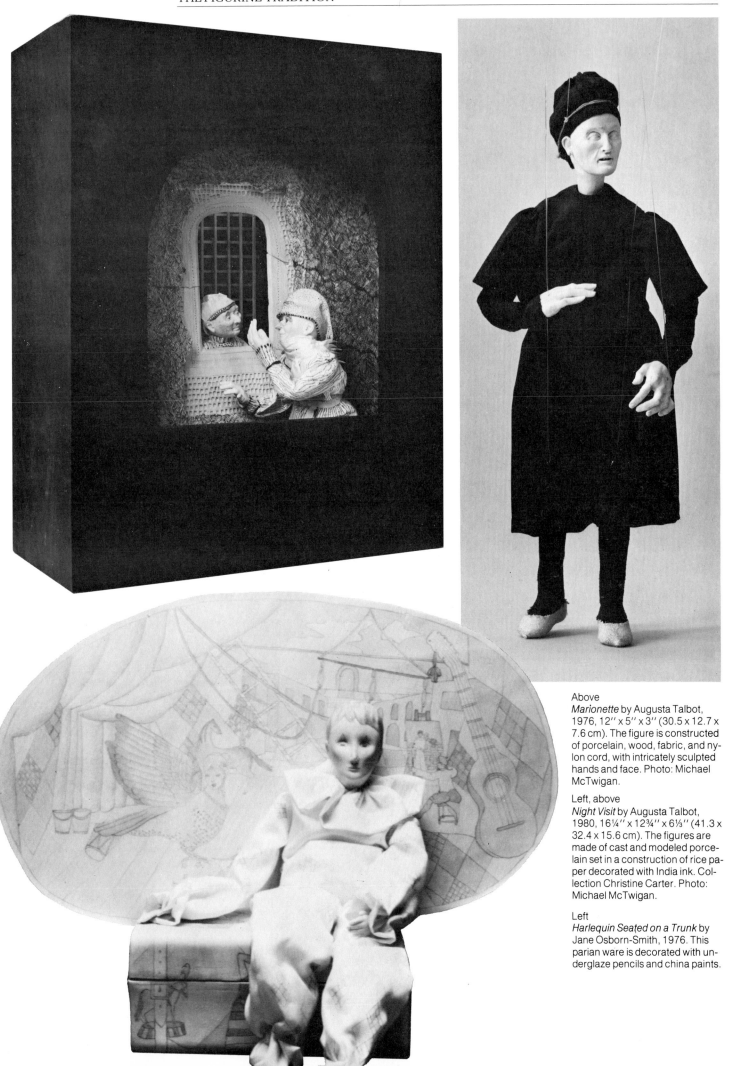

Above
Marionette by Augusta Talbot,
1976, 12″ x 5″ x 3″ (30.5 x 12.7 x
7.6 cm). The figure is constructed
of porcelain, wood, fabric, and ny-
lon cord, with intricately sculpted
hands and face. Photo: Michael
McTwigan.

Left, above
Night Visit by Augusta Talbot,
1980, 16¼″ x 12¾″ x 6⅓″ (41.3 x
32.4 x 15.6 cm). The figures are
made of cast and modeled porcelain set in a construction of rice paper decorated with India ink. Collection Christine Carter. Photo:
Michael McTwigan.

Left
Harlequin Seated on a Trunk by
Jane Osborn-Smith, 1976. This
parian ware is decorated with underglaze pencils and china paints.

CHAPTER TWELVE

THE INDUSTRIAL LEGACY

INDUSTRY OFFERS its own tradition. Until the 1960s, it was one which repelled studio artists. They viewed industrial concepts as predictable, uniform—an invalid vehicle for personal expression.

The close of World War II had ushered in a flurry of activity in the United States—in the arts, in business, in science, in geopolitics—as this country became the world leader in nearly every field. It was the emergence of Abstract Expressionism that gave American artists—and ceramists—a new confidence and courage. Like jazz and beat poetry, art became an arena for risk and experimentation. Following the lead of Peter Voulkos, John Mason, Paul Soldner, Jerry Rothman, and others in Los Angeles, American potters came to see clay as a gestural, action-oriented medium not unlike the "Action Painting"[1] of the Abstract Expressionists. Their energetically formed pots (barely recognizable as such) were slashed, torn, pummeled, and painted; each work was considered a unique "event" or experience. No wonder the look-alike sameness of manufactured ceramics did not interest these pioneering artists.

All this was to change during the 1960s. As Abstract Expressionist ceramics evolved into the more representational imagery of Funk Art, humor and social commentary entered the ceramist's formal vocabulary. Along with this, perhaps it was the air-brushed, comic-strip look of Pop Art that enticed the clay artist to experiment with bright enamel colors, low-fire clay, and commercial imagery. The results were cool, cleaned up,

and precise—what came to be known on the West Coast as "fetish finish." For this new style of carefully considered work, the exacting methods of industry were entirely appropriate.

In 1971, Richard Shaw and Robert Hudson began an eighteen-month collaboration, which was the first thorough-going use of slip casting in a private studio. Some casting was evident before this, though not as the primary method of any artist. Jim Melchert, for example, cast faces as part of his work in 1964-65, and Shaw himself had minimally explored the method in 1969, though it was not until his experiments with Hudson that casting became his dominant ceramic process. Working in Shaw's Stinson Beach, California, studio, they gathered numerous objects—rocks, twigs, duck decoys, innertube-like forms, bottles—to serve as models for their forms. From plaster molds they cast clay replicas, which were used in their entirety or in parts. Combined with wheel-thrown and hand-built elements, the forms were assembled into three-dimensional collages. Most of these alluded to vessels in general configuration—teapots, cups, and the like—although they did not actually function as such.

Shaw and Hudson used the single most popular technique of industry (90 percent of industrial ceramics are cast), but they did so with a unique vision. Although the quality of their casting is superb, the artists purposely left seams visible (usually smoothed away in industry) so that the process is plainly evident.

Pot by Nicholas Homoky, 1978, 5" x 4" (12.7 x 10.2 cm). The somewhat severe appearance of this wheel-thrown and polished pot is enhanced by the inlaid abstract design. Collection Daniel Jacobs. Photo: Jan Axel.

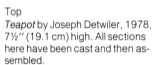

Top
Teapot by Joseph Detwiler, 1978,
7½'' (19.1 cm) high. All sections
here have been cast and then assembled.

Center left
Untitled #44 by Robert Hudson,
1973, 8'' x 7'' x 4.5'' (20.3 x 17.8 x
11.5 cm). This trompe l'oeil piece
was cast and assembled, underglazed, and painted with china
paint. Courtesy Hansen Fuller
Goldeen Gallery, San Francisco.

Bottom
Untitled #17 by Robert Hudson,
1973, 8½ x 13½ x 5 (21.6 x 34.3 x
14 cm). This cast and assembled
abstraction has been underglazed
and decorated with china paint.
Courtesy Hansen Fuller Goldeen
Gallery, San Francisco.

Right
Covered Bottle by Richard Shaw,
1973, 16½'' x 9½'' x 5½'' (41.9 x
24.2 x 14 cm). This piece was cast
and assembled, glazed, and
painted with china paint. Courtesy
Braunstein Gallery, San Francisco.

Multifired Slipware Tea Service by Lynn Turner, 1980, teapot 7″ x 8″ x 4″ (17.8 x 20.3 x 10.2 cm). Although molds allow only limited variations, the changes in color contributed by the underglaze make each of these cast and assembled pieces special and keep the design alive. Photo: Colin C. McRae.

Pencils and Funnels by Karen Thuesen Massaro, 1977, 6″ x 18″ x 10″ (15.2 x 45.7 x 25.4 cm). All pieces are cast black-and-white porcelain and have been left unglazed.

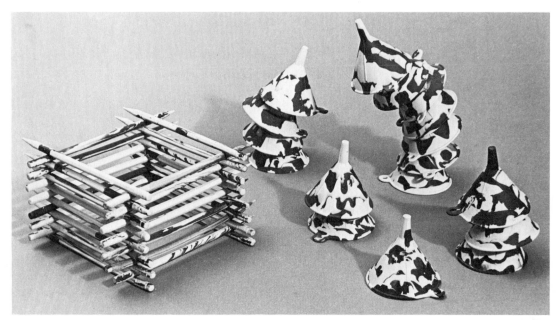

In addition to its ability to replicate forms, casting produces an extremely smooth surface particularly suitable for underglaze and china paints. For Shaw, this experiment with casting opened the way to a new aesthetic, namely his recent trompe l'oeil images. The ability of these images to mimic reality and thereby fool our eye would be less believable were they not visually accurate. Casting allows Shaw to capture the reality of an object, and porcelain, because of its physical strength and fine texture, is unique among clays in being able to render delicate yet stable forms. But in reproducing objects accurately, such as a pencil, Shaw does not merely take a mold from an ordinary pencil. Because the clay shrinks anywhere from 10 to 20 percent in firing, he must first carve a pencil that much larger in order to end up with one life-size. After firing, the separate parts are arranged and the surface is "illustrated" in keeping with the form's literal imagery.

Both the plaster used in mold making and the liquid porcelain used in casting have a seductive quality. The ease and almost magical power of the process is so compelling that from the outset of its popularity in the early seventies many ceramists used it unthinkingly. Five-and-dime, grocery, and hardware stores became the fountainhead for familiar, all-too-easy imagery. British ceramist Jill Crowley bitingly characterized this American school as one operating by the tenet of "if it moves, cast it." While Richard Shaw and Robert Hudson's cast work took the country by storm and cut a new path for modern ceramics, it also spawned a host of imitators whose art was often merely facile.

Like Shaw, Karen Massaro also casts everyday objects. Her intention is not to trick the eye, however, but to suffuse her objects with a "reality" of their own. This is accomplished by employing all-over surface patterns and by juxtaposing a series of various elements into a single work. She gathers her models from around the house: bars of soap, irons, funnels, and pencils. Multiple castings of the same form are grouped, stacked, and assembled into irregular, patterned configurations. Though the forms are representational, their surfaces are abstract, often marbleized or colored in "unrealistic" ways. These surfaces circumvent normal associations; we perceive an entire tableau, rather than individual objects. Massaro aims for the nonsensical pose of common objects to serve as a point of departure: bars of soap and funnels become vehicles for abstractions of form, color, and pattern.

Repetition is the gift of industry. In the studio repetition offers uncommon artistic possibilities, including the chance for making precise forms where mechanical regularity is intended. Like Massaro, Robert Milnes depends on the sameness and duplication of casting. His sculptures are made of exact, tubular shapes of porcelain combined with copper or steel tubing and joints. Milnes's interest lies in "the interior structuring of the walls on which the pieces are mounted, including the wiring, plumbing, and skeletal structure." He reinforces the structural nature of his work by exposing the joints supporting the porcelain tubes. The forms and surface treatments remind us of radio parts, electronic circuitry, and porcelain electric insulators.

While Milnes uses casting for its uniformity, Jacqueline Poncelet of England adopted the technique in order to produce limited editions of her very supple, unique forms. She casts a set number of pieces from each mold—say five to ten—and then destroys the mold to insure that only a "precious few" of that image exist. Casting allows her to make bone china forms with paper-thin walls. Their rounded contours—linked by process and aesthetic to industry—are most efficiently formed through casting.

Examining Poncelet's work illustrates a point about industrially produced forms. In factory production, the product requirements and manufacturing process dictate a specific kind of form, an example being the porcelain products of a plumbingware factory. Plumbingware forms must meet safety and sanitary standards, that is, all fixtures must have rounded edges to facilitate safe movement around them for easy cleaning. At the same time, gently curved shapes allow the plaster molds to be easily removed from the clay pieces once they have set.

Though paper thin, Poncelet's delicate bone china forms share a common technique and rounded profile with the products of a plumbingware factory. Both result from the same forming process and demonstrate the truth of Herbert Read's statement that "the

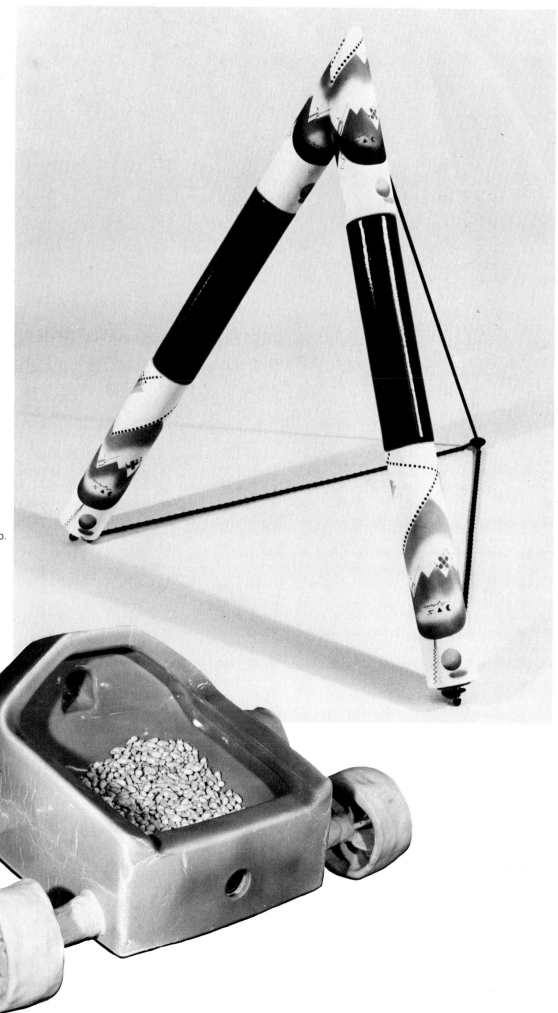

Left
Monte Alban II by Glenys Barton, 1976–77, 14″ x 8″ (35.5 x 20.3 cm). Made of cast bone china with a pressed slab base, this sculpture is burnished and left unglazed. Photo: Richard Davies.

Below left
Untitled by Jacqueline Poncelet, 1974, 3″ (7.6 cm). This shell-like bone china vessel was cast and assembled. Collection Karen McCready. Photo: Michael McTwigan.

Right
Cambridge Triangle by Robert Milnes, 1978, 36½″ (92.7 cm) high. This construction is made of underglazed and glazed porcelain combined with steel.

Bottom
Good Tooth Fairy Car by Tom La-Dousa, 1974. The pieces of this cast and hand-built urinal-turned-cart, made of vitreous china, are sprayed with opaque glazes and joined with epoxy. © John Michael Kohler Arts Center, Sheboygan, Wisconsin. Photo: Bayens Photo Co.

These commodes are drying in the casting area of the Kohler Company after they have been taken from molds and the seams have been cleaned. Courtesy Kohler Co. Photo: Jan Axel

laws of least resistance and of economy of effort make it inevitable that similar activities shall always lead to similar forms."[2]

The Factory as Artist's Studio: Wedgwood

Wedgwood, of Stoke-on-Trent, England, has invited artists to submit designs for production since the eighteenth century, when founder Josiah Wedgwood commissioned sculptor John Flaxman and painters William Hackwood and George Stubbs to design for the company. In 1976 Wedgwood invited Glenys Barton to use its facilities as she would her own studio. She created forms by modeling in plaster and reproducing multiple works by casting. Such industrial methods were then becoming popular among British ceramists and were even advocated and taught in the educational system. Also at this time, bone china was championed as an appropriate material for studio ceramists, a development symbolizing a rebellion against all that the followers of Ruskin and Morris in the nineteenth century and Bernard Leach in our own said should be avoided. For bone china was the "veritable child"[3] of the Industrial Revolution—a total departure from the essence of what these three reformers felt clay should embody.

Both Glenys Barton and Wedgwood seek total control and perfection in their work. "They both wanted the forseen, regular, predictable result which would express a concept already fully formed before the piece was ever modelled or went into the kiln."[4]

The outcome of Barton's participation at Wedgwood was a body of work produced by the firm in limited editions. These images of man tend to be precise and sterile, reflecting her concern with the themes of isolation and loneliness. Their singleminded expression of isolation is heightened by Barton's clinical approach to materials, for pristine geometric landscapes and relationships are the work's formal context.

The Factory as Artist's Studio: Kohler

The Arts/Industry program sponsored by the John Michael Kohler Arts Center, Sheboygan, Wisconsin, is uniquely conceived. In 1973, Ruth DeYoung Kohler, director of the arts center, organized a national ceramics exhibition entitled "Plastic Earth." The exhibiting artists were invited to a one-day seminar at Kohler Company to view the facilities. Their enthusiasm for a collaboration between artists and the factory led to the establishment of an artist-in-residence program the following year.

While in the factory, artists may utilize the massive facilities and expertise of one of the nation's largest manufacturers of plumbingware in order to explore the potential of industry in their own work. The factory parts have an inherent vocabulary of form—softly rounded corners, uniform surface, glossy glaze—with a particular aesthetic content bound by the products' usefulness and method of manufacture.

The Kohler Arts/Industry residencies span

#4920 Altered by Jan Axel, 1979, 30″ x 87½″ (76 x 223.5 cm), vitreous china, stained, cast, and assembled; iron rods and hardware. The walls consist of altered forms cast from a section of a urinal (Kohler Co. mold # 4920). Altered setters were used to create the floor. © John Michael Kohler Arts Center, Sheboygan, Wisconsin. Photo: Bayens Photo Co.

from four to twelve weeks in length and there have also been intensive, two-week workshops. The factory provides the ideal environment for exploring new concepts: Isolated from the concerns of everyday life, visiting artists can focus completely on the scale, pace, and facilities of the factory. Because they can participate in every aspect—from plaster modeling to kiln loading—there is unparalleled opportunity for growth.

Jack Earl and Tom LaDousa took part in the first program at Kohler and were instrumental in shaping subsequent sessions.[5] The idea of an artist entering a factory to create individual works of art is, of course, antithetical to the very nature of industry, where standardization, speed, and productivity are of utmost importance. To thousands of factory workers who use tons of clay producing household fixtures, art made of the material may seem superfluous. The artists, on the other hand, were confronted with the overwhelming scale of the factory and its machine-governed regularity: where kilns span a city block, where multifaceted molds require up to four workers to maneuver their weight and bulk, where hundreds of the same form lined up in rows crowd the artist's mind with tempting images.

The works to come out of the Kohler residencies are as diverse as those who have participated. Among the variety of expressions, though, several consistent qualities can be observed, scale and multiplicity being the most obvious. Because artists bring to the in-

dustrial setting their own perceptions of what industry is and what it offers, it is clearly a learning experience whose influence may be seen not only in those works created at the factory, but in works produced later. Tom Rippon is the only artist participating in the program who worked exclusively by hand in plastic clay, as he felt no kinship to the industrial methods at his disposal. However, the sheer scale of the factory and its production had a singular effect on Rippon's work. For the first time his forms expanded beyond the tabletop to include the table itself, a format he continued to develop after leaving Kohler. His works are now life-size vignettes comprising tables, chairs, and tiled floors.

Many of the ceramists who have participated in the program used the slip-cast parts that were available in the factory. These they cut, reassembled, carved, or used almost like canvases for their paintings and drawings. Often the fixtures themselves turned into visual puns: LaDousa's urinal-turned-cart, *Good Tooth Fairy Car*, 1974, Earl's *Sitz Bath Chair*, 1974, Clayton Bailey's *Toilet Teapot*, 1979, or Joe DiStefano's series of sinks transforming and disintegrating, 1974, to name a few. Even though the existing factory parts were natural as subject matter, in retrospect many of these humorous interpretations seem obvious and too easy.

Although Jack Earl began by playfully using forms taken from the production line, in later visits to the factory he extended his sub-

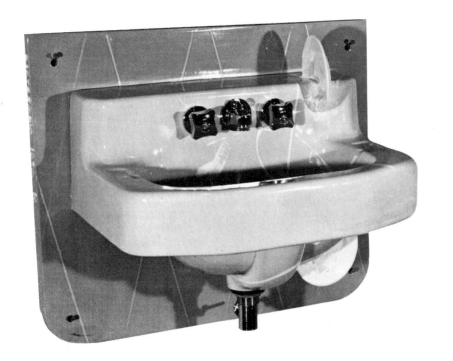

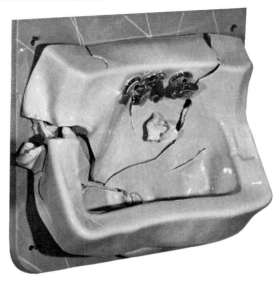

Above
Saturday and Sunday, two from a series of seven from *Soap Opera* by Joe Di Stefano, 1977, each approximately 20″ x 25″ (50.8 x 63.5 cm). The pieces are made of vitreous china, cast, soaked, smashed, incised, glazed, and chrome-plated with cast brass. © John Michael Kohler Arts Center, Sheboygan, Wisconsin. Photo: Bayens Photo Co.

Left
Ohio Boy by Jack Earl, 1977, 16″ x 18″ x 12″ (40.6 x 45.7 x 30.5 cm). Underglaze pencil and glaze were used to decorate this cast, hand-built construction of vitreous china. © John Michael Kohler Arts Center, Sheboygan, Wisconsin. Photo: Bayens Photo Co.

Top right
Untitled by George Mason, 1977, 145½″ (369 cm). The form is vitreous china that has been cast, glazed, and then blasted with an air-chipper. © John Michael Kohler Arts Center, Sheboygan, Wisconsin. Photo: Bayens Photo Co.

Bottom right
Setters (detail) by Terry Rosenberg, 1979, each tile 20½″ (52.1 cm). Made of vitreous china, the entire work contains 125 tiles that have been cast, incised, and then glazed. © John Michael Kohler Arts Center, Sheboygan, Wisconsin. Photo: Bayens Photo Co.

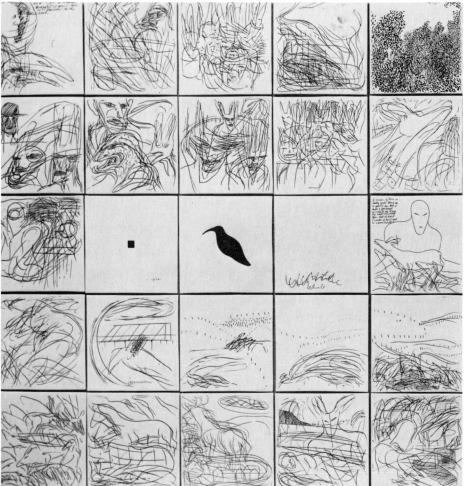

jects to include human portraiture, such as *Ohio Boy*, 1976, and animals. Both he and Richard Notkin, another resident artist, worked with expert modelers to construct very complex, multiparted molds they might never have attempted in their own studios. The minute detail (to the studio ceramist, complexity often translates into detail) they strove for and achieved amazed the factory workers, who were accustomed to the simple contours of bathroom fixtures. For though factory parts are quite complex internally, they appear outwardly simple.

Whereas in the studio slabs of flat clay are generally rolled out by hand or slab roller, in the factory even these are cast in molds. Such cast slabs are called setters. Large plumbingware is fired upon them, so they may shrink along with the forms and thereby prevent cracking and warping. Setters are extremely stable slabs, ideal for making large walls and murals. George Mason did just that during his residency, incorporating graphic and calligraphic imagery. He used available factory glazes and at times sandblasted specific areas to produce contrasting dull and glossy finishes. The works are meticulously crafted, and their clarity and austerity reflect the aesthetic of industrial finishes.

Terry Rosenberg also successfully used setters. After experimentation, he accepted the flat setters with their glossy, slick, industrial finish. He scratched quick, linear drawings into the slabs that were expressive of the factory's pace. Black glaze was then embedded into the incisions and the surface scraped clean—a Korean technique called *mishima*. This left a smooth surface, revealing precise linear drawings that were then clear glazed. Rosenberg made 300 such "drawings," using the setters like pages of a sketchbook. Once they were fired, he assembled 125 of them into a 45-foot wall installation. Until that time, the impetus behind the work was his belief that somehow the quality of line and pattern in the drawings would culminate in a cohesive work—"a conglomerate of two months of sporadic thought."

During her two residencies at Kohler, Karen Massaro used setters as canvases for single- or multi-unit "glaze paintings." She experimented with standard industrial glazes, building up layers of patterned color, which she then drew through at various levels with a sharp tool. These works were well received in the factory, where the potential for the standard glazes was seen afresh. The management was so taken by Massaro's use of them, in fact, that she was commissioned to create a mural for the Kohler Village sports center.

During several residencies, Robert Sedestrom established a system for himself equal to that of the factory, but did not want to succumb to its repetitive aesthetic. He cut strips and slabs of plaster with a jigsaw into numerous irregular shapes. They were then assembled into enormously complex volumetric forms, all parts held together with many clamps, and then cast. Because of their complex construction (which could never be exactly repeated) and variety of the elements' shapes, there was no duplication of form. Sedestrom mixed half slip with half factory glazes to achieve fired surfaces that were dull-colored, matte, and pebbly.

For some artists the factory acts as a catalyst for new ideas, for others the experience is an opportunity to continue in established directions. Clayton Bailey used the factory's products to make large-scale ceramic robots for his "Wonders of the World Museum," a compilation of "scientific" explorations into "kaolinism" and the origin of life. Beginning in the 1960s, he began to accumulate creatures, fossils, skeletons, machinery—all of his own making—many of which he buried and later "discovered" as evidence to support his wacky scientific creation theories and to stir up local authorities. Bailey houses and exhibits the collection at his home in Porta Costa, California (with himself in the guise of "Dr. Gladstone"), as a singular, ongoing work-performance.

Bailey fulfilled his intention to use only factory parts, meticulously assembling works from toilet tanks, plumbingware parts, and scraps and castings of oversize tools from the factory's machine and repair shop. Toilets were transformed into a giant teaset, to which he added proportioned handles and spouts, using toilet seats as lids. Bailey's humorous interpretations were true to the aesthetic of his previous work, while taking full advantage of the factory's unique facilities.

Plaster is as much a part of industrial ceramics as is clay. It is used to make the molds from which clay forms are cast, for when the mold is filled with liquid clay slip, it absorbs water and allows the clay to solidify inside. John Toki has a background in ceramics and his involvement with casting led him to turn from clay to plaster—making the process itself an art. When Toki arrived at the Kohler factory, he was interested not in its ceramic processes or even in the model shop where plaster molds are made. Instead he sought discarded scrap molds—known as "cull" in the factory—to use as elements in his massive, stacked and cemented sculptures.

Though Toki's work at the factory shared a substance—plaster—with his previous work, his process was markedly different. The sculptures made at the factory were like quick sketches, the antithesis of his usual

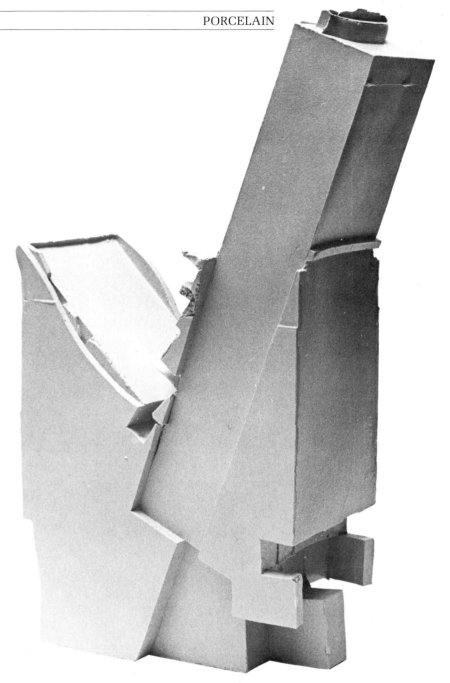

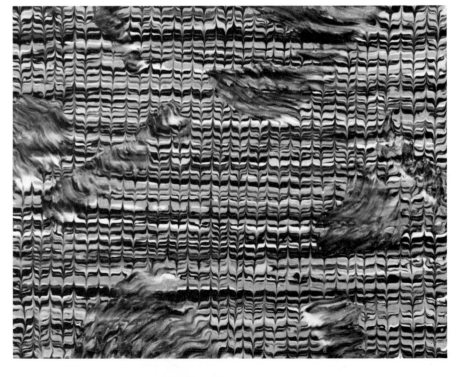

Left
Transitional Composition Six
by Robert Sedestrom, 1980, 23½″
x 15″ x 6½″ (59.7 x 38 x 16.5 cm).
This piece is made of cast vitreous
china with a matte glaze.

Below left
Glaze Painting # 4 by Karen Thuesen Massaro, 1979, 19½″ x 23½″
x ½″ (49.6 x 58.4 x 1.3 cm). The
construction is made of cast slabs
with factory glazes.

Right
White Autumn by John Toki, 1979,
85″ (215.9 cm). The cast plaster
elements of this piece were constructed, chiseled and then com-
pleted with iron rods and epoxy.
© John Michael Kohler Arts Center, Sheboygan, Wisconsin. Photo:
Bayens Photo Co.

Far right
Robot by Clayton Bailey, 1979,
55″ (139.7 cm). All porcelain
pieces are vitreous china; they
were cast and assembled with
hardware, electricity, light, and
epoxy. © John Michael Kohler Arts
Center, Sheboygan, Wisconsin.
Photo: Bayens Photo Co.

working method in which large, interlocking
masses of plaster are carefully executed. The
ability to freely assemble readymade plaster
forms at the factory allowed him to work
more spontaneously than before.

Upon entering the massive environment of
the factory, each artist must gain a new perspective on the artistic process. Both artist
and industry must realize the potential of an
exchange that enriches both product and
producer, both art and artist. The program
offers a rare form of patronage. But more
than financial support, it is the tangible exchange of fertile ideas and concepts. There
has been gradual progress in the inherently
difficult communications between artists and
their industrial counterparts. Artists have
clearly reaped benefits from the factory experience, but they must reciprocate by lending their aesthetic attitudes and technical
knowledge to industry if real progress is to be
made and such patronage kept alive. Otherwise the artist is only a passive beneficiary of
the industrial world, instead of an active par-
ticipant in it.

CHAPTER THIRTEEN

TRADITION DEFIED

ANY ARTIST working within a given medium develops an intimacy with, even loyalty to, that material. Nevertheless, artists may choose to defy the traditions and inherent qualities of their medium as they search for new forms of expression. This is as true of porcelain as it is of any material, despite its rather weighty heritage.

The Issue of Scale

Ceramics have traditionally been constructed on a table-top scale, notwithstanding the life-size terra-cotta soldiers unearthed recently in China or the six-foot storage vessels of Africa and Asia. Modern ceramists wishing to overcome the limitations of scale often do so by assembling individual components or modules into a larger, overall composition, as does Tom Rippon in his life-size tableaux, oversize portrait heads, and still lifes. Using many of the accouterments of art as his subjects—easels, palettes, artists' portraits—he draws with clay in space. Though his work is three-dimensional, it utilizes one of the conventions of two-dimensional drawing and painting—perspective. He cuts slabs of clay into shapes that incorporate the elongated appearance of objects viewed at a distance. Simple, solidly colored, these shapes lend the work a whimsical quality. His handling of spatial relationships is similar in feeling to paintings by Jim Nutt and Gladys Nielson.

The intimate scale of ceramics originates in the vessel tradition, as does the ceramist's concern with the interior and exterior of forms. The majority of ceramic works, whether abstract or representational, allude to the notion of containment or cavity, as opposed to the conventional vocabulary of sculpture, such as mass and volume. Ruth Duckworth's abstract ceramic wall murals are an excellent example. The clay is handled in thick slabs, juxtaposed in such a way that light from an exposed surface is bounced into an interior pocket, thereby drawing the viewer's attention to the mysterious, unseen surface. The very fact that Duckworth simultaneously expresses herself in large bowls, small footed bowls, and abstract murals with equal ease and in a similar fashion is evidence of this underlying preoccupation with interior and exterior among ceramists.

Toshiko Takaezu carries our perception of the interior mysteries of ceramic objects one step further by adding a small bit of clay to the inside of an enclosed form as she makes it. Once fired, the tiny clay ball rattles inside—her conception of the spirit contained by the form. She groups these large-scale spheres together, nesting them in hammocks suspended in an open space. Thus assembled, these two- to three-foot spheres comprise a sculptural and spatial environment.

The Need for New Terminology

Even with the dissolution of functional concerns, as seen in many modern porcelain works, the development of the hybrid vessel or more abstract forms does not easily as-

Facade by John Rogers, 9″ x 6″ (22.9 x 15.2 cm). This abstract was hand-built.

Above
A Tea by Tom Rippon, 1979, 54″ x 37″ x 45″ (137.2 x 93.9 x 114.3 cm). This life-size tableau is hand-built and colored with lusters on unglazed clay. Private collection. Photo: Anita Douthat.

Left
Cocks Fighting Over Art by Robert Arneson, 1970, 6″ (15.2 cm) long. Courtesy Hansen Fuller Goldeen Gallery, San Francisco.

Above right
Honk by Robert Arneson, 1973, 18″ x 13″ (45.7 x 33 cm). Courtesy Hansen Fuller Goldeen Gallery, San Francisco.

Right
Untitled by Sylvia Netzer, 1976, 54″ x 66″, each strip 2″ wide (137.1 x 167.6 x 5 cm). These pinched porcelain slabs have been fired on wood and sand and are held in place with silk pins. Photo: Robert Brooks.

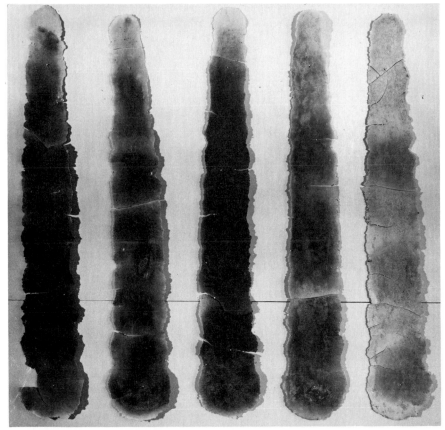

sume the mantle of sculpture. Those objects that straddle the line between conventional sculpture and traditional ceramics have been designated "ceramic sculpture." This curious category includes many objects exhibiting dissimilar substantive concerns. Ceramic sculpture, which traditionally meant figures and figurines, has now become a convenient term for lumping together objects as disparate as hybrid vessels; poetic, narrative, and figurative art objects; and sculpture—all of which may have only one thing in common: they are made of clay. Surely this serves none of the objects well. The strength of these images deserves to be recognized for its own virtue—outside those whose historical lineage is conventional sculpture. As the field of ceramics evolves and both maker and viewer demand critical analysis, alternative criteria are emerging along with a new vocabulary for aesthetic understanding. This kind of care and consideration should be applied to not only ceramics, but all art forms undergoing redefinition today.

The Unique Qualities of Ceramic Sculpture

Most ceramists embrace the qualities of clay and its specific history in their work. If not these, then the special transformational aspect of ceramics is called into play. Some of the strongest clay works proudly display their "ceramicness" while simultaneously carrying the artist's individual message.

Robert Arneson's work has long combined the qualities of the ceramic medium with a highly developed aesthetic sensibility—one so potent it has influenced a generation of Northern California art students. A salient example of his combined concern with the innate qualities of clay and the petulant content of his art is found in *Cocks Fighting Over Art*, 1970. As with most of Arneson's work, meaning comes partly through visual-verbal wordplay, in this case the proverbial "cock fight." The art here comes not from its imagery but from semantic designation, in the Dada sense that anything can be art if it is so designated. The cocks fighting over art works aren't the battered, flea-bitten ones encountered in a down-home cock fight, however. They are the traditional porcelain roosters normally seen on knickknack shelves with other "precious" figurines and curios. Their substance—celadon-glazed porcelain—evokes associations of treasured *objets d'art*. This analogy is reinforced by the fact that birds (roosters included) were popular forms among modelers at Meissen during the eighteenth century. Today our associations with this form lead not only to historical examples but to mass-produced hobby-shop figurines. By depicting the figurine as a debased, sentimental reminder of past fancies, Arneson

Top right
Exile Series # 2 by John Roloff,
1975, 8″ x 14″ x 36″ (20.3 x 35.6 x
91.4 cm). Private collection.

Center right
Untitled # 57 by John Roloff,
1978, 7″ x 36″ (17.9 x 91.4 cm).
The boat form is made of colored
porcelain, slip, and glaze. Courtesy Hansen Fuller Goldeen Gallery, San Francisco.

Bottom right
Shoreline Piece # 64 by John Roloff, 1978, 12″ x 192″ x 48″ (30.5
x 487.7 x 121.9 cm). This piece
is made of porcelain, perlite, porcelain slip, and volcanic ash. Courtesy Hansen Fuller Goldeen Gallery, San Francisco.

Below
Seven by Sylvia Netzer, 1979, 13′ x
28″ (10 m x 71.1 cm). This airy
curtain is made of die-cut porcelain pieces suspended on stainless
steel cable. Photo: Jan Axel.

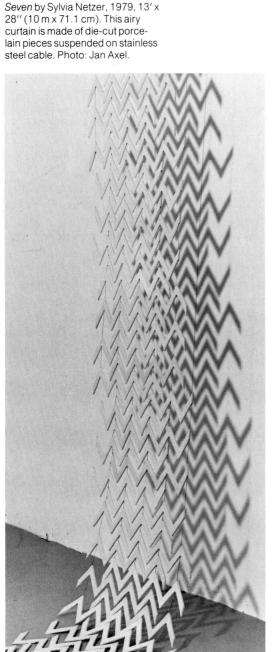

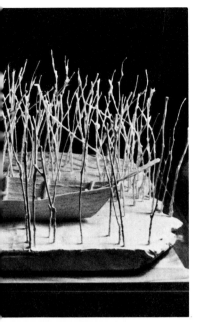

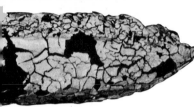

scoffs at this tradition; and "good taste," long associated with fine porcelain, is relegated to the level of a cock fight.

In this work Arneson is questioning the whole art-craft conundrum. The roosters, with their rich historical content, have picked a fight with art works and destroyed it without so much as ruffling their feathers. Perhaps this work symbolizes the problem of acceptance for an artist working in clay today. As aesthetic content has grown in ceramic works, the general view of them as craft still prevails.

Since 1965 Arneson has explored myriad ideas, attitudes, and states of mind using his self-portrait as a format. With naturalistic clarity and vigor he places himself on a pedestal, sometimes defying all propriety, as in *Honk*, 1973, where he depicts himself suggestively thumbing and blowing his nose. This gesture, intended to cause a visceral reaction, is beautifully executed in celadon-glazed porcelain—the ultimate putdown of the ware's inherent connotations of good taste and elitism. In the guise of a neoclassical bust (what could have more reverence for history), he at once embodies the height of tradition, celadon porcelain, while simultaneously sweeping away its potency with a common, repugnant gesture.

Like many ceramists who use one of porcelain's qualities as the central motif of their work, Sylvia Netzer uses it for its fragility and density. Thin skins of smoked porcelain hang together in a group in *Untitled* (about 1976). They have the fragility of insect wings and, in fact, their shape and texture recalls sun-dried snake skins. In another work, *Seven*, Netzer combines die-cut, zigzag porcelain shapes in a 13-foot curtain suspended from the ceiling and draping onto the floor. The shadow falling on the wall behind this piece lends it a beautiful, airy quality, while the tension of up and down movement created by the zigzag shapes keeps the work suspended visually in space.

John Roloff's transmutation of hard, dense porcelain into a seemingly soft, porous substance parallels the gradual evolution of his subject matter—the sailing vessel—which over time has become less and less literal. In his early work, Roloff began making recognizable boat forms which he fired to maturity. The porcelain surface was often glazed and had a dense, glassy finish which lived up to the conventional standard traditionally accepted for the material. As time passed Roloff's boats have become less literal in both image and obvious connection to clay. The

material is taken to extreme in work which is underfired, broken down into a chalky, powdery state, though it appears at the same time like sharp, jagged ice. Its outward appearance sharply contrasts with the notion of porcelain as stony and glassy, as seen in Roloff's earlier work, and though he still uses the material in his more recent pieces the form of the boat has become ashy or barklike. The newer forms poetically embody remnants of time and process—the transformational element required when working with clay. For Roloff, the substance has become the art form where process dictates product. Firing the kiln, which for many is predictable, is for him the unknown, the romantic mystery of the voyage. In several conceptual works he has disembodied the firing process by removing the containing boundaries of the kiln. By constructing kilns over segments of the earth, he has fired the earth itself, documenting the event in photographs. In the final analysis of these works Roloff found the process to be more important to him than the finished piece.

Roloff states that the indirectness of working with clay allows time for contemplation. The passage of time in the kiln, which usually indicates hardening and fixing of substance in a permanent state, for him suggests the passage of a much longer period of time in which transformation of the work takes place. His images express an abiding interest in fossils, also the trace or impression of something from another time.

Roloff's use of porcelain may seem arbitrary, but he manipulates it in that particular way to formalize his ideas. While at the same time he expresses a powerful vision, his work is true to that property which is porcelain's alone—the ability to maintain the desired form while undergoing changes possible only with the phenomenon of such high temperature.

Though artists like Arneson, Netzer, and Roloff, to name a few, thoroughly defy traditional forms of porcelain, they exemplify an extreme attitude by using the material as a point of departure. But even for those who follow in the tradition of vessel making, literal function has often been taken over by aesthetic function—instead of containing food to nourish the body, these vessels now hold ambrosia for the senses. Whether porcelain is explored as straightforward pottery or used for its innate qualities to expand traditional boundaries, in the end the medium is a blank sheet for recording the artist's creative impulses.

CHAPTER FOURTEEN

THE COLLECTOR AND THE OBJET D'ART

PORCELAIN HAS always occupied center stage in the arena of collecting. For centuries porcelain *objets d'art* have been valued for their beauty and ability to capture the spirit of each passing age, as though the spirit were embodied in the very nature of the material itself.

No historical figure better illustrates the passion and discerning taste of a porcelain collector than Augustus the Strong (1670–1733), Elector of Saxony and King of Poland. Augustus so loved porcelain that in 1717, after much negotiating, he gave Frederick William I, King of Prussia, a regiment of 782 soldiers in exchange for 117 pieces of Chinese porcelain. (The 359 children Augustus sired are evidence that his compulsions were not restricted to collecting porcelain.) We can't be too certain of Augustus's motivation for acquiring as many Chinese wares as he could, but we can be certain about his taste. The Chinese pots he collected possess an enduring beauty that continues to inspire contemporary ceramists and collectors. When Augustus founded the Meissen factory in 1709, his first modelers were likewise inspired by these Chinese examples, which they copied in form, glaze, and decoration.

Madame de Pompadour (1721–64), the favorite mistress of Louis XV, also exercised great influence on the tastes of her time. Through the 1750s and '60s she more or less dictated which poems were read, which plays were attended, and which art objects were collected. In the sophisticated era of the rococo, the age of "preciousness," Madame de Pompadour was the glittering hub around which the art and decoration of that day revolved. Porcelain was a favorite of hers and she was considered as grand a patron of the art as Augustus had been.

Each year de Pompadour and her king displayed and sold the best pieces from Vincennes (which moved to and adopted the name of Sèvres in 1756) in the royal apartments. As the king sometimes acted as salesman for the factory, French nobility bought the expensive porcelain wares often. Some grumbled, out of earshot of the king, about the pressure to buy porcelain, to which de Pompadour once retorted, "a man who would not spend his last sou on porcelain [is] neither a good courtier nor a good Frenchman."[1]

Madame de Pompadour's love for porcelain guaranteed the Sèvres factory much royal support; by 1753 Louis XV had taken over almost complete management of its operation. This extensive patronage allowed the factory to maintain production at the highest artistic level. The importance of de Pompadour's support, both financial and aesthetic, is attested to by the number of occasions she herself was the subject of a Sèvres figurine such as the allegorical portrait modeled by Etienne-Maurice Falconet entitled *Venus of the Doves*. Though Falconet was renowned for his full-size marble sculptures, he modeled many pieces in Sèvres biscuit porcelain (*pâte de marbre*), an unglazed body that closely resembles English parian ware, a statuary material that became popu-

Vincennes Ranunculi, Vincennes factory, 1750, 3″ (8 cm) diam. Modeled flowers such as these were used both as applied decorations and in bouquets. They were one of the hallmarks of early French porcelain making. © Sotheby Parke-Bernet. Agent: Editorial Photocolor Archives.

lar during the nineteenth century.

Madame de Pompadour's own favorite porcelains were the two-inch (5-cm) flowers that accounted for 85 percent of the Sèvres factory's sales. They were either displayed on wire stems in vases, mimicking real blossoms, or used as applied decoration on porcelain objects. To the delight of the royal court, de Pompadour sometimes perfumed the porcelain blossoms and mixed them with cut flowers.

Despite de Pompadour's love for porcelain flowers, the ultimate bouquet was made not for her but for Maria Josepha, one of the three "porcelain princesses." On the occasion of her marriage to the heir to the French throne, the Saxon princess sent her father Augustus III (King of Saxony and grandson and successor of Augustus the Strong)[2] 480 magnificent porcelain flowers from Sèvres. Not only was this bouquet meant to be an expression of daughterly devotion, but it was also intended to display the exquisite quality of French porcelain, then chief rival to the Saxon wares of Meissen.

Functioning as a modern-day Madame de Pompadour, Joan Mondale, as wife of the former Vice-President of the United States, has done more than any other recent public figure to call the public's attention to the arts and crafts—a mission that has earned her the sobriquet "Joan of Art" by the media. She is probably the first potter in history to have received front-page coverage in the *New York Times*. She was shown demonstrating her wheel technique with painter James Rosenquist at Clayworks in New York City, which provides a unique grant program for artists of all disciplines to use clay.

Collecting Today

Today the passion for collecting is at a fever pitch; more than ever, the one word heard in connection with collecting (and not confined to ceramics alone) is *investment*. In today's marketplace, Chinese porcelain is one of the most collected and valued goods. It offers the second-best compounded annual rate of return on investment in the realm of collectibles, second only to gold, followed by stamps, rare books, silver, coins, old master paintings, and diamonds.[3] A Ming polychrome vase purchased in Philadelphia for $150 in the early 1940s was appraised at $450 by the end of the decade. That same vase, in 1976, was estimated to sell at auction for $100,000 by Sotheby Parke Bernet's porcelain expert. The prediction was incorrect; the vase brought $260,000—the highest price paid for any work of Chinese art to that date. The difference between the price originally paid and the eventual auction price not only reflects the effects of inflation and a changed perception of the value of a Ming vase but reflects people's desire to invest in more secure, more tangible assets.

Few collectors today purchase modern ceramics with the intention of salting them away in a warehouse and waiting until prices rise. Despite the low cost of ceramic art relative to that of painting or sculpture—for we're talking of ceramic prices ranging from $100 to $5,000, in the main—most people collect those objects they *love*. This is as true now as it was in Augustus the Strong's day. Furthermore, there are no firmly established auction values for contemporary ceramics; porcelain collectors are true pioneers. Both passionate buyers and investment buyers are needed to establish market values and eventually create a secondary market for contemporary porcelain. If a particular artist or stylistic school achieves great notoriety, a demand is created in the marketplace for those works. This allows any piece that becomes available to be sold for a higher price than before. When highly desirable works are sold—which generally means higher prices—giddy anticipation is generated in auction houses.

Contemporary Studio Porcelain

The use of porcelain by individual studio artists is a relatively recent turn of events, notwithstanding late-nineteenth- and early-twentieth-century art pottery. Traditionally, porcelain *objets d'art* were the products of factories like Meissen and Sèvres, where figurines, genre scenes, and tablewares reached their zenith of expression in the eighteenth century. Unfortunately, modern followers of this tradition—the factories of Boehm, Cybis, Lladró—who produce "limited editions" of flowers and fauna, fairy-tale figures, and children at play, do a disservice to porcelain with their emphasis on naturalism and sugary sentimentality. Although advertised to the public as examples of great craftsmanship and sure-fire investments (prices for these objects often begin in the low thousands), their characterless modeling, indifferent surface decoration, and banal subject matter do not capture the spirit of our own age.

Happily, modern studio ceramists are not content to copy historical models but instead have emerged from their relative isolation to explore the larger world of aesthetic concerns shared by painters and sculptors. There they have found artists more interested in ideas than objects (witness Conceptualism, Minimalism, performance art, and the impermanence of some earthworks) who often disdain art precepts, such as beauty or decoration, that have been traditionally identified with porcelain. Today's clay artists have likewise broken the rules of classical ceramics. This may be seen in the Funk

Ant Farm by Burton Isenstein, 1979, 12″ x 5″ x 1″ (30.5 x 12.7 x 2.5 cm). Underglazes and china paint decorate this modeled and carved piece. Photo: Tom Van Eynde.

Warm Currents by Eva Kwong, 1978, 26″ x 21″ x 2″ (66 x 53.3 x 5.1 cm).

movement of the 1960s, when San Francisco Bay area artists rejected the preciousness previously associated with ceramics by either shunning or parodying the porcelain figurine tradition. This opened the way for an unabashed use of porcelain in the studio.

Contemporary ceramics is a youthful field, and those in it have an openness not often found in more established art disciplines where prices for art are currently at a much higher level. The fresh aesthetic approaches of today's ceramists are ready for the overview that great collectors can bring to the field. Ceramic art can be refined, strengthened, and enhanced by sincere and intelligent interest on the part of collectors, who sometimes become as knowledgeable as museum curators and gallery directors. Collectors have an added advantage, however, in that they are totally free from institutional limitations and can indulge their passion by selecting any objects they please.

In order to collect ceramics, a knowledge of history and a sense of current directions are essential, of course, but technical understanding also can enhance aesthetic choices. On the other hand, no amount of factual information can replace passion and taste, on the part of ceramist or collector.

At times aesthetic judgments regarding ceramics come hard. Furthermore, contemporary work has suffered from the outmoded attitudes held by even some of our most prestigious institutions. Witness the fact that the Museum of Modern Art, New York, has never exhibited the work of any living clay artist in a major show. The MoMA Design Collection, which was established in 1934 and includes over 1800 manufactured and handmade objects, exhibits just a small number of functional objects on a permanent basis, although the museum was originally founded with the idea of removing the barriers between fine and applied art. The only ceramic pieces on display are commercially made dinnerwares and chemical porcelains. There are only a few handmade ceramic pieces in the collection, and even they remain in storage due to limited space and what is perhaps a prejudicial attitude toward "handmade designs" on the part of the museum.

When the purchasing patterns of museums and collectors are examined closely, all historical styles seem to be indiscriminately acceptable as collectibles, regardless of their artistic merit. That these pieces exist at all seems, to many collectors, reason enough to value them; often a collection reflects whim and fashion, rather than scholarship and keen perception. The priorities of museums as well as private collections seem to depend upon a number of variables.

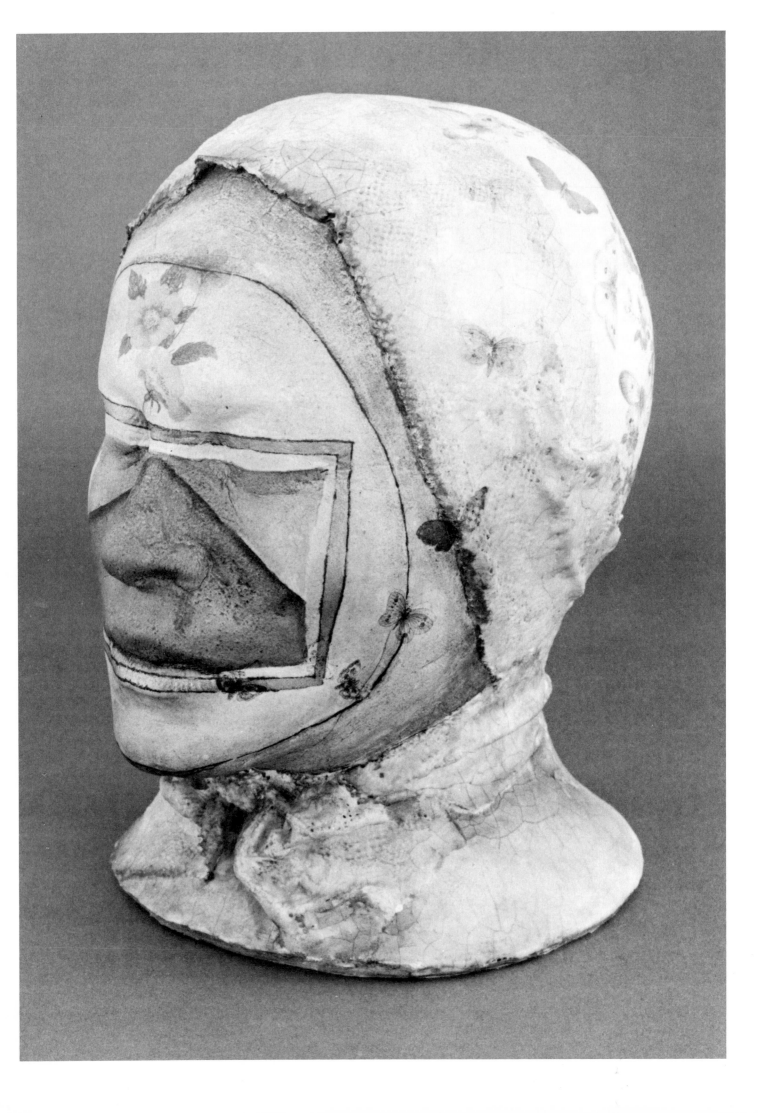

Beyond the general lack of interest in ceramics on the part of art museums, it is shocking that the one museum in the art capital of America devoted to contemporary crafts, the American Craft Museum (formerly the Museum of Contemporary Crafts), has a permanent collection of no more than 300 pieces in all media (and no permanent space in which to house it). Interest in crafts on the part of the general public is certainly increasing, and perhaps this will eventually lead to the establishment of significant public collections. The Biennial Exhibition at the Whitney Museum of American Art in 1978 included the work of ceramists Robert Arneson and Kenneth Price; the Metropolitan Museum of Art, New York, and the Renwick Gallery of the Smithsonian Institution, Washington, D.C., both have recently established acquisitions programs for contemporary ceramics. (A national ceramics museum to be located in Columbia, Maryland, is currently in the planning stages.)

Ceramists have found a more enthusiastic reception outside the environs of New York City—the Everson Museum in Syracuse, New York, which has been a showplace for modern ceramic art in this century. Its noteworthy Ceramic Nationals, begun in 1932, acted as a biennial barometer of the field for over forty years. The Ceramic Nationals consisted of a juried competition of work by ceramists around the country, culminating in an exhibition of 300 to 600 pieces. Ironically, the sheer breadth of the Nationals, which made them unique, caused their demise when the logistics and financing of such a large-scale exhibition became prohibitive in 1972. In 1978, however, the Everson Museum mounted an exhibition entitled *A Century of Ceramics in the United States, 1878-1978*. Accompanying the exhibition was the First International Ceramics Symposium, which brought together artists, teachers, dealers, critics, and historians for an exchange on issues of mutual concern.

Another watershed event for ceramic art took place at the San Francisco Museum of Modern Art in 1972, when the exhibition entitled *A Decade of Ceramic Art: 1962-72, from the Collection of Professor and Mrs. R. Joseph Monsen*, presented works by ceramic artists such as Robert Arneson, Irv Tepper, David Gilhooly, Richard Shaw, Howard Kottler, and Lucian Octavius Pompili, to name but a few. Through these works, one could see the development of strong, highly individual aesthetics among the artists represented. For curatorial convenience, the pieces were grouped in categories such as Abstract Expressionism, Funk, and Illusionism; but although certain pieces had similar aesthetic qualities, their variety and eccentricity stood out more than their commonality.

The most apparent bond between the works in the Monsen collection is visible on their surfaces, which are abrasive, inconsistent, colorful, and gloppy. They resemble the surfaces of Japanese ceramics more than anything that was current at that time in America. The Monsens' response to this kind of surface, and the appreciation they developed for California ceramic art of the 1950s and '60s, grew naturally from their actively collecting Asian art. Professor Monsen admits that during the late '60s it was startling to see the works of Jack Earl, Pat Probst Gilman, and Ann Adair—all carefully made of glistening white porcelain—within the context of the earthy, gestural work of Abstract Expressionist and Funk artists of the period.

The Desire to Collect

What is it that inspires people to become collectors or connoisseurs? The seeds of collecting may be sown quite early, beginning with a childhood accumulation of dolls, miniatures, matchbook covers, baseball cards, or postcards perhaps. These early "collections" often anticipate future interests. Almost all of us collect something, though we may not be conscious of it until we look around our homes and find many accumulated objects of the same genre.

The common ground of all conscious collectors is a grownup love affair with objects. As with everything else, there are changing fashions in collecting, but the collector of vision always stands out among the ever-increasing numbers of people involved in merely acquiring objects. Robert L. Pfannebecker's collection of over a thousand works made of metal, fiber, wood, glass, and clay reflects his unusually intimate approach, both as procurer and keeper of this extensive collection. His interest was born out of his friendship with Donald Wright, a local architect, jeweler, and sculptor who initially encouraged him. Pfannebecker's knowledge came by way of informal conversations and exchanging ideas with Wright. But he quickly developed his own personal method of collecting: bypassing the traditional sources of art—the galleries—he goes directly to the artist. Through a series of yearly trips that began in 1966, he has systematically visited leading art schools and universities such as Cranbrook Academy of Art in Bloomfield Hills, Michigan, the New York State College of Ceramics at Alfred University, and the University of Washington in Seattle, among others. This allows him to keep abreast not only of the work of the established artists who teach at these schools, but also of emerging talent. When Pfannebe-

Dream Sequence by Bruria, 1978, 10″ (25.4 cm) high. Draped and slip-coated cloth has been molded and modeled and then china-painted to create the surrealistic quality of this head. Photo: Eddie Owen.

cker makes a purchase, it is directly from the artist—sometimes paid out over a period of time, thereby providing the artist with a kind of stipend. And monies are sometimes advanced "on account," so to speak, for future purchases.

Pfannebecker's approach to procurement—developing an intimate rapport with artist and object—is also characteristic of the setting he has provided for his collection. Situated on forty-five acres in rural Pennsylvania near Lancaster, Pfannebecker built (with design help from Donald Wright) not only a home, but two out-buildings to house his collection. Rather than place the works on white walls or in cabinets behind glass, he has created "living" spaces in the A-frame buildings as a foil for them. Gray wood paneling creates a sympathetic atmosphere in which the Pfannebecker family and visitors may live with the pieces. The general public enjoyed a display of 150 pieces from the Pfannebecker Collection at Moore College of Art, Philadelphia, in 1980.

There are a variety of ways to become a dedicated collector. One way is through friendship, as Pfannebecker did. Another collector got started "through wishful thinking made tangible by the generosity of a friend." The story of that contemporary porcelain collector goes as follows:

Spotting an odd-looking teapot in the window of an antique (read junk) shop, I gave it a long, wistful look, but never considered buying it. [My] friend made the teapot a gift and it started my constant search for other unusual teapots. The expression "keeping an eye out for . . ." became a part of daily life as my "teapot eye" developed. Every walk around New York, every trip to a new area now became part of a search. Initially, my criteria for making new acquisitions were quite simple: unique form and an affordable price. The first teapots I collected were cast ones of the 1930s depicting nursery rhyme characters, but eventually a handbuilt contemporary teapot caught my eye in a craft gallery. It was modeled after the souvenir variety—but instead of commemorating a visit to a "vacation fun-spot," it included generalized farewell messages like "so-long," and "happy-trails" drawn on the teapot's surface in the manner of frosting on a cake. When I brought it home and lived with it for a while, I realized it had a vitality and individual character that was lacking in the manufactured ones next to it on the shelf.

The teapots described in the preceding story—some mass-produced, others handmade—were never intended to compete with one another, of course. We have room for both mass-produced and handmade ceramics in our lives, representing purely functional needs, on the one hand, and the recognition and encouragement of creativity, on the other. The spiritual message of that first handmade pot still speaks to the collector from between its pink and blue "frosting" layers, though since that time his taste has turned toward very refined, "precious" porcelains. Delicate enough to appear untouchable, they are a far cry, in form and aesthetic, from that sturdy first teapot. This collector's evolution in taste illustrates the aesthetic journey one can take when pursuing a passion for objects.

The seductive nature of collecting and the love of objects that develops from it is well demonstrated by the fact that many collectors often turn their avocation into a vocation.

Helen Drutt (Helen Drutt Gallery, Philadelphia), Rena Bransten (The Quay Gallery, San Francisco), Theo Portnoy (Theo Portnoy Gallery, New York City), and Florence Duhl (Florence Duhl Gallery, New York City, which closed in 1980) are only a few who wanted to share their passions for contemporary crafts by taking on the responsibility of gallery management. Not all fine galleries exhibiting ceramics, however, were started by former collectors. Braunstein Gallery began in 1961 in Tiburon, California, later moving to San Francisco. During the early 1960s Ruth Braunstein, a former dancer and dance teacher, found that the West Coast was not the ideal place to dance, and so she opened a gallery exhibiting paintings, drawings, prints, and ceramics. Another artist, former potter Alice Westphal, founded Exhibit A in 1971 in Evanston, Illinois. Westphal, who moved to Chicago in 1979, has established a reputation for showing works by the nation's leading ceramists. Nicholas Rodriguez, a teacher and collector, opened a gallery called The American Craftsman in 1973 in Greenwich Village, New York. When Warren Hadler, a former dancer for the Joffrey Ballet, joined him in partnership, the enterprise became the Hadler-Rodriguez Gallery. Although the gallery shows work in all media, it specializes in fiber works and ceramics.

The climate for collecting contemporary ceramics is slowly changing because of a few forward-looking museums and galleries. There are, however, still some practical stumbling blocks. While historical works abound in museums, private collections, and occasionally in galleries, contemporary ceramics have unfortunately not yet found a well-defined marketplace. In fact, the very diversity of showplaces is at times confusing. Craft shops, craft galleries, department stores, and craft fairs all show and sell a wide

.View of one of Robert L. Pfannebecker's minimuseums situated in the rural area surrounding Lancaster, Pennsylvania. Courtesy Robert L. Pfannebecker.

A portion of Daniel Jacobs' extensive collection of American and English ceramics, which includes both vessels and sculptural ceramics. Courtesy Daniel Jacobs. Photo: Jan Axel.

View of Jack Lenor Larsen's collection. Mr. Larsen designed his living environment to accommodate the extensive collection of ceramics and textiles for which he is known. Courtesy Jack Lenor Larsen.

range of craft works—in fiber, metal, wood, glass, and clay—that vary greatly in quality. Museums, fine-art galleries, and craft-art galleries are also exhibiting work. Ideally, it shouldn't matter what an object is made of, so long as it is good, but this enlightened attitude is not generally taken by all the factions of the art world. Aesthetic judgments are made even more difficult when craft showplaces assemble sculpture made of clay and functional wares together for no other reason than their common material.

Former gallery owner and collector Lee Nordness took a giant step forward toward creating public acceptance for crafts in 1970, when he organized a traveling exhibition called *Objects: USA* with the help of Paul Smith, director of the American Craft Museum. The show included the work of over 250 artists and was accompanied by a book that not only documented the pieces and artists in the exhibition, but also defined and discussed some of the issues still being grappled with today. One of those remains the semantic designation of works produced in craft-oriented media. Nordness said he pre-

ferred to call the pieces in the exhibition "art objects," as the word *handcraft* seemed to carry pejorative connotations "ranging from therapeutic to folksy."[4] While *art object* connotes a happy combination of creative energy and "objecthood" in a work, it does not require the piece to define itself as painting or sculpture in order to be valid as art. Ten years after the exhibition, *art object* still seems the most appropriate, sympathetic term for most works being made today.

Ironically, we are now witnessing a crossover between art and craft in both directions. "Just when many craftspeople—workers in clay, glass, wood, fiber, etc.—are beginning to see themselves and promote themselves as fine artists, a number of avant-garde 'fine artists' out of post-modernism and/or the patterning/decorative movement have been borrowing from the crafts (and design) or have actually invaded this alien territory of usable art."[5] Perhaps this crossing over will take place on all levels—in artists' studios, galleries, and museums alike.

When there is a relationship between collector and artist, it can be quite complex. Superficially, it is simply a matter of objects passing between people of mutual interest, though there is also an inherent antipathy between the two—for a well-to-do buyer in love with the object may shun the "bohemian" lifestyle of its maker. The other side of this is that the viewer may covet not only an object, but the talent that made it. For a collector, owning work can be a means of taking part in the creative process. As Robert Pfannebecker said, "We [collectors] all want to know the artist—it's a way to touch their soul."[6] The artist, in turn, needs patronage but may be at odds with the values of the collector. The artist also may feel contrary emotions when a piece, perhaps the favorite of a series, is purchased and taken. However, the artist usually admires the collector's vision and commitment and is often eager to be part of a respected collection. (Of course, an artist can create without either an audience or recognition and earn a living by some other means; but to live from one's work generates and continues the creative process.)

In the end, a committed collector may be an artist's most perceptive and appreciative audience; certainly an engaging, lively relationship is possible for both. Great collectors sometimes become great patrons, offering their unselfish support to artists—becoming, in effect, guardians of the creative process and its fruits. This form of support places the artist in the world at large. This is the height of involvement in the arts, the pinnacle of collecting. Individual collector-patrons may give the artist a stipend against future purchases, and galleries sometimes employ a similar system, accepting work on consignment and paying a "salary" or stipend to the artist against future sales. Implicit in this type of system is an ongoing commitment by both the artist and the collector or gallery. This allows an artist to develop, encouraged by both the necessary financial aid and spiritual sustenance from interested viewers.

Support from the individual collector is only one form of patronage. Museum purchases for permanent collections have always been an important means of support for artists, and it is to be hoped that museum budgets will expand to include contemporary crafts. Government organizations such as the National Endowment for the Arts support craft media, and this support is slowly but steadily rising to equal that provided for painting, sculpture, and photography. The Kohler Company, with its Artists in Residence program is an excellent example of the ways private industry supports the arts.

Other companies, such as Philip Morris, Inc., and Johnson Wax, have shown their support for specific craft media by sponsoring exhibits such as *A Century of Ceramics in the United States*, and *Objects: USA*. The patronage of such large corporations is equivalent to that provided by the Medicis in fifteenth-century Italy, just as government agencies now take over the patronage once given by the church. For today, only large corporations and public institutions can equal the support formerly provided by wealthy families and the church. Often government agencies and large corporations join hands to provide the necessary funding for an exhibition or event. Such was the case for the exhibition entitled *For the Tabletop* (assembled by the American Craft Museum), which was jointly funded by the National Endowment for the Arts and Rosenthal of West Germany.

Finding one's way as a collector through books on ceramic art is difficult because most books focus on historical wares—from T'ang dynasty China through nineteenth-century Europe. These books explain how to distinguish factories and marks to establish a work's origin and, ultimately, its value based on the established market prices. Though the books sometimes incorporate the history of both the wares and the period, they seldom offer advice in making aesthetic judgments.

Periodicals, on the other hand, are a good source of information for the collector. No matter what the scope of one's interests may be, it is possible to keep informed by joining the American Craft Council or NCECA (National Council on Education for the Ceramic Arts) and subscribing to magazines such as *Artweek, American Craft, Ceramics Monthly, Studio Potter, Art Forum, Art in America,* and *Art News*. Ultimately, however, the objects themselves are the best teachers—they speak directly through repeated handling and viewing, rather than through interpretive writing.

Collecting—on Any Scale

As the spirit of patronage develops in a collector, an object becomes less important for its own sake and more important as a vehicle for expressing the ideas, emotions, and dreams that are part of the creative force of the handmade object. Certain collectors think of themselves not as owners but as caretakers of their objects—seeing the eventual placement of their collections in public hands.

Accumulating a large collection or becoming a patron, however, may not be within everyone's means or even desires; nonetheless, art can be appreciated and enjoyed through ownership of one select piece. In our modern-day consumer society, where we are inundated by machine-made goods, the art object stands out as a beacon to the continuing power of the creative impulse.

NOTES

The Rise of the Ceramics Industry

1. Bevis Hillier, *Pottery and Porcelain, 1700–1914* (New York: Meredith Press, 1968), p. 22.

2. Simeon Shaw, *History of the Staffordshire Potteries* (1829), as quoted in Hillier, *Pottery and Porcelain*, p. 22.

3. Hugo Morley-Fletcher, *Meissen Porcelain in Color* (New York: Exeter Books, 1979), p. 46.

4. The development of the camera is credited to Thomas Wedgwood, Josiah's son, simultaneously with Frenchmen Joseph Nicéphore Niepce and Claude Niepce de Saint-Victor.

5. Anthony Burton, *Josiah Wedgwood* (New York: Stein and Day, 1976), p. 33.

6. Ibid., p. 31.

7. Herbert Read, *Art and Industry* (Bloomington, Ind.: Indiana University Press, 1961), p. 26.

8. Michael McTwigan, "Heirs to Wedgwood: Ceramic Art in the Post-Industrial Era," essay in *Contemporary American Ceramics: A Response to Wedgwood*, exhibition catalog (Philadelphia, Penn.: Helen Drutt Gallery, forthcoming).

9. John Steegman, *Victorian Taste* (Cambridge, Mass.: MIT Press, 1971), p. 277.

10. John Ruskin, *The Stones of Venice* (London: Smith, Elder, & Co., 1851–1853), vol. 2, p. 150.

11. Gillian Naylor, *The Arts and Crafts Movement* (Cambridge, Mass.: MIT Press, 1971), p. 26.

12. Harold Osborne, ed., *The Oxford Companion to the Decorative Arts* (London: Oxford University Press, 1975), p. 579.

13. Ibid., p. 577.

14. Naylor, *The Arts and Crafts Movement*, p. 7.

15. C. R. Ashbee, *Craftsmen in Competitive Industry* (London: Essex House Press, 1908), p. 10.

16. J. Bronowski, *The Ascent of Man* (Boston, Mass.: Little, Brown and Company, 1973), p. 280.

17. William Morris, *On Art and Socialism*, Holbrook Jackson, ed. (London: John Lehman, 1947), p. 21.

18. Van de Velde was Gropius's predecessor at the Weimar Academy of Art and Crafts, which was transformed into the Bauhaus in 1919.

19. Herbert Bayer, Walter Gropius, and Ise Gropius, eds., *Bauhaus, 1919–1928* (New York: The Museum of Modern Art, 1938), p. 10.

20. Ibid., p. 13.

21. Ibid., p. 16.

22. "The Evolution of Lump Clay—Coors U.S.A." (Golden, Colorado: Coors Porcelain Company, ca. 1957), p. 7.

23. The term *Rare Earth* is used by Kiehls Pharmacy, New York, New York.

24. This is a commercial product used to lighten the skin by fading blemishes.

The Nature of Porcelain

1. W. B. Honey, *The Art of the Potter* (New York: The Beechhurst Press, 1955), p. 6.

2. Ibid.

3. Ibid.

Whiteness

1. Suzanne G. Valenstein, *A Handbook of Chinese Ceramics* (New York: The Metropolitan Museum of Art, 1975), p. 174.

2. Rose Slivka, *Peter Voulkos: A Dialogue with Clay* (Boston, Mass.: New York Graphic Society and American Crafts Council, 1978), p. 123.

Translucency

1. Gustav Weiss, *The Book of Porcelain* (New York: Praeger Publishers, 1971), p. 69.

2. R. L. Hobson, *Chinese Pottery and Porcelain* (New York: Dover Publications, 1976), p. 42.

3. B. J. Mason, "The Growth of Snow Crystals," *Scientific American*, January 1961, p. 127.

4. Ibid.

5. Don Pilcher, "Values in Porcelain," *Studio Potter*, vol. 6, no. 2, p. 34.

6. Daniel Rhodes, *Clay and Glazes for the Potter* (Radnor, Penn.: Chilton Book Company, 1973), p. 18.

6. Refer to Mary Rogers, *Mary Rogers on Pottery and Porcelain* (New York: Watson-Guptill Publications, 1979) for a complete discussion of her work.

Fluidity

1. *Webster's Seventh New Collegiate Dictionary*, s.v. "fluidity."

2. Frank Hammer, *The Potter's Dictionary of Materials and Techniques* (New York: Watson-Guptill Publications, 1975), p. 226.

3. Marco Polo, *The Travels of Marco Polo*, rev. and ed. Manuel Komroff (New York: The Modern Library, 1953), pp. 251–52.

4. R. W. Binns, *The History of the Royal Porcelain Works, from 1751–1851* (London: Bernard Quaritch, 1865), p. 5.

5. Bernard Leach, *A Potter's Book* (New York: Transatlantic Arts, Inc., 1972), pp. 66–67.

The Surface

1. Gustav Weiss, *The Book of Porcelain* (New York: Praeger Publishers, 1971), p. 77.

2. This distinction has been made by Herbert Read, *Art and Industry* (Bloomington, Ind.: Indiana University Press, 1961), p. 91.

3. Harold Osborne, ed., *The Oxford Companion to the Decorative Arts* (London: Oxford University Press, 1975), p. v.

4. Read, *Art and Industry*, p. 22.

5. John Russell, *New York Times*, July 6, 1980, section 2, p. 1.

6. Read, *Art and Industry*, p. 22.

7. R. L. Hobson, *Chinese Pottery and Porcelain* (New York: Dover Publications, 1976), p. 41.

8. Rona Murray and Walter Dexter, *The Art of the Earth*, (Victoria, B.C., Canada: Sono Nis Press, 1979), p. 45.

9. Harris Deller (artist's statement), *American Porcelain: New Expressions in an Ancient Art*, exhibition catalogue, Smithsonian Institution (Forest Grove, Ore.: Timber Press, 1980).

10. Geoffrey Swindell (artist's statement), *Contemporary American Ceramics: A Response to Wedgwood* (Philadelphia, Penn.: Helen Drutt Gallery, forthcoming).

11. Jim Rothrock (artist's statement), *American Porcelain: New Expressions in an Ancient Art*, exhibition catalogue, Smithsonian Institution (Forest Grove, Ore.: Timber Press, 1980).

12. Mary Rogers, *Mary Rogers on Pottery and Porcelain* (New York: Watson-Guptill Publications, 1979), p. 86.

13. Philip Rawson, *Ceramics* (London: Oxford University Press, 1971), p. 164.

14. Garth Clark, "The Ceramic Canvas," essay in *Overglaze Imagery: Cone 019–016* (Fullerton, Calif.: California State University, 1977), p. 14.

15. Benn Pittman, *A Plea for American Decorative Arts*, pamphlet for Cotton States International Exposition, Atlanta, Georgia (Cincinnati, Ohio: C. J. Krehbiel, 1895).

16. Lee Nordness, *Objects USA* (New York: Viking Press, 1970), p. 117.

17. Adrian Saxe (artist's statement), *American Porcelain: New Expressions in an Ancient Art*, exhibition catalogue, Smithsonian Institution (Forest Grove, Ore.: Timber Press, 1980).

The Evolving Vessel

1. Claes Oldenburg, *Store Days* (New York: Something Else Press, Inc., 1967), p. 39.

2. H. Wakefield, "Artist-Potters from 1860," *World Ceramics*, ed. Robert J. Charleston (New York: The Hamlyn Publishing Group, Ltd., 1968), p. 314.

3. William Morris, "The Lesser Arts of Life," *Ceramic Art: Comment and Review 1882–1977*, ed. Garth Clark (New York: E. P. Dutton, 1978), p. 15.

Tea and Ceremony

1. Sōetsu Yanagi, *The Unknown Craftsman* (Palo Alto, Calif.: Kodansha International, 1972), p. 147.

2. Kakuzo Okakura, *The Book of Tea* (New York: Dover Publications, 1964), p. 17.

3. Rand Castile, *The Way of Tea* (New York: John Weatherill, 1971), p. 201.

4. Ruth Berges, *From Gold to Porcelain: The Art of Porcelain and Faience* (New York & London: Thomas Yoseff, 1963), p. 155.

The Figurine Tradition

1. Philip Rawson, *Ceramics* (London: Oxford University Press, 1971), pp. 29, 209.

2. As perceived by Michael McTwigan,

"Heirs to Wedgwood: Ceramic Art in the Post-Industrial Era," essay in *Contemporary American Ceramics: A Response to Wedgwood* (Philadelphia, Penn.: Helen Drutt Gallery, forthcoming).

3. R. M. N. McAusland, "Frank Fleming's Fantasy in Porcelain," *American Artist*, April 1979, p. 60.

4. Ibid.

The Industrial Legacy

1. *Action painting* is a term coined by art historian Harold Rosenberg in "The American Action Painters," *Art News*, December 1952.

2. Herbert Read, *Art and Industry* (Bloomington, Ind.: Indiana University Press, 1961), p. 108.

3. John Mallet, *Glenys Barton at Wedgwood*, exhibition catalog (London: Crafts Advisory Committee, 1977), p. 16.

4. Ibid., p. 9.

5. For a fuller discussion of the Kohler Residencies, refer to *Craft Horizons*, March–April 1964, and *Ceramics Monthly*, January 1975.

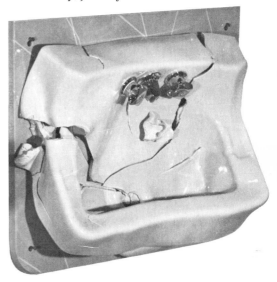

The Collector and the Objet d'Art

1. Gustav Weiss, *The Book of Porcelain* (New York: Praeger Publishers, 1971), p. 77.

2. Ibid., p. 78.

3. Jack Egan, "Bargain Days on the Stock Exchange," *New York Magazine*, July 9–16, 1979, pp. 9–16.

4. Lee Nordness, *Objects: USA* (New York: Viking Press, 1970), p. 7.

5. John Perreault, "This Price Is Right," *Soho News*, vol. 8, no. 2 (October 8–14, 1980), p. 7.

6. From a conversation with Robert Pfannebecker, October 1980.

MUSEUMS
WITH PORCELAIN COLLECTIONS

In addition to the special porcelain collections indicated below, many museums have comprehensive collections of all ceramic wares. At this time, no museum has an outstanding contemporary porcelain collection, although several have acquired a selection of contemporary ceramic works.

United States and Canada

American Craft Museum
New York, New York
Some contemporary special exhibitions

Art Institute of Chicago
Chicago, Illinois
Chinese, English, European

The Campbell Museum
Camden, New Jersey
Some contemporary, general

The China Institute of America
New York, New York
Special exhibitions

City Art Museum
St. Louis, Missouri
European

Cleveland Museum of Art
Cleveland, Ohio
Chinese, European

Colonial Williamsburg Museum
Williamsburg, Virginia
English

Cooper-Hewitt Museum
(Smithsonian Institution)
New York, New York
English, European

Cummer Gallery of Art
Jacksonville, Florida
Meissen (German)

Detroit Institute of Arts
Detroit, Michigan
English, European

DeYoung Memorial Museum
San Francisco, California
*Chinese, English, European,
French, Japanese*

Field Museum of Natural History
Chicago, Illinois
General

Henry Ford Museum
Dearborn, Michigan
American, English

Freer Gallery of Art
Washington, D.C.
Asian collection

Hispanic Society of America
New York, New York
Italian, Spanish

Huntington Library
San Marino, California
Chelsea (English), Chinese

John Michael Kohler Arts Center
Sheboygan, Wisconsin
Contemporary, special exhibitions

Los Angeles County Museum
Los Angeles, California
Chinese export, European

The Metropolitan Museum of Art
New York, New York
*American, Chinese, Chinese export,
English, European*

Mint Museum of Art
Charlotte, North Carolina
English, European

Museum of Fine Arts
Boston, Massachusetts
Chinese, Chinese export, English, European

National Gallery of Art
Washington, D.C.
Chinese

National Museum of History
and Technology
(Smithsonian Institution)
Washington, D.C.
English, European

Nelson Gallery
Kansas City, Missouri
Chinese

Newark Museum
Newark, New Jersey
American, English

Palace of the Legion of Honor
San Francisco, California
French

Peabody Museum of Salem
Salem, Massachusetts
Chinese export, Liverpool (English)

William Penn Memorial Museum
Harrisburg, Pennsylvania
Tucker (American)

Philadelphia Museum of Art
Philadelphia, Pennsylvania
*American, Chinese, European,
some contemporary*

Museum, Rhode Island School of Design
Providence, Rhode Island
Chinese, European

Seattle Art Museum
Seattle, Washington
European

Shelburne Museum
Shelburne, Vermont
Chinese, English

Taft Museum
Cincinnati, Ohio
American, Chinese

Wadsworth Atheneum
Hartford, Connecticut
French, German

Walters Art Gallery
Baltimore, Maryland
Chinese, English, Sèvres (French)

Henry Francis de Pont Winterthur Museum
Winterthur, Delaware
Chinese export, English

Great Britain

Ashmolean Museum
Oxford
Worcester (English)

Blenheim Palace
Oxfordshire
Chinese

Bristol City Art Gallery
Bristol
English

British Museum
London
General

Cecil Higgins Art Gallery
Bedford
English, European

Cheltenham Art Gallery and Museum
Cheltenham, Gloucestershire
English

City Museum and Art Gallery
Stoke-on-Trent
English

Derby Museum and Art Gallery
Derby
Derby (English)

Fitzwilliam Museum
Cambridge
English

Glynn Vivian Art Gallery
Swansea, Wales
Nangarw (Welsh), Swansea (Welsh)

Leeds Museum
Leeds
Contemporary ceramics

Liverpool Museum
Liverpool
Liverpool (English)

Luton Hoo House
Bedfordshire
English

National Museum of Wales
Cardiff, Wales
Welsh

Percival David Foundation
London
Chinese

The Royal Pavilion Art Gallery
and Museum
Brighton
English

Southampton Art Gallery
Southampton
Contemporary ceramics

Victoria and Albert Museum
London
Chinese, contemporary English, European

Waddeson Manor
Aylesbury, Buckingham
French

Wallace Collection
London
French, predominantly Sèvres

Williamson Art Gallery and Museum
Birkenhead, Cheshire
Liverpool (English)

Worcester Works Museum
Worcester
*Dyson Perrins Collection (English,
predominantly Derby and Worcester)*

York City Art Gallery
York
Contemporary ceramics

Europe

Bayerisches Nationalmuseum
Munich, West Germany
Meissen (German), Nymphenburg (German)

Capodimonte Museum
Naples, Italy
Italian

Espirito Santo Collection
Lisbon, Portugal
Chinese export

Grossherzogliche Porzellansammlung
im Prinz-Georg-Palais
Darmstadt, West Germany
Kelsterbach (German)

Gruuthusemuseum
Bruges, Belgium
Asian, European

Chinese Pavilion
Brussels, Belgium
Asian

Historiska Museet
Götenborg, Sweden
Chinese export

Kunstgewerbemuseum
(West) Berlin, Germany
German

Kunstgewerbemuseum der Stadt Köln
Köln, West Germany
German

Kunstmuseum der Stadt Düsseldorf
Düsseldorf, West Germany
German

Musée des Arts Décoratifs
Paris, France
French

Musée National de Céramique
Sèvres, France
Sèvres (French)

Municipal Museum of the City of Brussels
(Maison du Roi)
Brussels, Belgium
Chinese, Tournai (Belgian)

Museum für Kunst und Gewerbe
Hamburg, West Germany
Asian, Meissen (German)

Porzellansammlung der Staatlichen
Porzellanmanufaktur
(West) Berlin, Germany
Berlin (German)

Residenzmuseum
Munich, West Germany
Nymphenburg (German)

Rijksmuseum Amsterdam
Amsterdam, The Netherlands
Asian, Dutch, Meissen (German)

Museo del Palacio Real
Madrid, Spain
Buen Retiro (Italian-Spanish)

Saarland-Museum
Saarbrücken, West Germany
German

State Art Collections: Porcelain Collection
Dresden, East Germany
Chinese, Japanese, Meissen (German)

Asia, Eastern Europe, Middle East

Archaeological Museum
Teheran, Iran
Chinese

Hermitage Museum
Leningrad, U.S.S.R.
Chinese, French, Russian

Manila Museum
Manila, The Philippines
Chinese

National Palace Museum
Taipei, Taiwan
Chinese

Royal Ontario Museum
Toronto, Canada
Chinese

National Museum
Singapore
Chinese

Topkapi Sarayi Müzesi
Istanbul, Turkey
Chinese, predominantly Ming

Tokyo National Museum
Tokyo, Japan
Chinese, Japanese

GLOSSARY

Ball clay. A highly plastic clay of fine particles. When added to a porcelain clay body, it enhances workability, though it also adds iron impurities.

Bentonite. A highly plastic clay formed by the decomposition of volcanic ash that is used to enhance the plasticity of porcelain and to keep a glaze in suspension.

Biscuit (bisque) ware. (1) Unglazed ware that has been fired once at a low temperature. (2) Unglazed, high-fired ware used for statuary.

Bisque firing. Preliminary firing that hardens the clay body to permit handling and to allow it to receive a glaze. Glaze firing at a higher temperature usually follows.

Bone ash. Ground calcined bones, usually from cattle, used as a flux and to form the glass content in bone china.

Bone china. A soft-paste porcelain developed by the British in the eighteenth century. Because it contains as much as 50 percent bone ash, it has the translucency of "true," hard-paste porcelain.

Böttger stoneware. A dense brown stoneware produced by Johann Friedrich Böttger in 1706. It was modeled after Chinese I-hsing stoneware of the Ming period, and was called "jasper porcelain" by Böttger.

Burnishing. Polishing leather-hard clay to make the surface smooth or glossy.

Celadon. A type of glaze developed in China to emulate the character and color of jade; the best examples were produced during the Sung dynasty.

China paint. Colored enamel painted over a glaze for decoration; it fuses with the glaze at a low temperature (about 700°C).

Chinoiserie (lachinage). A European style (especially prevalent in the eighteenth century) in both the fine and decorative arts in which Chinese motifs and idealized scenes of daily life are depicted in an exotic, fanciful manner.

Clay body (body). A blend of clays and other constituents comprising the substance from which ceramics are formed. In the case of porcelain, these materials are basically kaolin, silica, and feldspar.

Copper red. A family of glazes developed by the Chinese during the Ming dynasty to emulate the character and color of rubies.

Crackle. A glaze with intentional cracks in its surface that are the result of the different rates at which the clay body and the glaze contract after firing. The pattern is often accentuated by rubbing color into the cracks.

Crazing. Undesirable crackles in the glaze that appear after firing. See Crackle.

Creamware. Cream-colored earthenware that was the forerunner of today's English white earthenware. It was developed during the early eighteenth century by the Astburys and was later perfected by Whieldon and Wedgwood.

Decal (transfer). A decorative motif printed in ceramic pigments on papers that is transferred onto the clay surface before glazing or to the glaze surface.

Deflocculant. A soluble material added to clay slip to increase its fluidity—a liquifier. It allows the slip to retain a high proportion of clay, fluid enough to be poured.

Earthenware. A low-fired (under 1100C) clay body that is porous. The opposite of porcelain in porosity and strength.

Feldspar. Any of a group of crystalline minerals used as the primary fluxing agent in clay bodies and glazes.

Feldspathic glaze. A glaze containing a high percentage (50–100 percent) of feldspar in its composition.

Flint. *See* Silica.

Flux. A substance that lowers the melting or fusibility point of a clay or glaze.

Frit. A glaze or glazelike substance that is melted and then reground; it is used as a flux in glazes and sometimes in clay.

Fusion. The melting of different ceramic materials into a homogeneous mass.

Glaze fit. A harmony of clay body and glaze achieved when the two have corresponding rates of thermal expansion and contraction during firing and cooling.

Greenware. Ceramics that have been formed but not yet fired.

Grog. Fired clay that is ground to various particle sizes and added to a clay body to give it strength, to open the body for even drying, and to reduce shrinkage. Only grogs of the finest particle size are added to porcelain in order to minimize the additional surface texture they create.

Hard-paste porcelain (pâte-dure). "True" porcelain, fired above 1350°C.

I-hsing ware. Fine-grained stoneware, developed in China during the Cheng-te period (1506–1521) of the Ming dynasty, used for making various utilitarian objects—most importantly teapots. These were exported to Europe during the seventeenth and eighteenth centuries and served as important models for Meissen and other European porcelain factories.

Jiggering. An industrial method of forming that uses a spinning mold and a template. Clay is placed in the mold and the template, attached to an overhead arm, is brought against the clay to shape the form.

Kaolin (china clay). The purest and most refractory of clays. Containing very little iron and therefore white, it is one of the major components of porcelain. Kaolin is named after Kaoling, the mountain pass "high on the hill" in China from which the clay was originally taken.

Kiln. A furnace made of refractory materials used to fire ceramics.

Leather-hard. A term used to describe clay that has dried sufficiently to be firm and can be handled without deforming but is still soft enough to incise and carve.

Luster. Metallic decoration applied to the surface of a glaze-fired object, which is fired again at a lower temperature.

Marbled ware (agate ware). Decorative ware with striations of color, achieved by partially blending different colored clays.

Millefiore (neriage). A technique that emulates millefiore glass in which various colored clays formed into pastilles are used as mosaic sections.

Oxidation firing. A firing atmosphere in which the kiln contains enough oxygen for the fuel gases to burn completely and for metallic oxides to achieve full coloration.

Oxides. Metallic oxides, such as cobalt, copper, iron, and tin, which add color to glazes.

Petuntse (from the Chinese *pai-tun-tzú*: "little white bricks"). This substance, along with kaolin, composed Chinese porcelain. It was a refined, nonplastic, feldspathic material derived from decayed granite and found only in China. After it was washed and prepared for use, it was dried in small white blocks.

Porcelaneous. The term used to describe ceramics composed of ingredients not as refined as those used in "true" porcelain. They are fired to temperatures in the upper stoneware and porcelain range.

Porcellana. Term for porcelain coined by Marco Polo in the thirteenth century. He named it for its resemblance to a white cowrie shell.

Primary (residual) clay. A clay found in its place of origin and therefore relatively free from impurities. Kaolin is a primary clay.

Proto-porcelain. A gray stoneware clay that receded Chinese porcelain; the wares made from it were covered with a feldspathic glaze.

Reduction firing. A firing atmosphere in which the kiln has insufficient oxygen to completely burn the fuel gases. The carbon monoxide and other hydrocarbon gases present in the kiln's smoky atmosphere "reduce" the oxides contained in the clay body and glaze, thereby changing the color and texture of the surface.

Refractory. Resistant to high temperatures. Kaolin and silica are refractory materials used in clay bodies and glazes. Because refractory materials can withstand both high and consistently changing temperatures, they are used for building kilns as well.

Saggar. A round fireclay box that protects glazed wares from ash and direct flame during firing. A saggar also helps to ensure even firing temperature and permits stacking the ceramic pieces on top of one another for firing.

Secondary (sedimentary) clay. A clay that has migrated from its original location because of natural forces. This clay has picked up impurities enroute and has been ground into fine particles.

Setter (kiln waster). A ceramic support that holds objects being fired in a kiln and helps prevent warping and cracking; setters are discarded after firing.

Short clay. A clay body lacking in plasticity.

Silica (flint). The glassy substance used in clay bodies and glazes.

Silica inversion. Sudden expansion and contraction in the lattice structure of silica that can occur at various points during firing and cooling. These inversions may result in cracks.

Slip (engove). (1) A liquid clay used for slip casting. (2) Liquid, colored clays brushed onto the surface of wet or leather-hard surfaces for decorative purposes.

Slip casting. A process of forming in which clay slip is poured into a hollow plaster mold, which absorbs water from the slip and leaves a dry, thin-walled object.

Soaking. Maintaining a particular firing temperature in the kiln to enhance translucency and fusion of clay and glaze or to achieve a particular glaze effect.

Soft-paste porcelain (pâte-tendre). Not as hard or as translucent as "true" porcelain, "artificial" porcelain was a product of Europe's attempts to imitate the Chinese clay body. It is fired to approximately 1100°C.

Temmoku. An iron-saturated glaze, usually brown and black with occasional rust patches.

Thermal shock. Stress created within a ceramic object caused by a great change in temperature; can cause cracking.

Thixotropy. The property exhibited by some gels of becoming fluid when shaken or stirred. Deflocculants bring about this characteristic in casting slips.

Vitrification. (1) The furthest point to which a clay body can be fired without deformation. (2) The formation of glassy, nonporous material in the clay body.

BIBLIOGRAPHY

Ashbee, C. R. *Craftsmen in Competitive Industry.* London: Essex House Press, 1908.

Ballinger, Louise Bowen, and Vroman, Thomas F. *Design: Sources and Resources.* New York: Reinhold Publishing Corp., 1965.

Barber, Edwin Atlee. *Artificial Soft Paste Porcelain.* Philadelphia, Penn.: Pennsylvania Museum and School of Industrial Art, 1907.

Barilli, Renato. *Art Nouveau.* London, New York, Sydney, and Toronto: Paul Hamlyn, 1969.

Bayer, Herbert; Gropius, Walter; and Gropius, Ise, eds. *Bauhaus, 1919-1928.* New York: The Museum of Modern Art, 1938.

Bennett, Ian. "British Twentieth Century Studio Ceramics." London: Christopher Wood Gallery, 1980.

Berges, Ruth. *Collector's Choice of Porcelain and Faience.* South Brunswick, N.J., and New York: A. S. Barnes & Co., 1967.

———. *From Gold to Porcelain: The Art of Porcelain and Faience.* New York and London: Thomas Yoseff, 1963.

Binns, R. W. *The History of the Royal Porcelain Works, from 1751-1851.* London: Bernard Quaritch, 1865.

Bloomer, Carolyn M. *Principles of Visual Perception.* New York: Van Nostrand Reinhold Co., 1976.

Bronowski, J. *The Ascent of Man.* Boston, Mass.: Little, Brown and Co., 1973.

Burton, Anthony. *Josiah Wedgwood.* New York: Stein and Day, 1976.

Cameron, Elisabeth, and Lewis, Philippa. *Potters on Pottery.* New York: St. Martin's Press, 1976.

Castile, Rand. *The Way of Tea.* New York: John Weatherill, 1971.

Charleston, Robert J., ed. *World Ceramics.* New York: The Hamlyn Publishing Group Ltd., 1968.

Clark, Garth, ed. *Ceramic Art: Comment and Review 1882-1977.* New York: E. P. Dutton, 1978.

Clark, Garth; Chicago, Judy; and Shaw, Richard. *Overglaze Imagery: Cone 019-016.* Fullerton, Calif.: California State University, 1977.

Clark, Garth, and Hughto, Margie. *A Century of Ceramics in the United States.* New York: E. P. Dutton, 1979.

Cushion, John P. *The Connoisseur Illustrated Guides: Pottery and Porcelain.* New York: Hearst Books, 1972.

Donhauser, Paul S. *History of American Ceramics.* Dubuque, Iowa: Kendall/Hunt Publishing Company, 1978.

Ducret, Siegfried. *The Color Treasury of 18th Century Porcelain.* New York: Thomas Y. Crowell, 1971.

"The Evolution of Clay—Coors U.S.A." Golden, Colo., Coors Porcelain Co.

Fleming, John, and Honour, Hugh. *Dictionary of the Decorative Arts.* New York: Harper and Row, Publishers, 1977.

French, Neal. *Industrial Ceramics.* London: Oxford University Press, 1972.

Godden, Geoffrey A. *British Porcelain: An Illustrated Guide.* New York: Clarkson N. Potter, Publisher, 1974.

———. *Victorian Porcelain.* New York: Thomas Nelson and Sons, 1961.

Goethe, Johann Wolfgang von. *Theory of Colors.* London: John Murray, 1840.

Gorham, Hazel H. *Japanese and Oriental Ceramics.* Rutland, Vermont, and Tokyo, Japan: Charles E. Tuttle, Co., 1971.

Hamilton, David. *Manual of Pottery and Ceramics.* New York: Van Nostrand Reinhold Co., 1974.

Hammer, Frank. *The Potter's Dictionary of Materials and Techniques.* New York: Watson-Guptill Publications, 1975.

Herman, Lloyd. *American Porcelain: New Expressions in an Ancient Art.* Forest Grove, Ore.: Timber Press, 1980.

Hillier, Bevis. *Pottery and Porcelain, 1700-1914.* New York: Meredith Press, 1968.

Hobson, R. L. *Chinese Pottery and Porcelain.* New York: Dover Publications, 1976.

Honey, W. B. *The Art of the Potter.* New York: The Beechhurst Press, 1955.

———. *Dresden China.* Troy, N. Y.: David Rosenfeld, 1946.

———. *English Pottery and Porcelain.* 5th ed. London: Adam & Charles Black, 1962.

Impey, Oliver. *Chinoiserie: The Impact of Oriental Styles on Western Art and Decoration.* New York: Charles Scribner's Sons, 1977.

Leach, Bernard. *A Potter's Book.* New York: Transatlantic Arts, Inc., 1972.

Lee, Sherman E. *A History of Far Eastern Art,* rev. ed. Englewood Cliffs, N. J.: Prentice-Hall and New York: Harry N. Abrams, 1974.

LeGro, Albert Leland. *Ceramics in Dentistry.* New York: Dental Items of Interest Publishing Co., 1929.

McFadden, David Revere. "Porcelain in the Collection of Cooper-Hewitt Museum." Washington, D.C.: Smithsonian Institution, 1979.

McTwigan, Michael. *Contemporary American Ceramics: A Response to Wedgwood.* Philadelphia, Penn.: Helen Drutt Gallery, forthcoming.

Medley, Margaret. *The Chinese Potter.* New York: Charles Scribner's Sons, 1976.

Metelli, Fabio. "The Perception of Transparency," *Scientific American.* April 1974.

Miller, Roy Andrew. *Japanese Ceramics.* Tokyo: Toto Shuppan Co., Ltd., 1960.

Morley-Fletcher, Hugo. *Meissen Porcelain in Color.* New York: Exeter Books, 1979.

Morris, William. *On Art and Socialism.* Holbrook Jackson, ed. London: John Lehman, 1947.

Murray, Rona, and Dexter, Walter. *The Art of the Earth.* Victoria, B.C., Canada: Sono Nis Press, 1979.

Naylor, Gillian. *The Arts and Crafts Movement.* Cambridge, Mass.: MIT Press, 1971.

Mallet, John. "Glenys Barton at Wedgwood." London: Crafts Advisory Committee, 1977.

Marryat, John. *Pottery and Porcelain.* London: John Murray, 1850.

Mason, B. J. "The Growth of Snow Crystals," *Scientific American.* January 1961.

McAusland, R. M. N. "Frank Fleming's Fantasy in Porcelain," *American Artist.* April 1979.

McCready, Karen. "8 for the 80's: California Clay." San Francisco, Calif.: Quay Gallery, 1980.

Nordness, Lee. *Objects: USA.* New York: Viking Press, 1970.

Okakura, Kakuzo. *The Book of Tea.* New York: Dover Publications, 1964.

Oldenburg, Claes. *Store Days.* New York: Something Else Press, Inc., 1967.

Osborne, Harold, ed. *The Oxford Companion to the Decorative Arts.* London: Oxford University Press, 1975.

Palmer, Arlene M. *A Winterthur Guide to Chinese Export Porcelain.* New York: Crown Publishers, 1976.

Patterson, Jerry E. *Porcelain.* Washington, D.C.: The Smithsonian Institution, 1979.

Perreault, John. "This Price Is Right," *Soho News,* vol. 8, no. 2, October 8–14, 1980.

Pilcher, Don. "Values in Porcelain," *Studio Potter,* vol. 6, no. 2.

Pittman, Benn. *A Plea for American Decorative Arts.* Cincinnati, Ohio: C. J. Krehbiel 1895.

Polo, Marco. *The Travels of Marco Polo.* Revised and edited by Manuel Komroff. New York: The Modern Library, 1953.

Rawson, Philip. *The Appreciation of the Arts/6: Ceramics.* London: Oxford University Press, 1971.

Read, Herbert. *Art and Industry.* Bloomington, Ind.: Indiana University Press, 1961.

Rhodes, Daniel. *Clay and Glazes for the Potter.* Radnor, Penn.: Chilton Book Co., 1973.

Rogers, Mary. *Mary Rogers on Pottery and Porcelain.* New York: Watson-Guptill Publications, 1979.

Rosenberg, Harold. "The American Action Painters," *Art News.* December 1952.

Ruskin, John. *The Stones of Venice,* vol. 2. London: Smith, Elder, & Co., 1851–1853.

Rust, Gordon A. *Collector's Guide to Antique Porcelain.* New York: The Viking Press, 1973.

Sandon, Henry. *Coffee Pots and Teapots for the Collector.* New York: Arco Publishing Co., 1974.

Savage, George. *Porcelain Through the Ages.* Harmondsworth, Middlesex, England: Penguin Books, 1954.

Schwartz, Marvin D., and Wolfe, Richard. *American Art Porcelain.* New York: Renaissance Editions, 1976.

Slivka, Rose. *Peter Voulkos: A Dialogue with Clay.* Boston, Mass.: New York Graphic Society and American Crafts Council, 1978.

Staehlin, Walter A. *The Book of Porcelain.* New York: Macmillan Publishing Co., 1966.

Steegman, John. *Victorian Taste.* Cambridge, Mass., MIT Press, 1971.

Valdenstein, Suzanne G. *A Handbook of Chinese Ceramics.* New York: The Metropolitan Museum of Art, 1975.

Ware, George W. *German and Austrian Porcelain.* New York: Crown Publishers, 1963.

Weiss, Gustav. *The Book of Porcelain.* New York: Praeger Publishers, 1971.

Weisskopf, Victor F. "How Light Interacts with Matter," *Scientific American.* September 1968.

Williams, Winifred. *White Porcelain.* London: Exhibition, June 10–27, 1975.

Yanagi, Sōetsu. *The Unknown Craftsman.* Palo Alto, Calif.: Kodansha International, 1972.

INDEX

Italicized page numbers refer to illustrations.